EVER A FRONTIER

Seal of Pittsburgh Theological Seminary

Ever a Frontier

The Bicentennial History of the Pittsburgh Theological Seminary

Edited by

James Arthur Walther

William B. Eerdmans Publishing Company
Grand Rapids, Michigan

For all the saints . . .
Alleluia!

Library of Congress Cataloging-in-Publication Data

Ever a frontier: the bicentennial history of the Pittsburgh Theological Seminary /
edited by James Arthur Walther.

p.   cm.

Includes bibliographical references and index.

ISBN 0-8028-3723-9

1. Pittsburgh Theological Seminary — History.   I. Walther, James Arthur, 1918-   .

BV4070.P689367E84   1993

230′.5′071073 — dc20   93-35442

CIP

□ CONTENTS □

☐ LIST OF ILLUSTRATIONS ☐

In editing this significant bicentennial volume on the history of Pittsburgh Theological Seminary, Professor Emeritus James Arthur Walther has placed us all in his debt.

Being both the oldest (1794) and the youngest (1959)[1] of the eleven Presbyterian theological institutions of the Presbyterian Church (USA), Pittsburgh Seminary is rightfully proud of its history of service to the church, which reaches from its early days on the expanding western frontier of the United States through today.

Globally viewed, the seminary's vision has reached all the major continents of the world. The seminary has inspired students, staff, faculty, and trustees to reach out and be "ever a frontier." This forward-looking and innovative spirit, always in touch with Reformed roots, shows clearly in the unfolding story of Pittsburgh Seminary, a story that is told with candor, humor, and humility throughout the chapters of this volume. The writers of this volume have themselves shared with the seminary a kindred spirit of adventure to the glory of God.

The history of Pittsburgh Seminary is actually a history of Presbyterians in the United States uniting among themselves. It also illustrates Presbyterian commitment to creating an ecumenical ministry through the seminary. The geographic landmarks in the school's history point to an underlying wish to be "ever a frontier." The seminary changed locations

---

1. The official date that records the consolidation of Western and Pittsburgh-Xenia Seminaries.

a number of times, residing in western Pennsylvania; Philadelphia; Xenia, Ohio; Newburgh, New York; Monmouth, Illinois; and St. Louis, Missouri. Geographic location was subordinate to fulfilling the needs of the church.

Pittsburgh Seminary was one of the earliest schools to grant a degree in theology to a woman — in 1893. The first African-American student of the seminary graduated in 1842. The Reverend Elisha Swift, associated with Pittsburgh Seminary, was the founder of the Western Pennsylvania Missionary Society in 1831, parent organization of the Presbyterian Board of Foreign Missions. Seminary graduates have ministered on the frontiers of China, India, Ethiopia, Sudan, and Egypt, breaking new ground as they faithfully carried out the challenge of spreading the message of John 3:16.

Through the years, the seminary's distinguished faculties have been recognized for their excellence in teaching, for their caring spirit, and for their committed scholarship, as well as for their close identification with the church, both denominationally and ecumenically. The school's contribution to archaeological research continues to be a vital part of its tradition and support of biblical scholarship.

In closing, I wish to express sincere thanks to all who have contributed to make this volume possible, especially to Professor Walther and to William B. Eerdmans, Jr., of William B. Eerdmans Publishing Company. I also wish to thank the Vira I. Heinz Endowment for underwriting costs related to this volume. My grateful thanks also to all members of the Board of Directors of the seminary, past and present, who have labored (in many cases unrecognized) as the silent heroes of the seminary.[2]

May you find in this book, as I have, new insights for ministry and a challenge to be faithful not only to our forebears but above all to our Lord, the Eternal Contemporary, who continually beckons us to even greater frontiers.

Carnegie Samuel Calian
President and Professor of Theology
Pittsburgh Theological Seminary

2. A list of directors, past and present, appears in the Appendix, pp. 273-74.

□   PREFACE   □

When the Pittsburgh Theological Seminary became a reality in 1959, it was at once the youngest and the oldest seminary in the American Presbyterian family. Its antecedent institutions had sprung up on the colonial frontier and seem never to have been permanently located. Today this "new-old" seminary appears to have a stable and enduring character. But the approach of a new millennium suggests that even now there is "ever a frontier."

A few years after President Calian assumed office, the bicentennial of Pittsburgh Seminary loomed on the horizon of the school's history. Even before planning for other parts of a celebration, it was expedient to prepare for publication of a written record of the past. Dr. Calian asked me to assume responsibility for such a book. Although retired, I am still active in the life of the seminary, and I have had some fifty years of association with the school and its predecessors. Since I am not a historian by trade, I solicited other professional help and became general editor of the project, writing only that portion of the history with which I have had closest contact.

Fortunately, resources are at hand to support this task. A very brief history was published in 1963 in an issue of the seminary journal *Pittsburgh Perspective,* a publication of which I was editor at the time. Other articles and books have also been published, containing pieces of the whole history. The seminary library contains rich archival materials that have been invaluable resources, and historical repositories of churches and judicatories involved have also been consulted.

I have been fortunate to enlist a team of writers who have important and functionally available relationships with various parts of this history. John E. Wilson, Jr., surveys the background necessary for understanding the denominational situation in American colonial times; he includes a discussion of church and state that is timely today. Dwight R. Guthrie provides much geographic, social, and political background on the Upper Ohio Valley, leading up to the chartering of Western Seminary. Wallace N. Jamison unravels the complicated histories of the antecedents of Pittsburgh-Xenia Seminary. Robert L. Kelley, Jr., picks up where Dr. Jamison leaves off and continues the history of the seminary up to the consolidation in 1959. Howard Eshbaugh and I cover the history of Western Seminary from its founding until the consolidation in 1959, and I continue that history to cover present-day Pittsburgh Seminary. Stephen D. Crocco brings together significant data about the seminary library's history and riches. Charles B. Partee provides, in biographical form, a significant sample of the seminary's role in missions. And Nancy L. Lapp reviews Pittsburgh Seminary's involvement with archaeology, past and present.

In a book such as this it is inevitable that some readers will wish for more details at this or that point. I have been guided by the judgment of the writers as to what should be included and what should be omitted. One of the writers declared to me that twice the number of pages allotted would hardly suffice to cover the assigned topic. Each chapter could certainly be expanded into a complete book. In this volume, however, we have had to work with the constraints of space.

The pictures included in this volume have been carefully selected from a large archival collection. Attention has been given to breadth of coverage and to what may prove of general interest to most readers. Visitors to the Barbour Library at the seminary may delve into the extensive treasure stored there.

As editor, I must take final responsibility for the book as it appears. I cannot, however, take final credit. It is quite evident that many people have contributed much labor to the volume. A special note of appreciation is due to President Calian for his initiative and support and in particular for his contacts with William B. Eerdmans, Jr., which led to publication. Thanks also to the editorial staff of William B. Eerdmans Publishing Company.

I would also like to thank several people who have been of particular assistance to me in preparing the volume. Mary Ellen Scott, volunteer archivist, managed the selection of the pictures, assisted by her husband, Harold E. Scott. Raymond F. Luber, who for a number of years was Director of Seminary Relations, gave administrative assistance. Dale R. Bowne, professor of religion at Grove City College, provided noteworthy aid with computer matters. Many thanks are also due to the Barbour Library staff and other administrative personnel for much ready help. And for much invaluable assistance, my wife, Janet.

In his first letter to the Corinthians, Paul admonishes his readers with these words: "What do you have that you did not receive?" (1 Cor. 4:7). A contemporary corollary might read: None of us is as smart as all of us. In looking back over the history of the Pittsburgh Seminary, these words seem to apply with particular aptness to the existence of the seminary today, to its history, and to the present volume.

James Arthur Walther

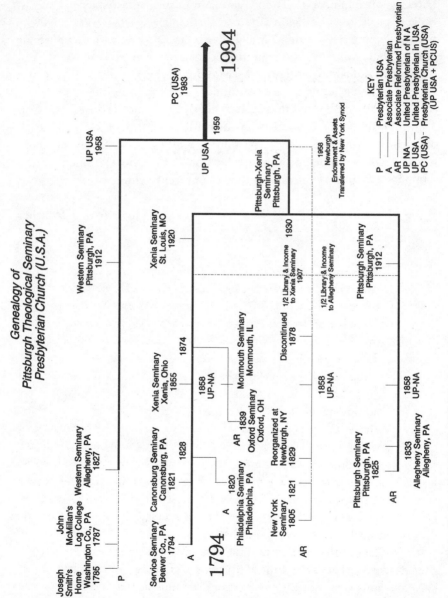

Genealogy of
Pittsburgh Theological Seminary
Presbyterian Church (U.S.A.)

1994

1959

PC (USA)
1983

UP USA
1958

UP USA

1958
Newburgh
Endowment & Assets
Transferred by New York Synod

Western Seminary
Pittsburgh, PA
1912

Xenia Seminary
St. Louis, MO
1920

Pittsburgh-Xenia
Seminary
Pittsburgh, PA

Western Seminary
Allegheny, PA
1827

Joseph
Smith's
Home
Washington Co., PA
1785

John
McMillan's
Log College
Washington Co., PA
1787

P

A

1794

Service Seminary
Beaver Co., PA
1794

A

Canonsburg Seminary
Canonsburg, PA
1821

1828

Xenia Seminary
Xenia, Ohio
1855

1858
UP-NA

1874

Monmouth Seminary
Monmouth, IL

Discontinued
1878

1/2 Library, & Income
to Xenia Seminary
1907

1930

A
1820

Philadelphia Seminary
Philadelphia, PA

AR 1839
Oxford Seminary
Oxford, OH

New York
Seminary
1805   1821

Reorganized at
Newburgh, NY
1829

AR

Pittsburgh Seminary
Pittsburgh, PA
1825

1858
UP-NA

1/2 Library, & Income
to Allegheny Seminary

Pittsburgh Seminary
Pittsburgh, PA
1912

AR

1833

Allegheny Seminary
Allegheny, PA

1858
UP-NA

KEY
P ————— Presbyterian USA
A ————— Associate Presbyterian
AR ————— Associate Reformed Presbyterian
UP NA ————— United Presbyterian of N A
UP USA ————— United Presbyterian in USA
PC (USA) - Presbyterian Church (USA)
          (UP USA + PCUS)

Prepared by James T. Vorhis & David W. Ross; revised 1992

xiv

Covenanters, Seceders, Moderates, and Evangelicals: The Scottish Origins of American Presbyterianism

John E. Wilson, Jr.

The Covenant Tradition

All of the Reformers insisted that only Christ can be head of the church, and beginning with Zwingli the Reformed tradition advocated the armed resistance of "the people of God" against tyrants who forbade the preaching of the gospel. Both of these elements were prominent in the Scottish Reformation, and both were points of serious contention. To recognize no human head of the church defied the English queen's claim to spiritual supremacy, and to recognize the right of the people to resist a religious tyrant made a claim that up to this point only the bolder humanistic thinkers had advocated. For the Scottish Reformers, political power did not derive from the people but from God's sovereignty. Christ was lord of all, including both church and civil government; therefore the church could and should clarify the law for the state and require justice from it. Should the king prove to be a religious tyrant, and should the lords prove to be unreliable opponents of his policy, then it fell to the people to resist him, for the lordship of Christ over the conscience of the Christian was the business of subjects as well as rulers.

The fact of the matter was that in Scotland it was largely the people, the commons, that carried the Reformation. For the Scottish Reformers the commons were not inherently more virtuous or trustworthy than the lords, but they were recognized as a political body capable not only of independent action but also of entering into a political contract or covenant with the lords and the king. Knox's ideal was to raise God and

1

the church to supremacy over all through the discipline of all persons by
the truth of the gospel. According to the Scots Confession of 1560, the
magistrate's part was to "purge" the church by suppressing "idolatry and
superstition" and, once that was done, to maintain and protect "true
religion."

George Buchanan was a distinguished Scottish humanist and classi-
cist and was to become the harsh tutor of the orphan prince, James VI;
he was also a moderator of General Assembly. In the midst of the Reformation he developed what was to be Scotland's most influential political
theory. *De Jure Regni apud Scotos* was printed in 1579, seven years after
Knox's death, although it had been written in 1569 and circulated as a
manuscript. Buchanan argued that the people possessed the historic right
"to create kings and keep them within due bounds." In basic agreement
with Knox, he argued that the king ruled by (constitutional) contract with
the people and in spiritual matters accepted the discipline of the church.
The theory lacked the working out of concrete rights, but it was clear
that the magistrate had to answer not only to God but also to the people,
and that the violation of the people's vital interests by a tyrant justified
his deposition. This was perceived as revolutionary and highly dangerous
by Elizabeth, who derived her magistracy from God alone. Reformed
churches of other countries lagged in their support, perhaps in deference
to Elizabeth, the most powerful and important monarch in Protestantism;
their view tended to be that the deposition of tyrants was the business of
the lesser magistrates, not the people.

Only in the concept of popular sovereignty did the Scottish Reformation initiate new thought in the relationship between church and state,
which was generally ordered along Calvinist and Presbyterian lines of
separate spheres of jurisdiction and discipline. Calvinist ideals of church
discipline found perhaps more success in Scotland than anywhere else,
especially in the Lowlands, where Reformation "from below" was most
evident. The remote Highlands remained Catholic, as did much of the
aristocracy. Among Protestants the new form of church discipline, including public repentance before the congregation, was not generally experienced as a loathsome imposition, and the final step of discipline, excom-
munication, was left to the church without serious question by the state.
The clear separation of the jurisdictions was to be of major importance
in later conflicts. "Erastianism," which advocated the civil magistrate as
the arm of discipline in the church — and which probably originated in
the Protestant city of Zurich — was repeatedly to be a temptation, and

for good reason: if the duty of the magistrate was to purge the church of idolatry and, once that was accomplished, to protect its freedom, then situations could and did arise when "purging" and "protecting" were difficult or impossible to separate.

Public covenanting in Scotland did not assume clear form and identity until the National Covenant of 1638 and the Solemn League and Covenant of 1643, but the later Covenanters found the origins of covenanting in the Reformation tradition. In the first place, the Scottish Parliament had "ratified and approved" the Scots Confession of 1560. Second and more importantly, in 1580-81 the king and his household signed, and thereby swore to, the so-called Negative Confession (King's Confession), which explicitly renounced doctrines not in agreement with the earlier Confession and indirectly endorsed the presbyterian form of government. In 1590 the General Assembly called for general popular subscription to the Negative Confession, and in 1596 it called for a public manifestation or "covenanting" of the people against the "popish lords."

James VI of Scotland, who in 1603 became James I of England, was never happy with the relationship between church and state in the Scottish Reformation. He feared the development of "democracy" in a church so independent of the state and so much rooted in the will of the people, and he worked, especially with the aid of a considerable part of the aristocracy, to control the church. He had two basic tools of domination: bishops as instruments of erastian control; and patronage, by which an aristocratic patron paid a good part of parish expenses, including the parish school and poor relief, in return for "presenting" or having the major part in the naming of a pastor. (Excepting the interval from 1690 to 1712, patronage was to last in Scotland till 1874.) Each of these violated the original intent of the Reformation, and especially patronage violated the will of the large majority of the people, who reacted to it by letting many a pastor preach to an empty church. Nevertheless, part of the Church of Scotland agreed with James's policy and accommodated itself to episcopacy. Most of the church hoped for a political solution that would establish the governance of the church according to the ideals of the Reformation.

James I was followed by Charles I, who, together with his Archbishop of Canterbury, William Laud, tried to extend the power of episcopacy and to impose on the Scottish Church a new and obviously Catholic book of worship as well as a supportive system of laws. Not all the people were against the new forms, but the large majority in the Lowlands clearly was. This majority, led by the chief ministers and nobles in Edinburgh, signed the National Covenant of 1638, which included references to the Negative Confession of 1580-81 and to historical acts of church and state against "popery." It included swearing by the name of God not only to uphold the Reformation but also to remain loyal to the king, who was implicitly included in the covenant as the party of the state.

In five years the Scots were to make another covenant, this time together with the English Parliament: the Solemn League and Covenant of 1643. The kings' policies had led finally and unavoidably to the "Puritan Revolution," which covenanting Scots called the "Second Reformation," partly because through it the Westminster Confession, its catechisms, and the Directory for Public Worship were written and adopted by the Scottish Parliament and General Assembly. The Solemn League and Covenant swore before God to extend Westminster Protestantism in Britain, to "extirpate" Catholicism and Catholic elements in the Church of England, to support the respective Parliaments, and to preserve and defend the king and his "power and greatness." Thus the king continued to be included in the covenant although he did not participate in covenanting. Before his final defeat, the king in desperation recognized Presbyterianism as the religion of Scotland, an act the Scots accepted as covenant.

But the king was soon to be killed by Cromwell and the English Parliament. For the Scots this was a serious breach of the covenant, and it led them to give their loyalty to the king's son, Charles II. To gain the support of the Scots, who went to war for him, he was willing enough to swear the covenant with hands lifted to heaven; once in power, however, he turned against them and the covenant. The Scots lost their battles against Cromwell, whose subsequent governance of Scotland was hardly resisted by all; indeed, major Covenanters took posts in the administration. Under Cromwell Scotland experienced the first religious toleration it had ever known.

The end of the Puritan Revolution and the restoration of the monarchy in 1660 brought Charles II to the throne of England and Scotland. He proceeded to try to force the Scots to conform to episcopacy, as his son James II did after him. Ministers were deposed; conventicles, or house meetings, and meetings in the fields — both of which had become common — were prohibited. Finally, in the terrible "Killing Time," in some areas of Scotland nonconformists or Covenanters were hunted down and murdered by Highlanders under the command of the infamous Stuart-loyalist Claverhouse. Not all Scots at this time were Covenanters or even

Presbyterians; some few areas continued to be loyal to episcopacy, and the Highlands were still remote and largely Catholic. The persecution ended finally with the "Glorious Revolution" of 1688-89, when the last of the Stuart kings, James II, fled from England and William and Mary were crowned king and queen.

During the entire seventeenth century, as the Scottish Church endured injury and persecution, there grew up a theology of the publicly sworn covenant that found its model chiefly in the Old Testament, especially in Nehemiah 10 and in Exodus 24, both of which have to do with the swearing of the people of God to uphold the law. Humanist ideas of power being derived from the people were combined with the image of Israel covenanting with God in the wilderness, as in Exodus 24, or of the exiles returning to Jerusalem, as in Nehemiah, to produce the concept of the public covenant as the act that constitutes government. The concept was weak at two points: the Scottish covenants represented the Protestant majority but not the Catholics and Episcopalians, and the concept of political power being derived from the people was not a biblical idea, as the Covenanters tried to argue. Furthermore, in a fashion typical of that century (but not the next), the Scottish covenants were conceived as having apocalyptic dimensions of significance: the Scottish Church was the true church, destined to lead the world to covenanted Reformation; Scotland was the new Israel.

But why, then, did God not lead the Scots to victory? Instead of experiencing a Davidic conquest, they lost battle after battle, and many suffered miserably. Samuel Rutherford found the cause in God's anger at the covenant-breaking especially of the English Parliament. He consoled a commander in the Scots' army with the assurance that the Lord was now only waiting for the increase of the guilt of the English and the resolve of the Scots before he reversed the course of events. "I had rather be in Scotland beside angry Jesus Christ, knowing that he mindeth no evil to us, than in any Eden or garden in the earth."[1] God's favor lay with those who kept the holy covenant. The Covenanters advocated the covenant of grace for salvation, but the public covenants stood beside the covenant of grace as a second, resolutely political and historical, theology of works. Historical life — providence itself — swung like a pendulum between glory and annihilation according to the keeping or breaking of the public

---

1. *Letters of Samuel Rutherford* (Edinburgh, 1863), vol. 2, pp. 335, 359, 369; cf. Rutherford, *A Survey of the Spiritual Antichrist* (1648), p. 9.

covenants. As in England in the previous century, a popular Covenanter literature especially about the martyrs during the terrible "Killing Time" hallowed the cause far into the next century.

There was another way in which the experiences of the seventeenth century made a long-standing impression on the lives of Scottish Presbyterians. The people found their own ways of getting around the unpopular encroachments of the Stuart kings on the church. Beginning early in the century, a tradition grew of traveling from miles around to gather for field meetings and at particular churches for Communion. Large Communion gatherings became a distinct sign of Scottish Presbyterianism, and a full century before the Great Awakening of the eighteenth century they were to include the first instances of large-scale awakenings both in Scotland and among the Scottish immigrants in northern Ireland. Like the later revival gatherings, they also became social occasions and popular events.

With the Glorious Revolution Scotland breathed a great sigh of relief, but for the Covenanter tradition a crisis ensued. Although Presbyterianism was reinstated in Scotland and the patronage system abolished (temporarily, as it turned out), no new public covenant was sworn, nor were the historic covenants renewed. In its will to make peace, the government — still controlling the church in an erastian way — and the General Assembly opened the way for Scottish Episcopalians to enter the Presbyterian system. The large number of ministers who had been placed in parishes under the Episcopalian Restoration were allowed to stay in their charges if they could accept the new system; only in some cases did mobs turn them out. To the satisfaction of almost all Presbyterians at the time, an act of Parliament fixed the Westminster Confession as the standard of faith for the church, and subscription was required of every minister. Not until 1910 was the law changed, the new law calling for subscription to "the fundamental doctrines of the Christian faith contained in the Confession."

The small number of Covenanter ministers who refused the settlement returned finally to the Church of Scotland, so that the remaining loosely organized Covenanter groups or societies strewn about the country were left without ministers. Later they received a minister and a new lease on life in the person of John Macmillan, who had been ordained in the Church of Scotland. Through personal study of the Covenanter tradition, Macmillan came to view the Church of Scotland as a desertion from the true church of the covenants. Because of his defiance of Presbytery procedures and the summons of the General Assembly, he was deposed from his pastorate in 1705. Yet he continued in pulpit, pay, and manse, obviously protected by his congregation and the local powers, according to one reliable report until 1727. Macmillan kept contact with the Covenanter societies and, through itinerancy, provided them with the sacraments. He refused loyalty to the civil government because it was noncovenanted and, in the persons of King William and Queen Mary, not Presbyterian. Had Macmillan formed the government, the "divine right" of Presbyterianism would have wiped away all toleration.

It may seem odd that, given such views, Macmillan and the several thousand scattered Covenanters found they were unable to form a presbytery and to ordain ministers. They held to the rule that at least two ordained ministers were required to form a presbytery. Not until 1743 was this condition fulfilled, when Thomas Nairn defected from the Associate Presbytery (Seceders) and joined the aging Macmillan. The Reformed Presbytery then came into being, which in time became the Reformed Presbyterian Church. The distinguishing mark of this tradition is the perpetual validity of the covenants, especially the National Covenant of 1638 and the Solemn League and Covenant of 1643. The period between the Glorious Revolution and the establishment of the Reformed Presbytery shows no theological development in this tradition, which had been completely focused on the problems addressed by the public covenants. New theological reflection only began with theologians, that is, the group of ministers that slowly grew up after 1743.

In America the Reformed Presbytery or Reformed Presbyterian Church came into being through scattered groups of Scots who identified themselves with the covenanting movement and wrote the new Presbytery in request of ministers, the first of whom arrived in 1752. He was joined in 1774 by a second minister, at which time the Reformed Presbytery in America was formed.

The Problem of the Persecution of Witchcraft

The "progress" that the Enlightenment everywhere wrote on its banner clearly brought great benefits, one of which was the repeal of laws against witchcraft, of which chiefly women had been accused and for which they had been persecuted. Witchcraft consisted not only of Christian belief in the devil, combined with fear, but also of remnants of pagan magical practices, usually helpful magic, at the lowest level of society. Such marginal people, usually families that passed on the traditions, were the most likely to be left out of the movements that formed the mind of Christian Europe. In rural Europe magical practices survive still. A clairvoyant can be paid a small sum to help locate a lost article, or someone bothered by "evil spirits" can seek the aid of someone knowledgeable in ways of keeping spirits away, and they can be perfectly satisfied with their success. In Scotland in the seventeenth century, either could have provided grounds for an accusation of witchcraft. Where there was good magic, it was believed, there was generally also at least the knowledge of bad magic — for example, how to curse an enemy. In the seventeenth century people generally believed far more in the power of oaths and curses than today, perhaps not only as belief in the Old Testament power of the word but also as a remnant of pagan times. A Covenanter might curse his executioners by calling out that his blood was on their heads. Of course, one must not take expressions of genuine evil lightly, but in Scotland persecution was apparently caused by irrational fear. What makes for a witch-hunt is, however, not only the fear and panic that a witch is out to do harm in covenant with the devil; witch-hunts are also related to a law. All witchcraft laws were survivals from medieval times and in one way or another based on Exodus 22:18, which states that a sorceress should be killed. (Deuteronomy 18:9-12 makes no reference to gender and only speaks of banishment.) There is some documentation that devil worship did take place; if true, this was probably also a remnant of pagan practices. But the accusations that people were in league with the devil were mainly matters of irrational fear and led to terrible consequences. Here was no Christian freedom.

One characteristic of the seventeenth century across Europe was the occurrence of witchcraft panics and persecutions. Christina Larner's excellent study *The Enemies of God: The Witch-hunt in Scotland* documents the sad course of events. She estimates that from the time of Reformation until the abolition of the law against witchcraft about one thousand people were killed, only one-fifth of them men, among them ministers and nobility. It is interesting to note the peak years of witch-panic: 1597, 1629, 1649, 1652, 1661, and 1662.[2] The worst years by far were 1649 and 1652. All of those dates can be related to high points on the roller

2. Larner, *The Enemies of God: The Witch-hunt in Scotland* (Baltimore: Johns Hopkins University Press, 1981), p. 61.

coaster of political and religious tensions and probable hysteria in Scottish public opinion. The year 1597 was an especially tense year for the church in its contest with James VI; it began with the rumor that the Catholics were coming to massacre the Protestants. The year 1629 was part of an equally tense period in the relationship between the church and the new king, Charles I, who tried with force to break the Scots' resistance to prelacy. The years 1648 and 1649 were a time of alarm throughout Protestant Scotland at the breaking of the Solemn League and Covenant by the English Parliament and the execution of Charles I, after the Scots had made a separate agreement with him in 1647 involving the recognition of Presbyterianism. The years 1661 and 1662 followed the Restoration, when Charles II rescinded recognition of Presbyterianism in Scotland, had the books of Covenanters such as Samuel Rutherford, the great Westminster divine, publicly burned, and initiated the persecution of those who refused to conform.[3] It was as if in the witch-hunts the people internalized the violence of these larger panics, finding their victims all too naturally among their own weakest members.

Everywhere in Western Europe the persecution of witches began to disappear like the shadows of the night with the dawn of Enlightenment. In Scotland the law against witchcraft was repealed in 1735. To their discredit, the Seceders of the Associate Presbytery in their second or "Judicial Testimony" against the condition of church and society in Scotland, delivered in the year 1737, charged that one of the "many evident signs and causes of the Lord's departure" — a Covenanter theme — was the repeal of "the penal statutes against witches . . . contrary to the express letter of the law of God, 'Thou shall not suffer a witch to live.'"[4] In his comprehensive *History of the Secession Church,* John McKerrow apologetically calls this statement "unworthy of the excellent men who penned it."[5] He does not deal with the problem of the "express law of God" as stated by the letter of the biblical text. Other than McKerrow's disclaimer, after the single brief mention in the Testimony of 1737 the subject of witchcraft seems to disappear in Seceder literature altogether.

3. The correlations can be made easily by using W. M. Hetherington's *History of the Church of Scotland,* 1st American ed. (New York and Pittsburgh, 1844), where the history is chronologically arranged by years.

4. Adam Gib, *The Present Truth: A Display of the Secession-Testimony* (Edinburgh, 1774), vol. 1, p. 144.

5. McKerrow, *History of the Secession Church,* rev. and enl. 2nd ed. (Edinburgh and London, 1854), p. 104.

Enlightenment and the Age of the Moderates

The Enlightenment and its revaluation of "natural reason" came to Scotland from England. It had two natural bridges into Scotland: the Episcopalians, who throughout the seventeenth and on into the eighteenth century maintained close contact with the Church of England, and the Scottish universities. In English theology the Enlightenment covered a rather broad spectrum of possibilities, stretching from Locke to the Deists. In Scotland the spectrum must have been similar, but it is more difficult to see and identify clearly. In the Church of Scotland representatives of Enlightenment gravitated rather naturally to the party in the church that came to be known as the Moderates, unquestionably the party of the Enlightenment. What they moderated was the old orthodoxy, but with a concealment of personal opinion that was to be a distinguishing mark of Scottish Enlightenment.

What the *Book of Common Prayer* was to the Church of England, the Westminster Confession was to the Church of Scotland, which is to say it was the symbol of unity. Among the Moderates, adherence to the Confession could and did mean a hypocrisy of convenience. The legal establishment of the Church of Scotland included subscription to the Confession, and the Moderates never wanted to upset establishment. In the first place, the Confession was a guarantee of order. If Moderates had difficulty, for example, with the Confession's doctrine of the Trinity or of the divinity of Christ, they had far greater difficulty with the chaos that would result from throwing the Confession out. One can observe the same kind of conservatism in the Church of England with regard to the prayerbook and the Thirty-Nine Articles. There was another political reason for conformity: by the laws of establishment the church supervised and controlled access to the universities. All university professors were required to be church members. Through this circumstance the Moderates were to be the actual carriers of the Scottish Enlightenment.

Finally, the Confession also served a religious purpose for the Moderates. For typical Moderate thinking, the Christian religion was a matter not of personal confessions and sworn oaths but of propositions that were either reasonable and Christian or unreasonable and not Christian. Moderates interpreted the Confession from the principle that God is a rational and benevolent Creator who has created a rational world and who communicates with humanity by reason. As the new thinking viewed it, the Westminster Confession was already a system of religious propositions stating the truth of Christianity as extracted from the Bible — this was remarkably similar to the way scholastic Puritan orthodoxy had intended it to be viewed — and the Confession was the product of some of the best minds of the previous century. The Moderates did not doubt that the Confession was "substantially" true; all it needed was a degree of revision in the concepts and some reordering of the priorities.

The contradiction between private and public faith seems to have taken its toll on the official theological faculties, at least at Edinburgh, the center of the Scottish Enlightenment. In *The Story of Edinburgh during Its First Three Hundred Years,* published in 1884, Alexander Grant reported that in 1741 there were four professors in the area of "divinity." The Hebrew professor listed all his courses as belonging to the arts and sciences faculty, and they were not taken by most theological students. The Principal of the University held a chair in divinity, but did not teach. Of the two remaining professors, one taught church history, which was not an indispensable qualification for students' probationary trials, so most students did not attend these classes either. That left one extended series of required classes in dogmatics that was attended by all students studying for the ministry. It was taught by John Gowdie, who lectured during the whole series on Pictet, a Genevan defender of Reformed orthodoxy, and on "some parts of the sacred text." For the students Gowdie was a dull and tedious lecturer. According to Grant's quotation of the reminiscence of a major Moderate, Alexander Carlyle, there was one advantage to attending the classes of such a dull professor, namely, "that he could form no school, and the students were left entirely to themselves and naturally formed opinions far more liberal than those they got from the professor." From these students came, according to Carlyle, a superior generation of ministers that "excelled in useful accomplishments and liberality of mind." Assuming that all this is true — and no facts contradict it — then the only real learning took place outside the theological faculty. At all Scottish universities the study of divinity required prerequisite studies in the classical languages and in arts and sciences, and in these studies as well as in extracurricular "clubs" at the universities students enjoyed the fruits of Enlightenment.

An important perspective on the position of the Moderates is given by John Witherspoon, the future president of the College of New Jersey, who was their most notable opponent. His method was literary satire, a Swiftian anomaly among traditionalists, which lends Witherspoon the appearance of being a Moderate; but he demonstrates the influence of the Enlightenment in other ways too. He followed Locke's rule: The truths of the Bible are either evident to reason or above reason, but not contrary to reason. Believing the Westminster Confession to be a true extraction of biblical revelation, he expounded it as a body of truth compatible with reason; or, where there was apparent incompatibility, he said that the truth was presently above reason, but that it might in the future be shown to be entirely reasonable. He argued that the Deists' propositions — such as that a Creator exists and that the Creator is good — depended on extractions from revelation such as the Confession; once the truths had been discovered, it was easy to show that they were reasonable "and boasted of as the productions of unbiased reason."[6] In all of these ways, including the relatively friendly judgment of the Deists, Witherspoon's theology shows the increasing influence of Enlightenment on the traditionalists in the church. But it would be wrong to include Witherspoon's views in the Moderate understanding of Christianity. The Moderates are better characterized by a Christianized "religion of nature" and even Scottish Freemasonry (founded in 1767) than by any genuine attempt to be orthodox.

In comparison with the different parties in the Church of Scotland, English Presbyterianism in the eighteenth century generally parallels the Scottish Moderates. Presbyterianism was tolerated in England under the religious settlement of the Glorious Revolution, but without being a member of the Church of England one could neither hold civil office nor attend the universities. The Presbyterian Church remained a small yet elite and rather prosperous middle-class group that represented progressive ideas not only in theology but also, with firm determination, in politics. English Presbyterians were in the first rank of those who supported the independence of the American colonies. They developed a number of excellent "dissenting academies" that produced some of the finest scholars of the age. In contrast to the Scottish universities, dissenting academies openly taught Arian, Socinian, and Unitarian theology; this, however, did not go unopposed by traditional Trinitarians. One cannot question the sincerity of English Presbyterians, since at any time they could have conformed to the Church of England and enjoyed the benefits of conformity.

6. Witherspoon, *Works* (Edinburgh, 1805), 8:30, as quoted by Douglas Sloan, *The Scottish Enlightenment and the American College Ideal* (New York: Teachers College Press, 1971), p. 121.

In Scotland, as in England and America, Enlightenment was essentially the affair of a new middle and upper-middle class that came to prominence through education and advances in technology developed by the surge of scientific effort. Upward mobility was a concept and a reality, if not a word, especially in the last half of the century. One historian writes of the period:

> People moving up the social scale from one environment [lower-class traditionalism] to the other [the relatively upper-class milieu of the Enlightenment] may have found a remarkable momentum from the contrast: the traditionalists equipping them from childhood with the ability and wish to seek a definite object in society through disciplined effort, and the Moderates opening up to them an enormous range of possible objectives of which their society approved other than the purely religious one — especially in the spheres of intellectual, artistic and economic achievement, in which so many Scots excelled at the turn of the 18th and 19th Centuries. Robert Burns and Thomas Carlyle, for example, had poor, infinitely pious fathers who carefully and gently instructed them as children in a traditionalist religious environment, and then, when launched as adults into a world of middle- and upper-class approbation, these children were able to maximize their enormous literary potential in a purely secular way.[7]

The most important teacher of the early Moderates was Francis Hutcheson, professor of moral philosophy at the University of Glasgow from 1730 until 1746. His father was a traditionalist Scots-Irish Presbyterian minister, and he too trained for the ministry, but he chose to teach instead. In the story of Hutcheson's climb toward an academic position one senses the yearning of a new generation of Scots for the wide horizons of free thought, experimental science, and unlimited historical and cultural studies that had already opened in England and on the Continent. As professor at Glasgow he kept his personal beliefs to himself, although here and there, such as in his efforts to have Moderates placed in the University, he advocated Moderate ideas in theology. It was said among his students that he was a Socinian. In his public work he developed a moral philosophy focused on the means and ends of a good and happy life, which is what Moderate ministers taught their congregations. Hutcheson's concept of

7. T. C. Smout, *A History of the Scottish People 1560-1830* (London and Glasgow: Collins, 1969), p. 239.

benevolence without self-interest was widely discussed, providing even Jonathan Edwards with a position to dismantle. For Hutcheson the greatest good and therefore the greatest interest of the self is happiness. Edwards demonstrated that benevolence in Hutcheson's system must be an expression of self-interest; for Edwards, true benevolence is a quality of life in Christ.

In the developing Scottish Enlightenment "usefulness" became a hallmark, and it made the Scottish Enlightenment a much-admired ideal in the American colonies. The Scottish Enlightenment excelled in technological advances — for example, in the areas of medicine, agriculture, and economics. The Universities of Edinburgh, Glasgow, and Aberdeen were suddenly among the foremost of Europe. Even David Hume's skepticism can be regarded as a technological examination of reason and therefore as "useful." Its effective result can perhaps be seen in Hume's own life. He was quite at home in the Edinburgh of the ruling Moderates, where he provided his servants with church pews, although he did not himself attend. He was regularly in the company of Moderates, who considered it an honor to name him as a friend. They interpreted his portrayals of the conflicts of religion and reason — including his statement that skepticism, for the educated person, is the first step toward sound faith — as so many good reasons to be a Moderate. If Hume disagreed with them, he found it unnecessary to correct the mistake. Thomas Reid, a Moderate minister in the Church of Scotland, soon produced a suitably useful answer to Hume's skepticism in Common Sense philosophy. It was to provide the philosophical basis for technological science not only in Scotland but also in America for a century and more. The Moderates produced no important theologians but many notable scientific specialists.

The Moderates gained and exercised political control over General Assembly, the most powerful body in the church, a control that endured beyond the end of the eighteenth century. This they were able to do, first of all, through holding sway in Edinburgh and in the wealthy and populous lands within comfortable traveling distance from the capital. They repeatedly designated Edinburgh as the meeting place of General Assembly, and the delegates to General Assembly from distant areas often had difficulty traveling to the city for the Assembly's meetings. The Council of Assembly, which had considerable power in dealing with business from the presbyteries, came to be composed entirely of Moderates. Furthermore, in the conflict on patronage, the Moderates, by the end of the first quarter of the eighteenth century, came to side entirely with the patrons, not with the congregations, who tended to be traditionalist and whose brand of religion the Moderates neither liked nor trusted. The open alliance of patrons and Moderates signals the class-identification of the Moderates, who saw patronage not only as the way to positions that paid well but also as the way to exercise control over the church.

In the Moderate view, the masses were in need of a firmly patronizing government. Of course, the congregations once again found ways to resist, usually the old ways of conventicles and worship in the fields. They occasionally tossed an unwanted appointee in the pond, which moved General Assembly, in the face of indifference at the presbytery level, to have its own enforcement agency, a traveling group outfitted with the right to induct ministers in hostile churches. The Moderates were never able to control the whole church, and other, traditional elements maintained a good share of pulpits. These elements were sometimes collectively called the "Popular Party" in the Church of Scotland, a designation with an anti-Moderate sting. The Moderates saw themselves as an elite minority in a world of powerful ignorance, but they knew they were the representatives of ideas that were destined to lead the way to a bright new age of science, culture, and wealth.

During the eighteenth century the church did little to alleviate the situation of the poor in the growing industrial areas. Migrant workers from Catholic Ireland, considered the poorest of the poor and most ignorant of the ignorant, had to endure the worst of conditions. In accordance with the Reformation, poor relief was the business of the parish, but in the new and growing industrial areas parishes were not able to cope with the situation. Not until the next century, under the leadership of Thomas Chalmers, did the church make a real effort to better the situation of the industrial poor. While the Moderates notably produced significant theoretical arguments against the utility of slavery in modern societies, they did not oppose the use of or trade in African slaves, in which Glasgow's wealthy tobacco industry participated. When Scots did turn against African slavery in the 1780s, it was the traditionalist and evangelical elements who led the attack.[8]

---

8. C. Duncan Rice, "Archibald Dalzel, the Scottish Intelligentsia, and the Problem of Slavery," *The Scottish Historical Review* 62 (1983): 121-26. See p. 125 on David Hume.

The Secession of the Associate Presbytery

The early part of the eighteenth century saw secessions in practically all parts of Protestantism. Beginning before the turn of the century, congregations in New England separated from the Congregational establishment in rejection of the Half-Way Covenant, which marks the beginning of the remarkable growth of the Baptist church in the colonies. At the beginning of the eighteenth century German pietist groups, separating from the increasingly nontraditional yet repressive establishments of Lutheran and Reformed Churches in Germany, began migrating in search of freedom, first to sanctuaries in Germany and then to Pennsylvania and New York. The Scottish Seceders were not the only secession movement in Scotland, but they were the first and the most important.

The withdrawal of the Seceders from the Church of Scotland took place in 1733. The movement was from the beginning theological and led by ministers, although it carried considerable popular appeal, and the secession came about directly as a result of conflict with the growing Moderate party at General Assembly. Although initially only four ministers seceded, the traditionalists in the church were generally sympathetic, there was much sympathy among the people, and the secession grew rapidly. The essence of the conflict between the secession and the church included serious disputes about the questionable orthodoxy of teachers and ministers, patronage, and the political methods of opponents at General Assembly. The ministers who were leaders of the protests were deposed by General Assembly, whereupon the ministers seceded from the church. As earlier in the case of John Macmillan, they continued to be supported by their parishes. One of them, the highly respected Ebenezer Erskine, was even elected moderator of his presbytery. In organizing they gave themselves the name "Associate Presbytery" because they did not see themselves as seceding from the church entirely, but principally from its ruling party.

The people of the Lowlands flocked to hear them, and this success itself finalized the secession. The Associate Presbytery or Synod, as it was soon to be called, found an important following in the respectable and financially solid middle class of the Lowland towns, where it came to have its major centers and where its ministers eventually lived, as did those in the established church. But there were many congregations gathered among the rural poor. The Seceders made no deliberate attempt to missionize the country, but their ministers were often invited by congregations. There were many reasons for those who sympathized with the Seceders to remain in the church, however, among them the fact that some presbyteries were strong and relatively independent of General Assembly and that in many places patrons and congregations worked closely together or patrons were inactive. Furthermore, being sympathetic did not necessarily mean complete agreement, and a difference of opinion with the strict Seceders meant for many that the Church of Scotland was the safer alternative. And there were considerations such as incomes and manses, the local parish school, and the poor who were pastored by the parish minister without having to pay.

The Seceder practice of closed or restricted Communion was not only a consequence of their rigorous Westminster orthodoxy. It was generally understood that to celebrate Communion in the Church of Scotland one had to be a member, and religious qualifications were common. Not restricted Communion but the declaration of open Communion was the innovation, and it came in the eighteenth century with another separatist movement, the Relief Presbytery, which came to be identified with the evangelical or revival group whose theology was similar to that of George Whitefield. Another usage of the Seceders in worship was singing only Psalms, because they were the biblical word of God, without instrumental accompaniment. Both were common features of the churches of the Reformed tradition during and after the Reformation. In the Church of Scotland only Psalms were sung until 1781, when General Assembly placed a book of paraphrases of Scripture beside the metrical psalter. Instrumental music was not allowed until 1866.

The orthodoxy of the Seceders was invigorated by an understanding of the covenant of grace that the Moderates and even many traditionalists rejected. Prior to the secession, before 1720 and after, General Assembly was the scene of great controversy about this understanding and found itself deeply divided over it for years to come. Through the use of an English book from the period of the Puritan Revolution — namely, Edward Fisher's *Marrow of Modern Divinity* — a group of theologians had revived and preached the unity of faith and joyful assurance, apparently in considerable contrast to the typical preaching of the time, which is reported to have been legalistic to the point of morbidity, perhaps as a result of the Covenanter struggles in the last part of the previous century. Seceder theology made the *Marrow* its own; some Seceder leaders had been involved in the controversy about the book from the beginning. The Seceders also affirmed the traditional doctrines of Dort, including the

18 JOHN E. WILSON, JR.

doctrine that Christ died only for the elect. As was not unusual in federal or covenant theology, however, they did not place a theology of election in the foreground; rather, they emphasized the offer of salvation to all who would accept it. The proclamation of the joy of faith in Christ was a major reason for their popularity. In 1720 General Assembly found the "Marrow Men" guilty, unjustly, of teaching antinomianism and universal atonement, and, justly, of teaching that the assurance of salvation belongs essentially to faith. But this in itself cannot be labeled error. The *Marrow* emphasizes Christ as the center of faith and therefore of assurance, even if it also includes the characteristic Puritan charge to test the genuineness of one's faith by examining the subjective human act.[9] The unity of faith and assurance can be claimed for the former, but not for the latter.

In Seceder theology the message of the *Marrow* was coupled with covenant theology, both for the individual person and for the collective, which could give congregations the appearance of being not at all joyful but very grave and severe. "The Covenant of Grace . . . lays us under much further obligation to duty and service than the Covenant of Works. . . . And our obligation to vow and to pay our vows, to covenant and perform to keep our covenants of duty and service to God in Christ, is yet more strengthened and furthered."[10]

In the years 1733 to 1743 the Seceders wrote a "Display" or Testimony in five separate "steps," which became the core statement of Seceder beliefs and of their theological orientation to specific problems. The ordination vows for new ministers included acknowledgment of the "perpetual obligation" of the National Covenant and the Solemn League, but the covenant tradition was modified in a decisive way, above all by accommodating the continuing responsibility of covenanting to the situation of a minority that did not have the civil government as a covenant participant. This new understanding placed the Seceders in opposition to those who advocated the perpetual literal validity of the former public covenants, because that meant withholding loyalty to the civil government until all conditions were fulfilled, such as the rescinding of toleration and the revival of commitment to the "extirpation" of Catholicism. Those conditions belonged, as the Testimony said, to times past; to make the

9. Fisher, *The Marrow of Modern Divinity, with Notes by the Rev. Thomas Boston* (Philadelphia: Presbyterian Board of Education, 1876), pp. 234-37, and other points in the text. Boston was the first major Scottish advocate of the *Marrow,* and his notes are a definitive guide to the way in which the "Marrow Men" understood it.

10. Gib, *Present Truth,* 1:212-17.

old covenants literally binding would mean they would "still be valid in a hundred years." Only the words of Scripture have the stamp of divine authority.[11] Covenanting was understood as a continuing obligation of the church to examine the tradition, its own situation, and the condition of the world in which it lives, and then to make a public covenant for true religion in accord with what the examination perceived. The former covenants were by reference prefixed as historical preambles to the present Testimony, a practice the Seceders found in agreement with the earlier public covenants. The general content of the full Testimony includes the secession document of 1733, the history of the secession, a confession of sins and a statement of the sins of church and society, a theological statement on the covenant of grace and the moral law, an exposition of the understanding of covenanting, and the justification of the Seceders' position on the relationship of church and state.

The most interesting part of the full document is the teaching on church and state, which is the last of the five steps and was written in 1743. Without directly criticizing the earlier covenants and without reference to the Scots Confession of 1560, it offers a series of thoughtful reservations, for which it finds agreement in the historic confessions of the Reformed churches of Europe, especially the Second Helvetic Confession, which, as it notes, was ratified by the Church of Scotland. According to the Second Helvetic Confession, God ordains the magistrate, and the magistrate is to be obeyed in just and equitable commands. In agreement with the Bohemian Confession, the Testimony states that, if the commands of the magistrate are evil, we should obey God. Today the king is not the protector and preserver of "true religion" that he should be according to the earlier covenants, but this does not mean, as Thomas Nairn argued, that loyalty should be withheld from the civil government. The king's person and the laws of the government are not to be generally condemned as evil, even if they include elements that must be publicly criticized. In a reservation that goes to the core of the previous covenants' understanding of the magistrate as protector and preserver of true religion, the Testimony suggests that Nairn's position means the incorporation of true religion into the constitution of the civil government. It argues that, "if true religion became a part of the civil constitution," the church would become part of the state and the basis for erastianism would be given.[12] Yet the Testimony also affirms,

11. Gib, *Present Truth,* 1:260-61.
12. Gib, *Present Truth,* 1:275.

perhaps in contradiction of itself, the magistrate's responsibility to defend the church and to advance its interests.

The Testimony derives the authority of the magistrate from the "will and consent of the body politic" as established by God in natural life and confirmed by Scripture. What remains of the "natural light" after the Fall, "in moral dictates of right reason, is the natural and eternal law of God," through which the people establish civil government. "Therefore, wherever they voluntarily constitute or consent to any form of Civil Government . . . the deed itself, or the substance of the deed, is always in consequence of and agreeable to God's law."[13] The Testimony only once seeks a basis for the consent of the people in the Bible, namely, with reference to Luke 20:24-25, "render unto Caesar. . . ." By using Caesar's coins the Jews "consent" (de facto) to Caesar's rule.[14] The sense is that by natural law the people generally find themselves under magistracy to begin with, before the question of how it happened is asked. Where it has to do with popular consent, the argument of the Testimony is not from biblical but from natural law, and yet it obviously wishes to have biblical and natural law harmonize, like two pieces of a picture puzzle that form a continuous whole when put together in the right way.

The Testimony states that in the period of the Restoration Charles II, and James II after him, "revoked and rescinded the whole former deed of the body politic, investing him with magistracy: As instead of holding his office immediately by the will of the body politic, he, by consent of Parliament, renounced any holding of them [namely, the body politic] and (absurdly, against the very essential nature of magistracy) he arrogated a derivation of it from God immediately." Both kings became evil tyrants who tried by the passing of laws to draw Scotland "into a conspiracy against the Kingdom of Christ, and against their own rights and privileges as men," so that the Protestants acted correctly in rejecting and resisting the claims of the kings.[15] It should be noted that the elected Parliament participated in the tyranny. As in the earlier covenants, the Seceder Testimony ignores the problem of the natural rights not only of the large Highland Catholic minority, against whom many Seceders fought in the uprising of the Jacobites in 1745-46, but also of the Scottish Episcopalians.

13. Gib, *Present Truth,* 1:310.
14. Gib, *Present Truth,* 1:303.
15. Gib, *Present Truth,* 1:341.

According to the Testimony, although the legitimacy of government is derived from creation or nature and not directly from the lordship of Christ, Christ has a "right" to have secular governments "subservient and tributary to his spiritual kingdom in the visible Church. And so, in subserviency to his mediatory kingdom, the management of the kingdom of Providence, throughout the whole world, was put into the hands of Zion's king." In the following sentences no reference to Christ is made. All order in the world is by God's providence and therefore by his preceptive will; "the voice of reason and religion proclaims that all order of the world is by the efficiency of God."[16] In later discussions of the Associates this was to be a key passage of the Testimony, and it was understandably subject to differing interpretations. Neither the "right" of Christ to have governments subservient nor the manner of Christ's "management" of providence is clear. The problem that underlies these unclarities is that of the relationship between natural law and Christ's lordship.

After the turn of the century a serious debate arose among the Seceders (Antiburghers) on the separation of church and state. Both groups argued from natural law and from revelation, but in different ways, and both referred to the Testimony and especially to the passage we have just discussed. The larger group argued from a sharp distinction between "temporal" and "spiritual" for the separation of church and state. The rule of civil society is natural law, the "eternal law of righteousness," which stands "in subordination to the divine glory." According to McKerrow's presentation, this group placed the state entirely on natural law.[17] The main proponent of the nonseparation of church and state was Thomas McCrie, who is still known for his lives of Knox (1811) and Melville (1819). According to McCrie, revelation "confirms" what the law of nature or natural reason teaches, including the interconnection of religion and the state, although "the revealed law contains a more sure and full exhibition of the rule of righteousness." Plato and Cicero verify that in the history of states political regulations about religion are "the dictates of common reason, received and acknowledged among mankind; they are the voice of God speaking by men of all ages and countries."[18] They affirm

16. Gib, *Present Truth,* 1:333.
17. See McKerrow, *History of the Secession Church,* pp. 443-75, esp. pp. 443-44, 469-72.
18. McCrie, *On Church Establishments: Extracts from Statement of the Difference etc.,* 2nd ed. (Glasgow, 1833), pp. 6-14; the quotations are from pp. 14 and 8.

that (true) religion strengthens the state, so that the state has a vital interest in protecting and promoting it. McCrie was obviously using the concepts of Common Sense philosophy, but he was actually less modern than the other group, whose division between the spiritual and the temporal represents a break with the tradition that the magistrate must protect and advance true religion and oppose false religion, and that the state must learn the law from the Bible. McCrie warned against "the system that would equalize all kinds of religion in the eye of the law," for it would be like a Trojan horse, whose evils, issuing forth, would "soon lay the bulwarks and palaces of Christianity in the dust."[19] John Witherspoon's position is more like that of the former, larger group, but he insisted that the magistrate has the responsibility to punish profanity and immorality. The result of the conflict between the two Seceder groups was that in 1805 they split into separate presbyteries.

The Seceders were to experience several divisions into separate presbyteries or synods. The most important occurred much earlier, in 1747, when the Associates split into "Burghers" and "Antiburghers" in an intense conflict about the burgess or citizens' oaths that were required by townships for the exercise of citizens' rights. These were essentially loyalty oaths, and they usually contained a religious clause, as in Edinburgh's, in which the person swore "before God and your lordships that I profess and allow in my heart the true religion presently professed within the realm and authorized by the laws thereof; I shall abide therein and defend the same to my life's end." The "Antiburghers" found that the oath swore exactly what the Seceder Testimony had rejected, namely, the actually practiced profession of the religion of the Church of Scotland; that was why the Seceders had gone out of the church. The "Burghers" found the Antiburgher objection unwarranted, since the church officially professed the Westminster Confession and religious tests were for the good of the civil government.[20] One glimpses the later conflict about church and state standing, so to speak, in the shadows behind the dissension on the burgess oath.

Lay members of the Seceders came to North America from Scotland and Ireland after 1740. They soon wrote to both Associate Synods in Scotland requesting ministers. Two Antiburgher ministers were first to arrive, and the Associate Presbytery of Pennsylvania was formed in 1754.

19. McCrie, *On Church Establishments,* p. 52.
20. McKerrow, *History of the Secession Church,* pp. 208ff.

Soon Burgher ministers also arrived. Since the burgess oath played no role in America, after a brief period the Burghers joined with the Associate Presbytery. After the watershed event of the American Revolution, the Associate and the Reformed Presbyterians (Covenanters) united in 1782 to form the Associate Reformed Church. The union was rejected by some ministers and congregations on both sides. These were supported by the respective parent organizations in Scotland, so that out of the union came not one but three churches.

The platform or basis for the union of 1782 contains the following statement on the relationship between church and state: Civil government originates with the Creator, not with Christ, but magistracy "is rendered subservient *by* the Mediator, to the welfare of his spiritual kingdom, the Church."[21] That is an impressive interpretation of Seceder tradition for life in the new republic, and presumably one source for it is the Covenanter tradition's insistence on Christ as lord also of the state. The work of making the state subservient is Christ's work, and his mode of operation may be either open, through the church, or hidden in the secret ways of providence.

The Evangelicals

In 1741 the Seceders invited George Whitefield to preach in Scotland. They thought he shared their beliefs, and they expected that he would make common cause with them; he could strike a decisive blow for the reconquering of the Church of Scotland. Apparently influenced by White-field's reputation of being an advocate of Reformed theology, they mis-judged him from the beginning. Whitefield came to Scotland, but in a meeting with a large group of Seceder ministers he frankly stated his loyalty to the episcopal Church of England; hence he did not endorse the Scottish interpretation of the great events of the past century, all of which

---

21. *The Church Memorial: Containing Important Historical Facts and Reminiscences Connected with the Associate and Associate Reformed Churches Previous to their Union as the United Presbyterian Church of North America,* ed. R. D. Harper (Columbus, Ohio, 1858), p. 57. See further David McDill, ed., *Exposition and Defense of the Westminster Assembly's Confession of Faith: Being the Draught of an "Overture" Prepared by a Committee of the Associate Reformed Synod, in 1783* [written by Robert Annan] (Cincinnati, 1855), pp. 187-96 (on covenanting), pp. 197-202 (on civil magistrate).

completely ruined him, not only for the Seceders, but also for many a traditionalist minister in the Church of Scotland. Of course he refused to confine himself to their churches and went wherever he was welcome. The Seceders wanted to know how he could preach a revival without including the revived and converted in the discipline of a church, indeed, a true church, to which Whitefield replied that as an Anglican he had no control over that. The "strange signs" of the new awakening, such as fainting and loud rejoicing, had been a part of the awakenings of the previous century in Scotland, but the Scots had not witnessed them in a long time. The Moderates and the Seceders found them reprehensible. The Seceders took the alarm to a remarkably high level, insisting that the unchurched disorder was the church-destructive work of the devil. It is reported that in June of 1742, thirty thousand people gathered on a hillside at Cambuslang to hear Whitefield, and three thousand received Communion in the tents that had been erected.

The awakening that Whitefield represented did cut across what had been important differences among the confessional churches, an observation that is often made of the German Pietist movement. Such had not been the case with the Scottish awakenings of the previous century. Another similarity between the Great Awakening and Pietism is that both tended to reorder the priorities of the traditional confessions through emphasis on spiritual rebirth, and both tended theologically toward Arminianism, which Wesley, but not Whitefield, openly adopted. The scope of the Evangelical group in the Church of Scotland at the time of Whitefield's revival is difficult to determine, but these Evangelicals were present, and, as events of the nineteenth century proved, the future church would for a time belong to them. Like the Moderates, but for completely different reasons, they wanted neither to give up the Westminster Confession nor always to be held strictly to the letter in interpreting it; and like the Moderates they were not defined by covenants and federal theology. Their progenitors were among the "Marrow Men" who chose not to follow the Seceders into separation from the Church of Scotland. In the eighteenth century they definitely opposed patronage, in most questions they sided with the other traditionalists in the church, and they were the first Scottish Christians to advocate the separation of church and state. The Moderates apparently labeled both Evangelicals and Seceders "high flyers," perhaps with reference to the mythical Icarus, but the name better fits the Moderate view of the Evangelicals.

The only secession of Evangelicals from the Church of Scotland in the eighteenth century was unintentional. Thomas Gillespie, a kindly, inoffensive, and self-effacing pastor with an unusually large family, was ordered by General Assembly in 1752 to help induct a patron's appointee whom the congregation had refused. Gillespie did not appear, as two other ministers did not. General Assembly chose to make an example of him and deprived him of his pastorate. Unlike the aggressive Seceders, he quietly left his post. The people fashioned a church for him in a barn and helped the family survive. He did not join the Seceders because he could not identify with their theology. His identification was always far more with the Church of Scotland, which, in spite of patronage and the politics and scorn of the Moderates, provided the latitude in which the Evangelicals could thrive. Gillespie opened Communion to any Christian. Not until 1757 was he joined by another minister from the Church of Scotland, and later they were joined by a third. In 1761 a new presbytery, the Relief Presbytery, was formed, which in 1847 joined with elements from the original Seceders to form the Scottish United Presbyterian Church. Gillespie only reluctantly participated in the formation of the new presbytery, and before he died he recommended to his congregation that they return to the Church of Scotland. The relation of the Relief Presbytery to the Church of Scotland has been compared to that of the Methodists to the Church of England, with the difference that the Relief Presbytery stood in separation. The Seceders formed their own school for the training of ministers. The Relief Presbytery did not; they continued to send their students to the Scottish universities until well into the next century.

From Ireland to Pennsylvania

The Presbyterians in northern Ireland were of Scottish heritage and were in close contact with Scotland. Any Scot seeking to move up socially or economically had to conform to the established Church of Ireland (the Church of England in Ireland). Poorer Scots moved into Ulster especially after 1690 to work the plantations of mainly English landlords, who appreciated their presence as much as their labor: their numbers helped to quiet the hostile intentions of the native Irish. Nowhere in Ireland was the Presbyterian Church protected by establishment, but the congregations were free to call their own ministers, assuming they could afford one. As a poor group of tenementary workers they had difficulty paying salaries for ministers, who were educated at Scottish universities. Since they, too, had supported the Restoration of the Stuarts against Cromwell's government, Charles II had rewarded the Scots-Irish with a royal grant to help support their ministers; it was never enough to pay more than a part of salaries, however, and it ceased altogether in 1717. Under the Stuarts it came coupled with a silent and often meaningless indulgence from the king, not with official toleration. Presbyterians in Scotland were not officially tolerated until the Glorious Revolution.

The effect of nonestablishment in eighteenth-century Ireland was that the "enlightened" ministers in Ireland, such as the "Belfast Society," whose counterparts were the Moderates in Scotland, found themselves in running conflict with the tradition-oriented congregations. Here, too, class differences could be observed, with most of the congregations representing the bottom side. The conflict quickly focused on subscription to the Westminster Confession, and it was led on the subscriptionist side not only by traditionalist ministers but also and especially by the elders of congregations demanding subscription. They wanted the traditional faith of the Scottish Church, and they were not getting it from the enlightened clergy of the Moderate party. How were the laity to recognize the true church? That was the critical question asked and answered, for the time being, by the requirement of subscription. As the conflicts wore on, this lay element came finally to decide that subscription was not an efficient test, insofar as experience showed that some ministers could subscribe in a sophistic way, interpreting subscription in their own minds to mean, not what the traditionalist congregations wanted, but what they needed. Furthermore, subscription had never been able to screen out morally problematic people. In Ireland, from 1746 on, the result was an increasing turn to the Seceders in Scotland. Both branches of the Seceders, the Burghers and the Antiburghers, had great success in northern Ireland.

The reasons for the migration to America, which began on a large scale in the last years of the decade before 1720 and increased dramatically by 1730, were mainly economic. The Presbyterians had basically the same status as dissenters in Great Britain, which means that they had toleration but not full liberty, since only members of the established church could hold civil office and only the established church had the right to marry. This meant the possibility of harassment, such as in cases where bishops refused to recognize the heirs of Presbyterian marriages and awarded the inheritance to others. The reason for such behavior on the part of some of the bishops seems to have been the fear of Presbyterianism spreading.

The economic reasons for leaving Ireland were high rents and taxes and a series of poor crops. Scots-Irish shipped to America often on terms of the cost of passage for work on the other side, and they went by the tens of thousands. It is estimated that from about 1717 to the time of the American Revolution between 200,000 and 500,000 people migrated. There is evidence that many of these were native Irish who had converted to Presbyterianism, perhaps to follow the path of opportunity. They poured into New York and Pennsylvania and down the eastern seaboard into the Carolinas. Far fewer came directly from Scotland.

The Scots-Irish were a distinctly Scottish ethnic group with definite traditions, and as a large group they worked together to promote group interests. With smaller Reformed groups the situation was different; for example, the small groups of French Huguenots, who left France because of Catholic persecution, conformed relatively quickly to the surrounding culture, whether in Boston or Charleston or in the refuges they found in Protestant Germany. The one condition seems to have been compatibility of religious confession. German groups show a similar pattern: when their numbers were small, as in the seventeenth century, they conformed to their surroundings and disappeared as a distinct group. In the eighteenth century their ethnic strength and their ability to maintain their own language and religious forms increased with the numbers of immigrants, and they sought areas where they could settle farms together.

The conflicts in the colonial Presbyterian Church (the Synod of New York and Philadelphia) between the new Scots-Irish and the settled, mainly Puritan Presbyterians are the subject of Leonard Trinterud's classic work *The Forming of an American Tradition*. His evident dislike of the "Old Side" Presbyterians and their apparently irrational supporters, the Scots-Irish, perhaps stems from his involvement in the conflict between funda-mentalist and moderate Presbyterians in the twentieth century.[22] Marilyn Westerkamp's recent study *Triumph of the Laity: Scots-Irish Piety and the Great Awakening, 1625-1760* provides a helpful corrective.[23] As she points out, the support given by the Scots-Irish to the demand for subscription to the Westminster Confession, a support that did not relent until just before the middle of the eighteenth century, was in direct parallel to the

22. Trinterud, *The Forming of an American Tradition* (Philadelphia: Westminster Press, 1949).
23. Westerkamp, *Triumph of the Laity: Scots-Irish Piety and the Great Awakening* (New York: Oxford University Press, 1988).

demand for subscription in northern Ireland. But the tide did turn —
from the "Old Side" subscription party to the "New Side" party — at
about the same time that congregations in Ireland began inquiring about
ministers from the Scottish Seceders. In America the turn was not to the
Seceders, who did not appear in the colonies until the 1740s, but to the
Evangelicals and the Great Awakening. This became the answer to the
people's question about true religion, and it was to continue to be the
answer even when many Scots-Irish became Methodists and Arminians.
The New Side Presbyterians became the party of the Awakening. Jonathan
Dickinson himself, the very able leader of the New Side, became an
Awakening preacher. The New Side's position on subscription never re-
sembled that of the Scottish Moderates or the Irish "Belfast Club"; rather,
it anticipated and paralleled that of the Evangelicals in Scotland.

The most accomplished scholar in colonial Presbyterianism, Francis
Alison, knew Francis Hutcheson and taught his moral philosophy. Alison
graduated from the University at Edinburgh in 1732; in 1735 he arrived
in America. Throughout his life he was on friendly terms with English
and Scottish Presbyterian representatives of Enlightenment, and he
devoted his life to the cause of developing high-quality educational institutions in America. Alison was much respected by Benjamin Franklin and
was called the best classical scholar in America by Ezra Styles, the president
of Yale College. He opposed the Awakening, and he strongly opposed the
Log College because he did not believe its ministers were adequately
qualified for the Presbyterian ministry. The odd thing was that Alison, an
apparent Scottish Moderate, was a leader of the Old Side Presbyterians,
the group that advocated subscription to the Westminster Confession. In
view of such apparent inconsistency, Trinterud accuses Alison of lack of
character.[24] Alison clearly advocated subscription, yet he also led the effort
for conciliation with the New Side, which included accepting the mod-
eration of subscription, the Adopting Act of 1729. It is possible that Alison
was just a Scottish Moderate who came to America not only with the
Moderates' distaste for evangelical "high flyers" but also with the Moderates' duplicitous attitude toward the Westminster Confession. It is also
possible that he, like Witherspoon, genuinely believed in representing
both the Confession and the Enlightenment, although on the side of
Enlightenment he seems to have been more open to the liberals than
Witherspoon. In comparison with others, Alison represents the ideal —

24. Trinterud, *Forming of an American Tradition,* p. 142.

however problematic it may be — of church and liberal university thriving together, and he did not want Presbyterian theological education separated from the university.

In Ireland the Scottish immigrants of the eighteenth century did not establish theological seminaries, but they did found academies that were led by university-educated pastors, and in some few instances ministers were trained locally by other ministers and examined by the presbytery. In making the transition to America the Scots-Irish took these possibilities with them, so that the development of a seminary such as the Log College (1735) was only relatively new. One professor sufficed, and the copying of lectures provided a substitute for unavailable textbooks. The point was not to avoid the universities but to train ministers (and provide the prerequisites) where a university education was impossible. The ability of the church to keep up with the frontier was to depend largely on how flexible it was willing to be on theological education.

In separating their theological education from that given in the divinity schools of the Scottish universities, the Seceders maintained the standard requirements for ordination. Provision was also made for prerequisite work, especially in languages, by the establishment of academies, although soon students were accepted for divinity studies who had their prerequisites from the universities.[25] The Seceders founded both kinds of schools in America, yet students were also allowed to attend the universities. Seceder schools lacked the liberality of university arts and sciences, and for that reason they would probably not have met with Alison's approval.

Seceder traditionalism was to be sorely tested by the many forms of Christianity in the New World. All Presbyterians in the mid-Atlantic states were keenly aware not only of each other but also of the other denominations. The *Display of the Religious Principles of the Associate Synod of North America,* whose narrative part was first published by the Associate Presbytery in 1784, contains a long catalog of errors of the other churches. Error and apostasy were everywhere. The narrative also complains about the position of the larger Presbyterian group on the Confession:

> The adherence to the Westminster Confession required of ministers belonging to the synod of New York and Philadelphia is with an exception of what not only the Synod itself, but any presbytery . . .

25. McKerrow, *History of the Secession Church,* pp. 778ff.

may judge "not essential or necessary in doctrine, worship or govern-ment." And who knows what this may be? Were the articles, deemed not to be essential or necessary, specified, it would then appear, what was the public confession made in the church; but while they are not, we cannot say what this is.[26]

It was a valid point, and one that was to bring the mainline Presbyterians as much confusion as freedom.

One could imagine that the Seceders, like the Amish Mennonites, might have been driven to seek peace in withdrawal from the surrounding culture. The Seceders never withdrew into isolation but continued the covenant tradition of engaging the situation of church and world. They were among the first denominations to condemn slavery, and in 1830 they excommunicated slaveholders. Occasionally the *Display* allows one to see something of their positive feelings about life in America. In the midst of a lamenting confession of sins one finds this sentence: "The Lord hath given us a large and good land, and hath preserved us in the enjoyment of many valuable privileges, the continuance of which is the more to be esteemed, as it is a remarkable instance of divine goodness, and long-suffering toward a very guilty people."[27] In the Scottish covenant tradition, guilt was usually matched with the anger of God, not with his goodness.

John Witherspoon entertained friendly relations with the Seceders and for several years tried to unite the Synod of Philadelphia with the Associate Presbytery. After a long history and many moderating develop-ments, these two currents of American Presbyterianism were finally joined in 1958, in the union that produced the presently existing Pittsburgh Theological Seminary.

Selected Secondary Literature

Secondary sources on the history of the Covenant tradition used in this essay include the following: S. A. Burrell, "The Apocalyptic Vision of the Early Covenanters," *The Scottish Historical Review* 43 (1964): 1-24; J. D. Douglas, *Light in the North: The Story of the Scottish Covenanters* (Grand

26. *Display of the Religious Principles of the Associate Synod of North America,* 7th ed. (Philadelphia, 1850), p. 56.
27. *Display,* p. 217.

Rapids: Eerdmans, 1964); J. G. Vos, *The Scottish Covenanters: Their Origins, History and Distinctive Doctrines,* 2nd ed. (Pittsburgh: Crown and Covenant Publications, 1980); *Testimony of the Reformed Presbyterian Church in Scotland: Historical and Doctrinal* (Glasgow: G. Gallie, 1866), a reprint of the original documents of 1837 and 1839. Discussion of the significance of George Buchanan can be found in the standard work by James Bulloch, *The Kirk in Scotland* (Edinburgh: St. Andrew, 1960).

The best single source on the general church history of Scotland in the eighteenth century is the book by Andrew L. Drummond and James Bulloch, *The Scottish Church 1688-1843: The Age of the Moderates* (Edinburgh: St. Andrew, 1973). Richard B. Sher's recent work, *Church and University in the Scottish Enlightenment: The Moderate Literati in Edinburgh* (Princeton: Princeton University Press, 1985), has filled a gap in published work on the Moderates. A very commendable recent collection of essays, which extend into cultural and religious history, is M. A. Stewart, ed., *Studies in the Philosophy of the Scottish Enlightenment* (Oxford: Clarendon Press, 1990); see also R. H. Campbell and A. S. Skinner, eds., *The Origins and Nature of the Scottish Enlightenment* (Edinburgh: J. Donald, 1982); and R. W. Schmitz, *Hugh Blair* (New York: King's Crown, 1948). I have found nothing that contradicts Alexander Grant's report on the deplorable state of theological studies at Edinburgh, in *The Story of the University of Edinburgh during Its First Three Hundred Years* (London: Longmans Green, 1884); Andrew J. Campbell confirms Grant's view in *Two Centuries of the Church of Scotland* (Paisley: Gardner, 1930), pp. 100, 134. To make a comparison with Oxford University, see E. G. W. Bill, *Education at Christ Church Oxford 1660-1800* (Oxford: Clarendon Press, 1988), pp. 301-7. V. L. Collin's *President Witherspoon: A Biography* (Princeton: Princeton University Press, 1925) needs supplementation, especially in the area of Witherspoon's theology. Current general histories of Scotland include social history.

A short treatment of Seceder history can be found in G. Slosser, ed., *They Seek a Country: The American Presbyterians* (New York: Macmillan, 1955). David C. Lachman has recently published a dogmatic study of *The Marrow Controversy 1718-1723* (Edinburgh: Rutherford, 1988).

For the history of the Scots-Irish and their transition to America, see also M. A. Armstrong, "English, Scottish and Irish Backgrounds of American Presbyterians, 1689-1729," *Journal of the Presbyterian Historical Society* 34 (1956): 3-18. The evidence for large numbers of native Irish among the Scots-Irish migration is given by Leroy V. Eid, "Irish, Scotch and Scots-Irish: A Reconsideration," *American Presbyterians: Journal of Pres-*

byterian History 64 (1986): 211-25. On Reformed immigrant groups from Europe see Jon Butler, *The Huguenots in America* (Cambridge: Harvard University Press, 1983). Douglas Sloan, *The Scottish Enlightenment and the American College Ideal* (New York: Teachers College Press, 1971), is very informative on the development of Presbyterian schools and contains excellent sections on Witherspoon and on Francis Alison.

□   CHAPTER TWO   □

Presbyterian Beginnings in the West

Dwight R. Guthrie

The Presbyterian Church (U.S.A.), like other churches named "Presby-terian," for the most part had its beginnings across the seas, chiefly in Scotland and in the northern six counties of Ireland. James I of England — also known as James VI of Scotland — set up those six counties as the Plantation of Ulster. Presbyterian settlers from Scotland moved west-ward across the Irish Sea and joined Presbyterians who were already residing there, thus giving credence to the term "Scotch-Irish."

The happy estate of these Presbyterians in Ulster fluctuated under Charles I, Charles II, James II, and William and Mary, but when in the early 1700s a change for the better had not come, the word "migration" spread from person to person. Sailing conditions made emigration to America possible from different locations in the British Isles, and "safety considerations" were becoming more acceptable. "The year 1710 marks the beginning of the great migration; ten years later it became a steady stream averaging three to six thousand emigrants a year."[1]

Some of the emigrants came to Boston, but there was a lack of hospitality there; many soon moved southward to the Delaware River towns of Lewes, New Castle, Wilmington, and Philadelphia. Later many came directly to these towns. It may be added here that the town called New Castle became well known among those emigrating from the north of Ireland and Scotland. "Largely because there was a line of ships sailing

---

1. W. W. Sweet, *Religion in Colonial America* (New York: Charles Scribner's Sons, 1943), p. 251.

with some regularity from Londerry to New Castle, the little town on the Delaware became the principal port of Presbyterian entry. From it Presbyterians fanned out north and south, but especially west, wherever cheap land could be had."[2]

The Movement Westward over the Alleghenies

Many of the Presbyterians who flooded New Jersey, Delaware, and southeastern Pennsylvania heard stories of the frontier west of the Allegheny Mountains that could be theirs for occupancy. They joined with others to move west in caravans. The arrival of so many from across the seas and the mixing of many with different religious and cultural backgrounds made living a great deal easier, and an overland trip to the west did not seem to be too much for them. They had heard stories about Indians, but thoughts of forts, neighbors, and self-sufficiency negated many of their fears.

The turning point that convinced many settlers to move west came with the fall of Fort Duquesne in 1758 and the establishment of Fort Pitt. Put another way, it was the rise of British power and influence in the west and the strong probability that Protestantism would have a chance to thrive "out there." With those odds in their favor — a new life beckoning and a strong determination to succeed — many Presbyterians made preparations to journey westward when transportation and other conditions were somewhat favorable.

It may be injected here that events happening among Presbyterians in Philadelphia led to more clergy action on the western frontier. Earlier there had been a schism between the Synods of New York and Philadelphia, but on May 25, 1758, the two bodies of Presbyterians — the Old Side and the New Side — were joined into one, the Synod of New York and Philadelphia. The newly organized Synod stood ready for action, and the happenings west of the mountains gave the emigrants the signal to move westward. The Synod went on record to deputize army chaplains and available ministers to go out and do what they could to give spiritual help to the settlers and to work among the Indians where possible. This

2. E. B. Welsh, "Westward, Ho!" in W. W. McKinney, ed., *The Presbyterian Valley* (Pittsburgh: Davis & Warde, Inc., 1958), p. 146.

took place in the ensuing months and years after 1758. The events west of the Alleghenies served to generate a new missionary spirit in the east.

Before the American Revolution there was also a strong stream of settlers moving into western Pennsylvania from Virginia. Paths and trails had been carved out from Frederick to Winchester to Wills Creek in southwestern Pennsylvania. "The Virginians believed that the whole of the Monongahela Valley lay outside the charter limits of Pennsylvania and hence within the boundaries of their colony. Acting on this belief they established their claims in accordance with the Virginia land system, and when in 1780 the boundary dispute was settled Pennsylvania agreed to recognize these claims."[3] In addition to the Virginia "trail" mentioned above there was one from the Natural Bridge in Virginia to Staunton westward and north up the Tygart Valley and the Monongahela and Youghiogheny River valleys to Fort Necessity, Redstone Old Fort, Peters Creek, Chartiers Creek, and on to Fort Pitt.

Putting Down Their Roots

There were many problems and tasks ahead for these Presbyterian settlers. The land was there, and the payments — if any — were not burdensome. A cabin made of logs and a barn would be raised by neighbors who would come from far and near. A cellar for storage was dug out under a portion of the house. Here potatoes, pumpkins, apples, and other foods and articles could be stored. A spring house was needed, as was a smoke house and a shed. A work horse or horses, cattle, and chickens would be purchased, with payments made in one way or another. Helping each other was the rule in all matters that were considered too much for one individual or a family to accomplish.

The physical aspect of getting a home and farm started rested mainly on the husband's shoulders, with some help from the wife. In most cases the children were small or not yet born. Trees and stumps had to be cleared from a portion of the land before a garden could be started or crops could be planted. The husband, wife, and often the children would toil through the summer to have potatoes, greens, cucumbers, pumpkins, etc., to put on the table and in the shed or spring house. Time would

3. Solon J. Buck and Elizabeth H. Buck, *The Planting of Civilization in Western Pennsylvania* (Pittsburgh, 1939), p. 138.

have to be found for "pay back in kind," repaying the hours of work or produce volunteered by neighbors. There would be church services, efforts for education, as well as other meetings to attend. Truly the pioneers were kept exceedingly busy.

Why the Early Presbyterians Settled in Certain Locations

The early 1700s saw a virtual wave of human beings surge westward. The first part of the eighteenth century was marked by the movement of settlers west from the coastlands to areas just east of the Allegheny Mountains. This was also true all along the Appalachian range from Pennsylvania south into the Carolinas. The first movement inland was primarily an effort to get away from the coastal communities and have acres of land in less populated areas. The defeat of the French and Indians with the fall of Fort Duquesne in 1758 became almost a rallying cry to British subjects in the east to move west to the vicinity of Fort Pitt. There were some Germans mixed here and there among the settlers, but the movement westward was made up mainly of the Scots, the Irish, the Scotch-Irish, and the English.

The settlers who came "up from Virginia" or who moved westward across Pennsylvania were often moving toward a determined destination, that of relatives, friends, or others who had gone "out there" at an earlier date. For example, visits to relatives are testified to in records such as these: "came to the house of his brother-in-law, John McElhenny" and "a visit to the Thomas McMillan's home on Peter's Creek" (a brother).[4] Early ministers were sometimes influenced into accepting calls to churches by the fact that relatives or friends had already settled in or near those church areas. The presence of these ministers, in turn, influenced others at a later time to settle near certain churches. These illustrations could be multiplied many times.

In the latter half of the eighteenth century, the people who surged westward had the problem of obtaining land and property rights. In some instances the successors of the Penns sold portions of the west to settlers. There were situations in which some Penn successors had sold land rights to the Indians and then in turn collected or tried to collect from the

---

4. Dwight R. Guthrie, *John McMillan: The Apostle of Presbyterianism in the West* (Pittsburgh: University of Pittsburgh Press, 1952), pp. 24, 25.

settlers. Some of the new settlers dared to challenge the successors, who lived mostly in the east, or the Indians, who were not considered stable and who remained in defiance of the landowners.

In Virginia the "headright" system granted fifty acres to each emigrant. A large portion of southwestern Pennsylvania was claimed by Virginia until 1780, and as many as one thousand land certificates were given to settlers. When an agreement was reached between the two states and the present western boundaries of Pennsylvania were established, each state recognized the land rights of the other. The period 1769 to 1774 was a time in which record numbers of immigrants rushed to occupy portions of southwestern Pennsylvania.

The matter of land purchase, rent, or lease was a factor in settling, but most settlers managed to cross over that hurdle. All settlers were looking for cheap land. The Commonwealth of Pennsylvania was active in land matters.

> The ownership of vacant lands, with the exception of manors and other private estates, passed from the Penns to the Commonwealth by the Divesting Act of 1779, and in 1784 when the Revolution was over, the land office was reopened. Quitrents were abolished and the amount of land that could be obtained on a single application was increased to 400 acres, but the price was raised to ten pounds for 100 acres. Settlers who had occupied vacant land were given the preemptive right to purchase but were required to pay interest on the value of the land from the date of settlement. By treaties of October, 1784, and January, 1785, the Indians gave up the remainder of their claims to land in Pennsylvania.[5]

Indian attacks were still a possibility in many areas, and this, combined with the fact that the price of land had risen to £30 for 100 acres, had a tendency to send a stream of immigrants through southwestern Pennsylvania to southern Ohio and Indiana, on into Kentucky, and later into the northern tier of territory south of Lake Erie.

In the early days much was made of settlements on waterways. References are made to rivers such as the Youghiogheny, the Monongahela, the Allegheny, and the Ohio, and also to creeks such as Cross Creek, Pigeon Creek, Peters Creek, Dunlap Creek, and Chartiers Creek. Waterways were essential for the settlers. The rivers and creeks provided for

5. Buck and Buck, *Planting of Civilization*, p. 146.

transportation and shipping. They were necessary in some instances for drinking water and for the trapping of small animals. They were used as maps or guidelines for travelers. Referring to early travelers who visited or came to the west to live, E. B. Welsh writes:

> McClure and Frisbie in 1772 followed up the Susquehanna, the Juniata and its Raystown Branch, then over the ridges beyond its headwaters, and down into the Ligonier Valley. Finley and McMillan on their first journeys were guided along the Potomac to its upper tributary streams, then over the watershed down to the Tygart or the Youghiogheny, and on to the Monongahela. With only the stars by night, and the moss on the trees by day to give directions, the flowing waters were their God-given guides.[6]

Another determining factor for settlement was the proximity of the intended home to a nearby fort, for example, Lindley's Fort in Washington County. Early accounts are replete with stories of a hasty run to the nearest fort.

Agriculture also played a role in the settlement process. As time, energy, and resources permitted, each family planned to clear large segments of land so that crops could be raised. Families were frequently large, and some of the produce was used or stored for later use. Some of the crops could be sold or exchanged for needed supplies or money. There was a military presence before and after the French and Indian War, and the troops often became a market for the crops that were raised.

Presbyterian Army Chaplains and Other Ministers Sent West

Army chaplains are mentioned in 1758, the same year in which the Synods of New York and Philadelphia were united. General John Forbes was in the west and about to move on Fort Duquesne (November 28). The French and Indians burned the fort and withdrew. This brought about the erection of Fort Pitt and a shift to Protestantism. Philadelphia Presbyterian leaders marked the change with a new emphasis on missions. Soon the Synod deputized army chaplains and ministers to survey the

6. McKinney, ed., *Presbyterian Valley,* p. 147. See also McMillan Journal, Part I, in Guthrie, *John McMillan,* p. 203.

situation in the west and to do everything possible to serve the early settlers and if possible to do work among the Indians. The change to a Protestant emphasis in the west was a clear signal to the Scots, Scotch-Irish, and English in the east, and to some still at home across the seas, to move westward. Presbyterians and other Protestants were poised in New Jersey, Delaware, and southeastern Pennsylvania to move out. McKinney states that "the year 1758 was the turning point in the developing history of Western Pennsylvania both from the religious and the political viewpoints."[7]

Among the Pennsylvania troops in the Forbes army was the Reverend Charles C. Beatty, who served as a chaplain in Colonel William Champlain's regiment. He is thought to have preached the first Protestant sermon at Fort Pitt. It was a Thanksgiving sermon. It can also be considered the first sermon by a Presbyterian minister in the west. The Reverend Hector Alison, a former moderator of the Presbytery of Philadelphia, was appointed by the new Synod of New York and Philadelphia to serve as chaplain at Fort Pitt. He is believed to have served at the fort in 1759 and 1760. Smith's *Old Redstone* says that the Reverend Alexander McDowell accompanied Hector Alison and that the chaplains petitioned the governor of Pennsylvania to "recover" the Indian captives in the west.[8] The trips from east to west took place during the summer months and took three to four months.

The Protestant emphasis in the west brought about a missionary emphasis in the new Synod. In 1762 a group recognized by the Synod as "The Corporation for Poor and Distressed Presbyterian Ministers" appointed several of its members to attend the next synod meeting with a plea "that some missionaries be sent to preach to the distressed frontier inhabitants, and to report their distresses, etc."[9] This request was acted upon and expense money allowed. The result was that the Reverend Messrs. Charles Beatty and John Brainerd were delegated to go as soon as possible. But there was an uprising on the frontier, referred to as Pontiac's War, and the trip of Beatty and Brainerd was postponed. When this Indian uprising was put down, thanks to Colonel Bouquet's victory at Bushy Run, the Synod

7. McKinney, ed., *Presbyterian Valley,* p. 9.

8. Joseph Smith, *Old Redstone, or Historical Sketches of Western Presbyterianism, Its Early Ministers, Its Perilous Times, and Its Early Records* (Philadelphia: Lippincott, Grambo & Co., 1854), p. 112.

9. Smith, *Old Redstone,* p. 113.

renewed its request (1766) that Beatty, now accompanied by George Duffield instead of Brainerd, carry out the previously scheduled mission.

They arrived at Fort Pitt in September and reported to the chaplain, Rev. Mr. McLagan, who arranged for room and board. The following year they reported back to the Synod that

> they found on the frontier numbers of people earnestly desirous of forming themselves into congregations . . . also they visited the Indians at the Chieftown of the Delaware nation, on the Muskingham, about 130 miles beyond Fort Pitt . . . that a considerable number of them waited on the preaching of the gospel with peculiar attention . . . that several other tribes of Indians around them were ready to join them in receiving the gospel.[10]

The Synod was pleased with this report and appointed Messrs. Brainerd and Cooper to spend at least three months among the frontier settlements and the Indians. This trip failed to materialize because of "discouraging circumstances."

In 1769 the Synod, eager but frustrated in its efforts to help out on the frontier, devised a new technique. It "ordered" the Presbytery of Donegal, the presbytery nearest to the frontier, to supply the west with ten sabbaths of ministerial service. This may or may not have been carried out, but it is known that the Reverend James Finley in 1771 met the Synod's request to supply sabbath services over the Alleghenies for two months. It is possible that he had visited the frontier settlers on previous trips. He may well have been the first Presbyterian minister, other than army chaplains, to cross the Alleghenies in the interest of the Christian gospel.

The minutes of Donegal Presbytery read that in April of 1773 a Mr. Ferrin was appointed to preach in Pittsburgh in November. During the next two years a series of men were given assignments in the west, including Pittsburgh. The Synod backed up its high resolve for missionary activity by granting Donegal Presbytery £15 for missionary expenses.[11]

About this time, David McClure and Levi Frisbee, Congregational graduates of Dartmouth College, were ordained and commissioned for service on the frontier. They were sent out to work among the Delaware

10. Smith, *Old Redstone,* p. 116.
11. G. S. Klett, *Presbyterians in Colonial Pennsylvania* (Philadelphia, 1937), pp. 78-79.

Indians on the Muskingum River in Ohio. Donegal Presbytery got in touch with them and authorized them to work in Presbyterian settlements. In 1773 they toiled among several congregations between Ligonier and Pittsburgh. Some settlers had not heard a sermon for fourteen years until these two ministers arrived.[12] The Presbytery of Donegal gave McClure and Frisbee a thorough examination in Presbyterian theology and received them as members. They were examined in the Larger and Shorter Catechisms and the Westminster Confession of Faith.[13] As ordained ministers in the Congregational Church they would have been familiar with these Presbyterian standards.

So it was that these two young ministers preached in and around Pittsburgh and among the Indian settlements to the west of Pittsburgh over a ten-month period — mostly along the Ohio River and its tributaries. Frisbee is reported to have had health problems and did not travel as much as his partner. He preached regularly at Pittsburgh and Long Run. McClure preached in many areas, including a five-point preaching field. Churches reached included Ligonier, Squirrel Hill, Jacob's Swamp, Proctor's Tent, Round Hill, and others, most of which have different names today. When Frisbee regained his strength, the two exchanged their fields of labor. Not long thereafter these two ministers, having finished what they believed was their planned tour of the frontier, reported to the Synod of New York and Philadelphia and returned to their native New England, where they continued in the ministry, never to return to the west.[14]

McClure wrote in his *Diary* during his stay on the frontier, "These people here in this new country are as sheep scattered upon the mountains without a shepherd. May the good Lord raise up and send forth faithful laborers into this part of His vineyard." Dr. McKinney adds this comment: "God heard their prayers. The answer came speedily in the arrival of the four men who made their permanent home in widely scattered parts of Western Pennsylvania and who petitioned the Synod to be permitted to organize themselves into the Presbytery of Redstone."[15]

12. Buck and Buck, *Planting of Civilization,* p. 104.
13. *Diary of David McClure,* ed. Franklin B. Dexter (New York: Knickerbocker Press, 1889), p. 112.
14. *Diary of David McClure,* p. 124; McKinney, ed., *Presbyterian Valley,* p. 12.
15. McKinney, ed., *Presbyterian Valley,* p. 13.

The Seven Presbyterian Ministers Who Came to Stay

John McMillan

John McMillan, the recognized leader of "the seven Presbyterian ministers who came to stay," was born in Faggs Manor, Pennsylvania, in 1752. His parents had come from County Antrim, Ireland, some ten years earlier and settled in southeastern Pennsylvania. John was educated in the Faggs Manor elementary school and had some training in the Log Cabin Academy presided over by John Blair, who had modeled the school after William Tennent's Log College (which Blair attended). McMillan went on to the Pequea Academy and studied under Robert Smith. Then it was on to the College of New Jersey (Princeton). After graduation he was encouraged to preach (do missionary work) in the settlements of Virginia. This preaching often led to a "call" to one of the churches.

John had a sister, Janet, and a brother, Thomas, who had gone out to western Pennsylvania. This led to an extension of his second missionary trip in Virginia on into southwestern Pennsylvania via "the Old National Trail" and up the Tygart Valley. He became interested in two churches, Chartiers and Pigeon Creek, and made a commitment to each of them. He was dismissed from the New Castle Presbytery to the Donegal Presbytery. Ordination followed on June 19, 1776, and he was married to Catherine Brown of Bradywine on August 6. It is thought that he made the promises to the Chartiers and Pigeon Creek Churches in the fall of 1775, with presbytery action to follow. After at least two trips over the mountains, he brought his wife and their firstborn child to his pastoral charge in 1778.

Parishioners gave assistance to McMillan as he built his log cabin home, barn, spring house, smoke house, shed, home furniture, etc. In addition to his preaching, he did tasks for presbytery and worked the land. In some twenty years he not only increased his holdings to one thousand acres, but he built a new and larger home. Catherine was left to raise and care for seven children. She is known to have housed and boarded students in the manse, and she did household work, gardened, and wove clothing, along with handling some church affairs. She died in 1819 after forty-three years of marriage.

McMillan's life and ministry had many facets, and in each of them he played a dominant role. He led the effort to establish Redstone, the first presbytery in the west, in 1781. In this he was assisted by Power,

John McMillan (1752-1833), who began to teach in his
Log College in the mid-1780s

Dod, and Smith. He was chosen as the presbytery's first moderator. In 1793 he gave up the work at Pigeon Creek because of the growth of the Chartiers church.

He labored as a teacher and trainer of theological students, and this may well have been his greatest glory. He built his own log cabin for the training of theological students. McMillan followed the examples of William Tennent, Robert and John Blair, and Robert Smith. About 1780 he set up a Latin and Greek school, having in mind the preparation of young men for the ministry. The term "seminary" was not in common use at that early date, but ingredients for such a school were there. It will be noted as we touch on Dod and Smith that they, too, had Latin and Greek schools. Some students transferred from school to school. In the 1780s the McMillan, Dod, and Smith schools operated in this way with respect to the training of theological students for the ministry.

In 1802 McMillan became professor of divinity in the newly established Jefferson College. Matthew Brown, the president, wrote of McMillan's theological efforts that "perhaps about one hundred ministers were trained, more or less, in his school of the prophets."[16] When the Presbyterian Church in 1822 planned the building of a "seminary in the west," the thought was to recognize and continue McMillan's work in Canonsburg, but large monetary and land grants by Allegheny Town on Pittsburgh's north side caused the seminary to be built there.[17]

McMillan did a great deal of presbytery work by preaching once a month in area settlements. This led to the establishment of at least a dozen churches, among them Bethel and Lebanon (1776). He was recognized politically as a dominant power in the west. He was a big man with a powerful voice. He had a rigid preaching style and a Jonathan Edwards type of message. He held to "the old ways," including the colonial type of clothes, and his humor was the Scotch-Irish brand. In 1794, during the Whiskey Insurrection, he withheld the Lord's Supper from those who opposed President Washington's excise laws. Politicians valued his friendship.

At his death in 1833, John McMillan was honored by the *Daily Pittsburgh Gazette* in these words: "The deceased was the Apostle of the Presbyterian Church in the west. The founder and father of her institutions in this section of the country."[18]

James Power

James Power was born in Nottingham in eastern Pennsylvania in 1746. He graduated from the College of New Jersey, and in 1772 he was licensed

16. Guthrie, *John McMillan,* p. 75.
17. Guthrie, *John McMillan,* pp. 74-76. See also pp. 133-34 below.
18. The 1992 General Assembly of the Presbyterian Church (U.S.A.) elected as its moderator a descendant of McMillan, the Reverend John McMillan Fife (Pittsburgh Seminary, class of 1967).

to preach by the New Castle Presbytery. He was of medium height, slender, erect, and neat in dress, and he possessed a distinct preaching style that featured a loud voice with clear and distinct enunciation. His memory was good, and he called all parishioners and friends by their names.

Power came over the Alleghenies in 1774, a year before McMillan, and spent three months in missionary work. His visits were in areas now known as Westmoreland, Allegheny, and Fayette counties. Two years after his first visit he returned to the west with his wife and four young daughters. He followed "Braddock's Trail." The husband and wife each rode a horse. Power had his oldest daughter ride behind him and the youngest on a pillow in front of him. The other two daughters rode in a hamper basket hung on the side of the lead horse.[19] One month after their arrival in the west a fifth daughter was born to Mrs. Power, the first child to be born in a manse in western Pennsylvania.

Power was the first of "the seven who came to stay" who settled his family in western Pennsylvania; the home was near Brownsville at Dunlap's Creek. He visited church groups at Laurel Hill, Mount Pleasant, Sewickley, Tyrone, and Unity regularly. The two churches that he served as pastor were Sewickley and Mount Pleasant in Westmoreland County. He surrendered the Sewickley church in 1787 due to the growth of the Mount Pleasant church. When Redstone Presbytery was established in 1781, he was one of the four organizers. He was then thirty-five years old.

Power, like McMillan, was a missionary pastor. He is referred to as the founder of several rural churches in Redstone Presbytery. He was something of a circuit rider, and once or twice he was reported killed by the Indians. Though thoroughly trained in theological studies, Power was the only one of the so-called "four horsemen" who is not referred to as having trained theological students. He confined his efforts to pastoral work, preaching, and missionary endeavors in the surrounding area. His health was not the best at all times, and this may have accounted for his desire to be on a horse and out of doors a great deal. He died in 1830 at the age of eighty-five, having given fifty-four years of preaching and pastoral work to the west.

19. Smith, *Old Redstone,* p. 225; Guthrie, *John McMillan,* pp. 48, 49.

Thaddeus Dod

The third of the Presbyterian clergymen who came to the west to stay was Thaddeus Dod. He was born in 1740 of English stock. His father's family were New England Puritans who settled in Connecticut in 1645. His parents migrated to New Jersey, and Dod was brought up in the hill town of Mendham. With specialized study in mathematics and Latin he may well have been the most scholarly of these pioneer preachers. As a young man he had a sense of sin that led him to search for salvation and inner security. Like McMillan, he entered the College of New Jersey, and he graduated a year after him, in 1773. He found the place stimulating, and by his thirty-third birthday he was looking forward to a career in the ministry. Soon after his graduation he married Phoebe Baldwin, and their home was in Patterson Creek, Virginia.

In 1775 he was licensed to preach by the New York Presbytery, and he is reported to have made his first visit to the west in that year. In 1777 he was in the west and thinking of staying. His first stops were Fort Lindley, Lower Ten Mile Creek, and Cook's Fort on the Upper Ten Mile Creek. About ten families from Dod's home area in New Jersey had come to the west around 1773 and had settled at Ten Mile Creek in south-western Washington County. These families are thought to have been a step higher on the cultural ladder than the average pioneer. Dod settled among them and organized the Upper and Lower Ten Mile Churches (ten miles from Washington and ten miles apart). Two respected elders, James Cook and Demas Lindley, had come from back east, and Dod was happy to have them and the others around him. The Indian problem had eased a little, and Dod's wife joined him in the west in 1778.

Thaddeus Dod was an excellent speaker. His keen mind made his sermons persuasive and attractive to his parishioners and especially to the young people. There were still occasional Indian raids, and there were times when his preaching services were changed because of them.

Dod's talents in Latin, Greek, the classics, and the natural sciences led him to build a Log Cabin Academy near his house. It is thought that this was done in 1782 at his farm on Lower Ten Mile Creek or at Amity. His son, Cephas Dod, wrote later that sleeping accommodations were made for students and that James Hughes, John Brice, Robert Marshall, Francis Dunlevy, David Smith, and David Lindley studied Latin there. The Dod school was discontinued in 1785, and some of the students listed above returned to the McMillan school where they had been earlier. Some students went to the newly opened school of Joseph Smith at Upper Buffalo.

In cooperation with McMillan and Smith, Dod opened what was chartered as the Washington Academy in 1787. Classes began in the upper room of the Washington Court House on April 1, 1789, and twenty or thirty students enrolled. Dod reluctantly agreed to serve as principal for one year, and he served an extra three months. Then David Johnston, his associate, took over. Dod had returned to his ministry at the two Ten Mile churches before fire destroyed the courthouse and caused the suspension of the Academy.

Thaddeus Dod was truly a great preacher and teacher. His untimely death in 1793 at the age of fifty-three ended a splendid ministry at both the Upper and Lower Ten Mile churches and brought to an end his excellent efforts in the field of education. Dod, McMillan, Smith, and Power were friends, but they were not intimate. Dod's stature as a preacher and educator may have drawn him a little apart from the others. He and McMillan exchanged students, supported each other in matters of education, had a joint ministry in an occasional serving of the Lord's Supper, and with Smith and Power founded Redstone Presbytery, the first presbytery west of the Allegheny Mountains.

Joseph Smith

Joseph Smith, sometimes referred to as "Hell-Fire" Smith, was another of the foursome that formed Redstone Presbytery and made their mark on Presbyterianism in southwestern Pennsylvania. He was the oldest of this group. He was born in Nottingham, Maryland, in 1736. He graduated from Princeton in 1764 and was licensed by the Presbytery of New Castle in 1767. He served a church or two in the east and then, at the recommendation of the presbytery, preached in the settlements before making up his mind to cross the mountains into western Pennsylvania. Following in the footsteps of McMillan, Power, and Dod, he accepted a joint call from the Buffalo and Cross Creek Churches in Washington County in 1779. He remained there until his death in 1792.

Smith joined with the other three in the formation of Redstone Presbytery in 1781. Probably around 1785 he opened a school in his wife's kitchen at Upper Buffalo and called it "The Study." Smith's son, also named Joseph Smith, stated in his *Old Redstone* that "this was the first movement [school] made for preparing young men for the ministry."[20] Messrs. McGready, Porter, and Patterson began study there, and James Hughes, John Brice, Robert Marshall, and John Hanna transferred from Dod's school to Smith's. Still later, Smith's school, by mutual agreement, became part of McMillan's school and then Canonsburg Academy in 1791.

Joseph Smith was a revival preacher, hence his nickname "Hell-Fire." His pattern was that of Jonathan Edwards and George Whitefield. He assisted other ministers in revival efforts. His strong voice and ability to use pathos in his sermons held his audiences in a state of rapture. Smith's son wrote of his father: "His voice was remarkable alike for the terrific and the pathetic and as Dr. Kirkland said of the celebrated Fisher Ames, 'Now like the thunder, and now like the music of heaven.'" Samuel Porter said of him, "I never met a man who could so completely unbar the gates of hell, and make me look so far down into the dark bottomless abyss."[21] He was a man of prayer and was often heard praying at night or at his church when no service was being held. His two sons became ministers, and his four daughters all married ministers.

Smith was tall, slender, and blonde. As a young man he had piercing eyes and was more than a little emotional. This temperament, along with his busy schedule of education and evangelism, drained his energies and may have contributed to his death at the age of fifty-six. He was the first of the western Pennsylvania "four horsemen" to ride triumphantly through the celestial gates of heaven.

James Dunlap

James Dunlap was born in Chester County, Pennsylvania, in 1744. He prepared for the ministry at Faggs Manor Academy and studied under Robert Smith at Pequea. He graduated from Princeton College in 1773 and then served for a time as a tutor in that school. He also had preparation for the ministry under James Finley at Nottingham. After finishing his theological training he was ordained by New Castle Presbytery in 1781. He may have known McMillan at Faggs Manor or Princeton, and perhaps he also knew of James Finley's trips to the west. These and other factors led him to go west. On October 15, 1782, after delays caused by travel

20. Smith, *Old Redstone,* p. 781.
21. Smith, *Old Redstone,* p. 66.

and Indian raids, the newly formed Redstone Presbytery met, and "the name of a fifth minister was added to the roll. The newcomer was Reverend James Dunlap, who had accepted a call to Dunlap's Creek and Laurel Hill, two churches in Fayette County."[22]

Dunlap has been referred to as "the fifth horseman" inasmuch as he was made the fifth member of the Redstone Presbytery. He had been a member of the presbytery for only a short time when he refused to take part in the ordination of a Mr. John Watson. He accused Watson of "unchristian conduct." There was a prolonged discussion, and Watson was rebuked by the moderator before they could continue. This was the presbytery's first action as a Court of Appeals.

Dunlap also began to teach a few young men who wished to become ministers. He was well qualified to teach languages and classical literature. The younger Joseph Smith said of him, "He was somewhat reclose in his habits, of amiable, cheerful spirit, but inclined to despondency. His person was small, his features pleasing and his manners popular. His health was not very robust, but his conscientious diligence in the discharge of his duties secured him the respect and affection of the trustees and students."[23] In 1789 he gave up his work as pastor of the Dunlap's Creek Church to give full time to the Laurel Hill Church.

After Jefferson College was chartered on January 15, 1802, Dunlap was elected a member of the Board of Trustees. Following the sudden death of the college's first principal, John Watson, the Board elected Dunlap as president in the spring of 1803. The presbytery permitted him to serve also as pastor of the Miller's Run Church, which was not far from the college. For a time he was a member of the newly formed Presbytery of Ohio, but later he returned to Redstone Presbytery. The history of Jefferson College gives many details of Dunlap's tenure and problems as principal or president. His health became a problem, and he retired as college head in 1811. Later he went to Abingdon, near Philadelphia, where his son, the Reverend William Dunlap, resided. He died there in 1818 at the age of seventy-five years.

22. W. W. McKinney, *Early Pittsburgh Presbyterianism, 1758-1839* (Pittsburgh: Gibson Press, 1938), p. 54.

23. Smith, *The History of Jefferson College, Including an Account of Early Log Cabin Schools and the Canonsburg Academy* (Pittsburgh, 1857), p. 67.

James Finley

James Finley was born in County Armagh in the province of Ulster, Ireland, in 1725 to pious parents of Scottish descent. James was brought to America at the age of nine. He began his education under the direction of Samuel Blair at Faggs Manor Academy. At the age of fifteen Finley had a revival experience under the Reverend Robert Smith. His interest in revivals led to the special experience of traveling some 200 miles in company with the great evangelist George Whitefield.

Finley was ordained by the Presbytery of New Castle in 1752 and installed pastor of the East Nottingham Church. He had the fiery zeal of a missionary and had many characteristics of his brother Samuel, who was called to be president of Princeton. In 1782, at the same meeting of Redstone Presbytery that accepted James Dunlap, Finley accepted a call from the united congregations at the Forks of the Youghiogheny for his pastoral services. He was now about to settle down in a place he had visited before, for, strange as it may seem, Finley had made three or four trips to the west in earlier years, possibly as early as 1765 as an army chaplain.

In 1771 the Synod of Philadelphia commissioned him to supply sabbath services over the Allegheny Mountains for two months. In 1772 he came west with his fourteen-year-old son, Ebenezer, to place him on a farm he had purchased in Fayette County near Dunlap's Creek.[24] As noted earlier, this gives Finley the honor of being the first Presbyterian minister, other than army chaplains, to cross the Allegheny Mountains.

These trips back and forth from East Nottingham seem to indicate that Finley was a restless person. He exuded energy and was mission minded. Dr. Welsh refers to these trips as a "busman's holiday."[25] Finley appears to have given spiritual life to the Forks of the Youghiogheny, churches now known as Round Hill and Rehoboth. In addition to these endeavors he preached in many settlements in southwestern Pennsylvania. Though his pastorates at Round Hill and Rehoboth began in 1782, it was not until 1785 that the details of his transfer to Redstone Presbytery were finalized. Finley was one of "the honored seven," all graduates of Princeton College, who carried the responsibility of spreading Christianity and Presbyterianism throughout the expanses of the west. This they did in

24. Smith, *Old Redstone,* p. 284.
25. McKinney, ed., *Presbyterian Valley,* p. 149.

their own way, so very successfully that the whole area was soon called their "Western Zion."[26] Finley died in 1795 at the age of seventy. He left a bequest to Canonsburg Academy, which became Jefferson College.

John Clark

John Clark was born about 1718 somewhere in New Jersey. He and his wife Margaret spent most of their lives in Maryland and had no children. They had taken a Welsh boy, William Jones, into their home, and he accompanied them on a trip to the west in 1781. He grew up in the manse and became a minister. In 1776 John McMillan had organized the eastern and western areas of Peter's Creek into church groups that were known as the Bethel and Lebanon Churches. Clark, though no longer young, appeared quite active when he arrived in the west and immediately took over the responsibility of these two churches. In New Jersey and Maryland he had been the spiritual leader of churches in which the tides of New Side had ebbed and flowed. "His mind and spirit had also been fed from Whitefield's ministry."[27] He wore a long white beard and was soon dubbed "Father Clark." He was also referred to as the "Nestor" (the oldest and wisest man) of the Presbytery of Redstone.

When Washington Academy was organized in 1787, John Clark was one of the original trustees. Joseph Smith tells of an "extensive revival of religion" at the Bethel and Lebanon Churches under Clark's leadership in the same year.[28] The next year he gave up his work at the Lebanon Church to give all of his time to Bethel. In 1793, with McMillan, Patterson, Hughes, and Brice, he formed the Ohio Presbytery because of the increasing number of ministers west of the Monongahela River to the Ohio River.

Time was running out for Clark, but he would yet be involved in one notable event, the Whiskey Insurrection of 1794.[29] Clark's church at Bethel was right in the midst of things, and even though he was an old man he made an impassioned plea to prevent violence and bloodshed.

26. McKinney, ed., *Presbyterian Valley,* p. 16.
27. McKinney, ed., *Presbyterian Valley,* p. 67. On the Old Side/New Side controversy, see pp. 8, 9, 124, 125, 160, and 161 in *Presbyterian Valley;* see also pp. 66-67 below.
28. *Old Redstone,* p. 301.
29. See further details below, pp. 60-61.

Years of experience had taught him that this type of action was wrong and could only lead to disaster. Almost literally Clark stood in the path of the insurgent army, gathered on July 17 at Couch's Fort. Because Clark was grave, sedate, wise, and venerable, he may well have been the one who defused this dangerous situation. Certainly Clark, McMillan, and others worked in their churches to quell this uprising and called on their people to vote "aye" for submission to federal laws and acceptance of amnesty. The Presbyterian ministers and churches were largely responsible for the successful settlement of this issue.

John Clark lived until 1797, but at the age of seventy-nine his very feeble health brought about his death. His library and money for an education were left for the boy he had raised, William Jones. Others like Dunlap, Power, and McMillan were to carry on the magnificent work of these "seven ministers who had come to the west to stay." The foundations of Presbyterianism in the west had been firmly laid.

The First Presbytery in the West and Subdivisions That Followed

The town of New Castle on the Delaware River had become sufficiently prominent to have its name used for a presbytery. This presbytery expanded in a few years, and in 1732 its western part (Lancaster and Dauphin Counties) was set apart as a separate presbytery called Donegal. Soon the western boundary of this new presbytery was thought to be "the setting sun." McMillan, Smith, and Power were "sons" of the New Castle Presbytery, and they, with Dod, served as missionaries of Donegal Presbytery. It was difficult for these ministers to attend presbytery meetings, however; hence the four of them petitioned the Synod of New York and Philadelphia to establish a presbytery west of the Laurel Ridge to be known as Redstone Presbytery. The request was granted, and the first meeting of the new presbytery was held at the Pigeon Creek Church on September 19, 1781. This presbytery, like Donegal Presbytery earlier, reached westward toward "the setting sun." The northern and southern boundaries of the presbytery were yet to be established.

The word "redstone" was known throughout southwestern Pennsylvania because of the burnt-out surface coal that had a reddish appearance and that could be found near waterways. The name attached to "Redstone

Old Fort" near Brownsville and to Redstone Creek. The Synod designated the Laurel Hill Church as the first meeting place of the new presbytery, but reports of Indian raids in that area changed the meeting place to the Pigeon Creek Church. Ministers present were John McMillan, James Power, and Thaddeus Dod (Joseph Smith was unable to attend). The elders were John Neil, Demas Lindley, and Patrick Scott. Dod preached the sermon from Job 42:5-6. McMillan was chosen to be moderator and Power to be clerk. Muddy Creek and South Fork requested ministers from both Redstone and Donegal Presbyteries. Presbytery adjourned to meet again the next morning. Another regular meeting was scheduled for October 25, 1782. An earlier meeting of the presbytery before that date was prevented by Indian threats. Presbytery met in 1782 as planned at Dunlap's Creek. Ministers Smith, McMillan, and Power were present, with Dod absent. Elders James Edgar, John McDowell, and Moses Latta were also present. Smith preached a sermon from Proverbs 8:4. Power was chosen to be moderator and McMillan to be clerk. Smith's reasons for missing the 1781 meeting were accepted, and presbytery received the Reverend Mr. Dunlap of New Castle to serve the Dunlap's Creek and Laurel Hills churches and the Reverend James Finley to serve churches at the Forks of the Youghiogheny.

Early Subdivision of Redstone Presbytery

In 1793 Redstone Presbytery had grown from four to twelve ministers. A recommendation for a subdivision was made, and the Synod approved the dividing line to be along the Monongahela River, the Ohio River, and areas west of the Allegheny River. The new name was to be the Ohio Presbytery. There were five original ministers: John McMillan, John Clark, Joseph Patterson, James Hughes, and John Brice.[30] The first meeting was to be held at Upper Buffalo, in Washington County, October 23, 1793.

McMillan was the only one of the five who had been an original member of the Redstone Presbytery. He was about to give up Pigeon Creek and serve full-time at his Chartiers Church. Clark was seventy-five years old and about to give up his work at the Lebanon Church to serve full-time at the Bethel Church. Patterson had studied under Joseph Smith at the Buffalo Church and began to serve the united congregation of Raccoon and Montour's Run. Hughes had also studied under Smith and

30. Minutes of the Ohio Presbytery, vol. 1, p. 1.

was now installed in the Lower Buffalo Church in Washington County and the Short Creek Church (now in West Virginia). John Brice had been installed as pastor of the Three Ridges Church, West Alexandria, and the Forks of Wheeling Church (West Virginia).[31]

The Presbyteries of Redstone and Ohio in 1801 asked the Synod of Virginia for still further subdivision. The minutes read as follows: "At the united request of all the members present from the Presbyteries of Redstone and Ohio, the Synod [of Virginia] did, and do hereby establish a presbytery to consist of the Reverend Messrs. Thomas Hughes, William Wick, Samuel Tate, Joseph Stockton, and Robert Lee, including in their bounds all the churches north and northwest of the Ohio and the Allegheny River, to the place where the Ohio River crosses the western boundary of Pennsylvania and to be known by the name of the Presbytery of Erie."[32]

The very next year, 1802, the General Assembly declared that the Presbyteries of Redstone, Ohio, and Erie would become the Synod of Pittsburgh. At this time, the Ohio Presbytery included the churches of St. Clairsville, Crab Apple, Steubenville, and Two Ridges in what was to become the state of Ohio. Erie Presbytery had the Youngstown and Mount Pleasant churches (Beaver County), also to be included in the state of Ohio. In 1808 Erie Presbytery numbered sixty-five churches and nineteen ministers. Hartford Presbytery was then separated from it, and in 1814 the Grand River Presbytery was carved out of it. In Pennsylvania the Presbytery of Washington was established in 1819, Butler in 1820, and Blairsville in 1830. Other divisions followed, especially to the west. A period of rapid expansion among presbyteries took place in western Pennsylvania and Ohio in the early 1800s.[33]

31. McKinney, ed., *Presbyterian Valley,* pp. 21-23.
32. The Records of the Synod of Virginia, vol. 2, p. 74, and noted in McKinney, ed., *Presbyterian Valley,* pp. 20, 29, 148.
33. McKinney, ed., *Presbyterian Valley,* pp. 153-56.

Concerns

The Indians

Several tribes of Indians were in or near areas occupied by the settlers. There were the Delaware, the Shawnee, the Mound Builders, the Iroquois, the Ottawa, and the Senecas. Whole tribes were not the problem so much as were small groups or bands out of a tribe or tribes. These groups would go off on raids among the white settlers. The period before the defeat of the French and Indians and the erection of Fort Pitt was a difficult time; marauding Indians harassed the whole area of white settlers. Immediately before and after the fall of Fort Duquesne (1758) the French were thought to have encouraged Indian attacks on the English settlers. Before the purchase of the land from the Indians in 1758 the frontier had receded eastward to the vicinity of March Creek.[34] In the period 1758 to 1764 the famous chief of the Ottawa Indians entered into what has been called "the conspiracy of Pontiac," threatening to destroy all English forts and the undefended settlements. Eight of the twelve forts were destroyed, but thanks to Colonel Bouquet the Indians were dealt a decisive defeat at Bushy Run (August 15, 1763), and the defenses at Fort Pitt were bolstered. The next year Bouquet, with 1,500 men, attacked the main Indian villages along the Muskingum River and forced a peace.

From 1760 to 1794, however, the Presbyterian settlers in south-western Pennsylvania were constantly on the alert for Indian raids. Cattle were stolen, crops were destroyed, barns were burned, and individuals and even whole families were massacred. John McMillan wrote in his journal that Indian raids prevented him from moving his family "to my congregation until November, 1778."[35] In 1782 the wife of a Baptist minister, Rev. John Corbly, and three of his five children were killed. In 1783 a messenger interrupted a sermon by Thaddeus Dod at Caleb Lindley's house and reported that the Indians had just murdered a family named Heath.

The first meeting of Redstone Presbytery (1781) and two later meetings were delayed because of troubles with Indians. "The summer of '82 was a sorrowful summer on frontier inhabitants."[36] The county

34. Klett, *Presbyterians in Colonial Pennsylvania,* p. 74.
35. Guthrie, *John McMillan,* Appendix C.
36. Smith, *Old Redstone,* p. 240.

seat town of Hannastown "was completely burned by Guyasuta and his relentless warriors on July 13." James Power was preaching nearby at Unity, and his family thought that he had been killed, but he escaped.[37] In 1792 the Synod of Virginia cited trouble with the Indians as the reason for delaying the establishment of an institution of learning in Washington County, Pennsylvania.[38] It was not until General Anthony's victory at the Battle of Fallen Tribes (August 20, 1794) that the entire frontier felt safe from Indian raids. These Indian troubles were, however, only a small part of the miseries that the Presbyterian settlers of southwestern Pennsylvania experienced in the second half of the eighteenth century.

Homes and Home-Life Routine

Many of the early settlers who came to western Pennsylvania lived with relatives and friends for a short time until a dwelling of some kind could be erected. They had discussed matters with friends back east, and for the most part they knew what to expect. In the early days, needed supplies such as salt, nails, iron, etc., could be procured en route in towns such as Chambersburg or Hagerstown. By the late 1800s supply stores had sprung up at various places along the traveled pathways from east to west. Horses were a necessity, and they could carry loads of up to two hundred pounds each.

Once the destination had been reached and a home site selected, neighbors for several miles around would be contacted to work on a given day. Men called "choppers" would fell trees of a proper size and cut them into the desired lengths. The plan was to build a log cabin house. The log house idea is thought to have originated in the Scandinavian countries, the Swedish settlers bringing it to the Delaware Valley. Once the logs were cut, a team of horses would haul them to the designated place. Log would be placed on log, the corners would be properly connected, and the open spaces between the logs would be filled with a clay substance. A "straight grained tree" would be found so that clapboard could be made for the roof. All of this would take a full day, and often a second or third day would be given to finishing up such things as a clapboard table with round legs, a three-legged stool, or two clapboard shelves held up by wooden pins fitted into auger holes in the logs. If no pewter dishes had been

37. See McKinney, ed., *Presbyterian Valley,* p. 14.
38. Guthrie, *John McMillan,* p. 93.

brought, wooden bowls would be made. In a letter to James Carnahan, president of Princeton University (1832), John McMillan gave an account of the building of his home.[39]

McMillan himself was big and strong. He would have had some help, but the larger part of the building he would have done himself. Each family aimed to get ahead, to improve, to add to the house, and to add other structures. Every effort would be made to have a horse or horses, a cow or cows, and chickens. Crops were planted as soon as possible. If corn, wheat, or other crops were raised, they could be stored or exchanged for needed supplies. Homes were built near a creek or another source of running water. Some settlers set traps and shot deer, pheasants, and other wildlife to add to their food supply. The average man was a good farmer and assisted with the garden near the home. The wife kept the home in order, prepared meals, did some work in the garden, knitted or wove clothing, and helped here and there as time and energy permitted. She was often the mother of several children, who needed attention and care. In time sons and daughters could help around the house, in the garden, in the field, or wherever needed.

Some settlers looked forward to the time when they could have a new home with a stone foundation and perhaps log walls that were skillfully fitted together, especially at the corners. It would be a two-story structure with three or four bedrooms. It would be composed of different types of wood, with rafters of oak, floorboards of cherry an inch thick, black walnut trimming, and hand-worked molding. The filling between the logs would be carefully prepared, perhaps with small stones and mud. In time this log house might be covered with weatherboard sheathing, which added both decoration and insulation.

Land was cheap, and through frugal procedures money could be saved and more acres bought. The next step was to have a helper on the land and to have a servant, or perhaps a slave, to help in the house and to be considered a part of the household. If guests came for dinner, nothing out of the ordinary took place. The bill of fare might be "potatoes boiled in their jackets . . . pumpkins stewed and prepared with milk, lamb's quarter, greens gathered in the pasture in front of the door, with great bowls of fresh milk, cool and nice from the spring house at the foot of the hill. This was the entire meal; plenty of everything, and everything of the best . . . no apology was offered."[40]

---

39. The text of this letter can be found in Guthrie, *John McMillan*, p. 38.
40. Guthrie, *John McMillan*, p. 39.

Transportation

Consideration of transportation in western Pennsylvania must begin with the Indians. The fact that Indians lived in different areas, traveled from one Indian nation to another, did a great deal of hunting, and were by nature something of a restless people meant that they carved out trails and pathways in the vast wilderness. They used canoes and found shallow crossing places along the rivers. It was common for them to carry their canoes from one stream to another. They seldom put markers along the trails since these trails were a way of life for them and were "worn deep by innumerable footsteps that could easily be followed."[41]

The first white men who came west were traders. They carried trinkets and necessities, useful and attractive articles that might be traded for Indian furs, which would bring large sums at trading posts and back east. These traders were happy to follow the Indian footpaths. Some traders possessed horses; they not only rode themselves but also led packhorses. When the soldiers came in the 1750s, "packhorse trains" became the normal means of getting supplies from one campsite to another. These packhorse trains might consist of twelve or more horses, with one soldier leading or directing the train and another bringing up the rear. The average load for each horse was about two hundred pounds, loaded onto cleverly constructed wooden pack saddles.

There were short expanses in eastern Pennsylvania and Virginia where roads extended for a few miles westward. This meant that wagons could be used on the initial part of the journey. The movement of French and British troops soon caused these roads to be widened and extended a few miles here and there.

> The first road that opened into western Pennsylvania was used by the Ohio Company from the Potomac at Wills Creek (Cumberland) to the Youghiogheny, probably 1752, but it is doubtful if wagons were used on it before the French opened their portage road of 15 miles from Presque Isle to LeBoeuf in 1753. The Ohio Company's road was improved and extended to Gist's Plantation west of Chestnut Ridge by Washington in 1754 and wagons and can[n]on were drawn over it.[42]

41. Buck and Buck, *Planting of Civilization,* pp. 229, 230.
42. Buck and Buck, *Planting of Civilization,* pp. 231, 232.

Pennsylvania's legislature authorized a lottery in 1754 for building roads from Philadelphia westward toward Pittsburgh. Other monies were authorized by the legislature from time to time. John McMillan's first trip west (1775) began in Virginia; he traveled over trails and paths but not on any roads. McMillan's journal mentions what is now called "Natural Bridge." The journey led through mountainous country. Places mentioned include Warm Spring Mountain, Green Brier Mountain, the Allegheny Mountains, Elk Mountain, and Cheat Mountain. This brought him to the head of the Tygart valley and on into southwestern Pennsylvania.

The other way (from east to west) lay westward from Philadelphia via James Burd's Road, through Shippensburg to Bedford and over the Raystown Path to Fort Ligonier. General Forbes's troops opened much of this road. By 1759 the entire road from Philadelphia to Pittsburgh was laid out, but it was only in the beginning stages of development.

The settlers in the west kept one or more horses, if possible, and used them for farm labor and transportation to nearby farmhouses, to town, to meetings, to church, and for other trips. Roadways in and around communities and from one community to another soon developed, and wagons and buggies were used, but for years the main method of transportation was the horse and saddle.

Politics

The people of western Pennsylvania in the eighteenth century patterned their politics after the people who had settled east of them in the western parts of the Atlantic seaboard colonies. Easterners were traditionally conservative. Many of them were Quakers, Germans, or others who had recently arrived from their mother country. It was natural and to their advantage to hold onto the past. Their counterparts farther to the west had a democratic outlook. In the west there was (or seemed to be) a whole new world of problems, and a break with the past — or the east — seemed more desirable than holding onto the things of the past.

Once the counties of Allegheny, Washington, Fayette, Westmoreland, and Bedford were a part of the Commonwealth, the pendulum of assistance or control was more favorable to the west. In 1790 around 13,000 white families occupied these five counties. The leading politicians were Hugh Brackenridge, John Neville, and Thomas Scott (Allegheny County), William Findley (Westmoreland), John Smilie and Albert Gallatin (Fayette), and James Ross (Washington). These men wrestled with problems such as whether or not to have a strong central government, whether or not to adopt a proposed "Constitution," and whether or not to have an "ultra-democratic state constitution."

One hectic political situation thrust upon the frontiersmen of western Pennsylvania was the Whiskey Rebellion previously mentioned. In 1791 the government in Washington enacted an excise tax on spirits — that is, on whiskey. Many of the settlers had their own stills and made whiskey for their own consumption and for export to the east for profit. It was not altogether the money paid as a "whiskey tax" that was resented; rather, it was largely the idea of "taxation without representation" reminiscent of the Boston Tea Party. Many of the people in southwestern Pennsylvania became involved on one side or the other. The tax was difficult to enforce, and one or two inspectors had been "tarred and feathered." It has been said that the 1793 war between France and England stirred up the idea of democracy and led to the establishment of two democratic societies in Washington (Pennsylvania) and Mingo Creek.

Some warrants were served on violators without fanfare, but there was trouble in 1794 when General John Neville, an inspector, accompanied by a U.S. marshall, served a warrant on a farmer at the Mingo Creek settlement. "Shots were fired by a group of drunken harvest hands, and the Marshall and Inspector Neville were forced to flee. The next morning, forty or fifty men surrounded General Neville's house, Bower Hill, intending to seize and destroy the writs. Neville had fled, but the insurgents demanded his resignation as inspector."[43] A small army of five hundred men then gathered around Neville's house, and shots were fired by the insurgents. Soldiers had been brought in from Pittsburgh; those on duty returned the gunfire, and a skirmish ensued. James McFarlane, an assailant leader, was mortally wounded, and Neville's house was burned. Politicians Findley, Smilie, Gallatin, and Brackenridge did what they could to quiet the radicals.

Word was sent to President Washington, and he sent commissioners to the mouth of the Youghiogheny to read a proclamation that the U.S. militia had been called out to deal with the insurgents. Stormy meetings were held, and it was determined that a popular referendum be held. September 11, 1794, was set for a vote on submission to federal laws,

43. Buck and Buck, *Planting of Civilization,* p. 469; see this source for additional details.

the acceptance of amnesty, and the signing of a promise to submit to the laws of the United States. John McMillan was in the forefront of settling this serious problem. His former charge at Pigeon Creek was partly in the Mingo Creek area where the rebellion began, and some of his people were in need of amnesty. At his Chartiers Church, McMillan postponed the communion service until after the September 11th voting date, "purposing to refuse the sacrament to those who had not signed the agreement to follow the law." He also went to the polling place on September 11th and stood there as a witness to what he believed was right for his country. At the end of the day the vote was in the affirmative. The Synod of Virginia, the controlling church body at that time, set apart November 2, 1794, as a special day of fasting and prayer to confess the sins of the people and the land "because of the late very sinful and unconstitutional opposition which had taken place to some of the laws of the United States."[44] Politics could be difficult in the 1790s, as in any period of our land, but they could also give opportunities to choose new directions and new ways of doing things.

Education and Theological Training

The Earliest Stages of Education in the West

When the earliest settlers came to western Pennsylvania, they carried the seeds of education with them. Wherever they came from, these individuals had advanced to different levels of reading, spelling, writing, and other stages of education. Not many, aside from lawyers, ministers, and newspaper people, had much education. Families were, however, concerned about educating their children, and parents did what they could to bring this to pass. Where it was possible, a tutor would be hired and sometimes would be shared with the children of neighbors. The so-called wealthy families had a decided advantage in bringing in tutors.

The clear-cut path to an education was either the home or the "school," which was generally established by a minister who had moved into the area. Soon places like Pittsburgh had "school masters" and "school mistresses" who taught children for a fee. These teachers came

44. For these and other details, see Guthrie, *John McMillan,* pp. 162, 163.

from the homes of lawyers, physicians, ministers, editors, retired army officers, and other professional people. An important motivation for securing an education was to be able to read and better understand the Scriptures.

Schools Established by Ministers

We have already touched on ministers "who came to stay." At least three of these seven ministers established schools, and the others, to be sure, gave a helping hand here and there. The three ministers and their schools, in addition to teaching basic knowledge, had an eye turned toward training young men to become ministers.

John McMillan was the first of this group to conduct a school of education of this kind. We have noted the precedents. A "Log Cabin School" had been established by the Reverend William Tennent at Neshamminy near Philadelphia in 1726. Samuel Blair, a student of Tennent, started a similar school at Faggs Manor just west of Philadelphia in 1739. Robert Smith established a similar school at Pequea, nearby, in 1750. McMillan had attended the Faggs Manor and Pequea schools, and in setting up his school in the west he was following the advice of Robert Smith, his teacher.

The Log Colleges in eastern Pennsylvania served well and were sources of learning, influence, and usefulness to many young men. McMillan taught first in his home at Chartiers, near Canonsburg, and then in his Log Cabin School around 1780. His first school, along with books and other equipment, burned.[45] New books were brought in from the east, and a new log cabin school was built near his home.

There has been dispute among the descendants and followers of McMillan, Dod, and Smith as to which school preceded the others. It is generally agreed that McMillan's school was first, but a second dispute centers around what was taught in the schools. Joseph Smith's grandson contends in his History of Jefferson College that the honor of establishing the first Latin School (a school that trained young men for the ministry) should go to his grandfather. However, McMillan says in an account of his life's activities written in March of 1832 to Dr. Carnahan, President of the College of New Jersey, that soon after he settled at Chartiers he

45. For this and other details, see Guthrie, John McMillan, pp. 83, 84.

followed the advice of Robert Smith of Pequea and "collected a few who gave evidence of piety and taught them the Latin and Greek languages. Some of these became useful, and others eminent ministers of the Gospel."[46] There is abundant evidence that McMillan's school was indeed a Latin School, a classical and theological school.

The next phase in McMillan's interest in education was his participation in establishing academies. He was contacted by the Reverend Samuel Barr, pastor of Pittsburgh's First Presbyterian Church, and by Hugh Brackenridge of the State Legislature to sit as a trustee of the proposed Pittsburgh Academy, chartered February 29, 1787. In the same year, McMillan, along with Judge James Allison and John McDowell, was instrumental in getting Washington Academy chartered on September 24, 1787. As previously noted, this academy started classes in Washington Courthouse in 1789 with Thaddeus Dod as teacher and principal.

When the courthouse burned down within a year, there was lethargy about reestablishing the Washington Academy, so Colonel Canon, Judge Allison, John McDowell, and McMillan proceeded to establish an academy in Canonsburg. Colonel Canon offered land, and in July 1791 the decision was made to build the academy, with classes to start that fall. The charter came in 1794, and McMillan was named the honorary president in 1798. In 1800 McMillan, Allison, Cook, and Ritchie drafted a petition to the legislature to make the academy a college. The charter came on January 15, 1802, and the Canonsburg Academy became Jefferson College. McMillan was elected the first president, but he resigned and asked to serve instead as professor of divinity. The success at Canonsburg led to action that revived Washington Academy in 1793 and caused it to be set apart in 1806 as Washington College, with Matthew W. Brown as the first president. These two colleges became rivals and served separately until 1865, when they were finally united as Washington and Jefferson College.

Theological Training Schools

As we have noted, in addition to their preaching and pastoral work, McMillan, Smith, and Dod felt inclined to give attention to teaching and training young men who might someday be ministers of the gospel. We

---

46. The letter is quoted in full in Guthrie, *John McMillan,* pp. 274, 275.

have mentioned their teaching and theological emphases and their attempts to provide training for those who were planning to become ministers. Smith, Dod, and McMillan each provided some theological training for students.

Records show that Joseph Patterson was ordained in April 1789, John Brice in 1790, and James Hughes in 1791. It is believed that each of these men had some training under McMillan, Smith, and Dod.[47] Very little emphasis was placed upon the particular theological training school that each attended. The high point for these men was to be taken under the care of the presbytery, which included examination in Latin, Greek, metaphysics, logic, and natural theology. There was also a paper or thesis to be prepared and presented at a presbytery meeting and accepted by a presbytery committee. Brice is recorded to have preached four sermons before presbytery and to have passed further examinations in philosophy and systematic theology. It is hard to believe that the Presbyterians of "the old country" or those back east were more demanding of their licentiates seeking ordination than were those in southwestern Pennsylvania.

The founding of Jefferson Academy in 1791 established the first embryo theological seminary in the west. Redstone Presbytery was under the supervision of the Synod of Virginia, and in September of 1791 the Synod designated Washington County as the location of one of two centers of learning. It was to be "under the care of the Rev. John McMillan."[48] A year later the Synod designated Canonsburg as that "center of learning in Washington County." This academy flourished, and men in "Divinity, Law, and Medicine" received training there. When the Pennsylvania Legislature granted a charter to Jefferson College in 1802, Dr. McMillan, as professor of divinity, carried on his training of young men for the ministry. He did more than any of his colleagues to lay a foundation for a theological seminary in the west. His work in his Log Cabin School, in the Canonsburg Academy, and at Jefferson College had much to do with theological education. Matthew Brown, a president of Jefferson College, wrote about McMillan: "Perhaps about one hundred ministers were trained, more or less, in his school of the prophets; many of whom were eminently useful."[49] S. J. M. Eaton, in his history of Erie Presbytery, says

47. Details are given in Guthrie, *John McMillan,* pp. 107-17.
48. Minutes of the Synod of Virginia, vol. 1, p. 79.
49. Smith, *Old Redstone,* p. 209.

that in the first twenty years of Erie Presbytery, twenty-eight ministers were enrolled, and "no less than 18" studied at Dr. McMillan's log cabin.[50]

Much of this background lays the foundation for the official establishment of a seminary in the west by the General Assembly of the Presbyterian Church. The church fathers had long accepted both the idea that Princeton Theological Seminary was too far to the east and the fact that the Presbyterians in the west were ordaining young men to the ministry. Hence, why not have a counterpart to Princeton Seminary in the west? The Synod of Pittsburgh took action in 1821 with these words: "Resolved That a Theological School for the above purposes, be established by the Synod, the present site of which [is] to be at Jefferson College."[51] The plan was thus to build on McMillan's work, begun at his Log Cabin School and continued at Canonsburg Academy and Jefferson College.

A board of thirteen was chosen for the Western Theological Seminary of the Presbyterian Church. It was announced that they would receive bids from any town that wished the seminary to be built in it. Alleghenytown (across the river from Pittsburgh) promised $21,000 and eighteen acres of land worth $20,000, and this was considered the best of thirteen bids. Though the Western Theological Seminary was built in Alleghenytown and not in Canonsburg, all leaders of the church and others knew that John McMillan played a leading role in laying its foundation.[52]

Religious Attitudes in the Early American Church

The religious beliefs of the regular Presbyterians in New Jersey and eastern Pennsylvania in early colonial days conformed somewhat to those known and followed in the land of their birth. The tendency, however, was to become independent of Scotland and the "old country." Because a great many colonists who became "westerners" lived for some time in the east before moving west, they became indoctrinated in eastern religious thinking. Once an individual was a western settler, psychological factors there

50. Eaton, *History of the Presbytery of Erie, with Biographical Sketches of All Its Ministers and Historical Sketches of Its Churches* (New York: Hurd & Houghton, 1868).

51. For this and other documentation, see Guthrie, *John McMillan,* pp. 74-76.

52. G. J. Slosser, ed., *They Seek a Country* (New York: Macmillan, 1955), p. 307, gives 1785 as the founding date of Western Seminary.

tended to make him or her more religious or church-minded. Among these factors were dangers of several kinds, including the the Indians, the isolation of living often a mile or more from the nearest neighbor, and the associated element of loneliness. The church became the centerpiece in the struggle to face up to the realities of life.

The majority of the western Presbyterian churches had a Sunday morning service of singing, prayer, Scripture reading that addressed the needs of the parishioners, and pulpit preaching. The abilities and the style of the preacher had a major effect on the Sunday service.

In the early decades of the eighteenth century a movement developed back east that in time moved west onto the frontier. It started in New Jersey under the preaching of Theodore J. Frelinghuysen, who came to America in 1720. He was a German of pietistic beliefs, and he became the pastor of four Dutch Reformed churches in the Raritan Valley. Some people had little desire for his kind of preaching. "The last thing that they wanted was to have a religion that would stir the emotions and set up high standards of personal conduct."[53] The so-called rich people were the most unhappy, but the poor and the young were enthusiastic. Controversy developed and divisions took place among the Dutch churches.

Frelinghuysen's religious emphasis and revivalistic approach to religion reached over into the Scotch-Irish, more particularly among the graduates of William Tennent's Log College. A number of young men were trained for the ministry at this school, including several sons of Tennent. One of these sons was Gilbert Tennent, who fell under the influence of this revivalistic type of preaching. Soon five evangelical Presbyterian ministers founded the New Brunswick Presbytery. This style of religion received a boost from George Whitefield, who arrived from England in 1739 and had phenomenal success in winning souls to Jesus Christ. Several years after Frelinghuysen began his preaching, Jonathan Edwards began his revivalistic type of preaching in New England. This heightened evangelical emphasis in time found its way through Samuel and John Blair, Robert Smith, and others of the "log college" vintage to the Presbyterians in western Pennsylvania.

There were those of this "New Side"[54] who believed that a conversion experience was a prerequisite to entrance into the ministry and that it was an important factor in the worship experience of individuals. John

53. Sweet, *Religion in Colonial America,* p. 294.
54. For more details on the Old Side/New Side problem, see pp. 27-28.

McMillan, with his huge frame and his loud voice, was a natural in following his pastors at Faggs Manor and Pequea in the revivalistic approach to preaching, and he was characterized as a revival preacher. His first revival began on a Thursday morning in December 1781, "a day which had been set by Congress as 'a day of thanksgiving for the survival of Cornwallis at Yorktown.'" When the first service of this revival was held there were forty-five accessions to the church. The second revival was in 1795, the third in the spring of 1799. As McMillan commented, "The Lord again revived his congregation at Chartiers." The fourth revival was a part of the "Great Revival in the West" that took place between 1797 and 1805. For McMillan, from 1799 to 1802, especially in 1802, there was revival accompanied by "bodily affection." The revival in Kentucky, thought to have been started by James McGready, who had been a pupil under McMillan, was reported to include jerking, jumping, barking, and yelling.[55]

Many Presbyterians, particularly "the Associate Presbytery or Seceders," opposed revivals and labeled them "fanatical and of satanic origin."[56] McMillan and his colleagues, in contrast, accepted the actions of revivalistic followers as means to a worthy end. The summer of 1802 was memorable for revival fervor. McGready wrote an enthusiastic letter to McMillan about revivals. There were signs of revival at the Cross Roads and Upper Buffalo churches. The Reverend Elisha Macurdy at Three Springs reported that the spirit of revival began at his communion service on the last sabbath of September 1802. Members of his congregation were so heightened that they agreed to hold a service the very next evening and remained at church that night and until noon the next day. It was said of this revival, "This was a very solemn season; the people were almost universally bowed, some deeply affected and lying prostrate, their cries for mercy enough to pierce the Heavens, while they appeared to be on the brink of despair."[57] McMillan and most of his Presbyterian colleagues were not stampeded into fanaticism by the excesses attached to revivalism. They waited patiently for the excitement to subside and then "gathered up" those who still believed and instructed them in God's word, brought them before the Session, and welcomed them into the fellowship of Christian believers as church members.

55. Guthrie, *John McMillan*, pp. 67, 68.
56. Smith, *History of Jefferson College*, p. 202.
57. *Western Missionary Magazine*, 1802, p. 329.

Epilogue

It is fascinating to look back nearly four hundred years at some of the trials and tribulations of our forebears. Religion was not the only reason behind the move to the New World, but it is a main reason why Presbyterians and many others left their homes in the British Isles. They were willing to risk everything in a trip across the treacherous Atlantic; and later many gave up conveniences to live on the dangerous frontier. This was the price they paid for freedom. Starting out with almost nothing, through toil, ingenuity, perseverance, and faith they carved out for themselves a way of life that made them stand tall in the areas of education, politics, the church, statesmanship, and other areas where leadership was needed.

In examining the early history of American Presbyterians, we have seen many admirable qualities in them: poise, strength, leadership, and belief. They have left us a heritage of which they could be proud — one that challenged them every step of the way to resist oppression, to make the most of what life offered them, to improve their life-style, and to maintain their religious nature with a fundamental belief in God as heavenly Father, in Jesus Christ as Son and Savior, and in the Holy Spirit as ever-present Advocate. From the beginnings of Presbyterianism long ago across the seas to the founding of a Presbyterian theological seminary in Pittsburgh, it is a challenging and fascinating trip — a journey that descendants of those heroes and heroines of faith will want to read about, to retrace in their own lives, and to call their own.

□ CHAPTER THREE □

Associate and Associate Reformed Seminaries

Wallace N. Jamison

It may appear strange that in the history of American Presbyterian theological education the activity of Scottish splinter groups should bulk so large. But the reason is not difficult to determine. In the repeated splits within the established Church of Scotland, the members of the secession churches were the most at risk. Thus when the pressure from the establishment became most acute, it was the secessionists who were the most likely to emigrate to the New World. Not only did America promise economic improvement, which for poverty-stricken Scots has always been an attraction, but it promised religious freedom from the oppression of an established church. So Covenanters and Secessionists made the hazardous voyage to America during the eighteenth century in increasing numbers. Once established in their new homeland, they sought to organize churches within the tradition of their own particular denominations.

In the American colonies, moreover, there were none of the conditions that had caused church splits in Scotland. There was no established church, so the secession quarrel was irrelevant. No burgher oaths were required, so the Burgher-Antiburgher conflict was meaningless. Under those conditions, we might well ask why the scattered groups of Presbyterians did not at once unite. Virtually no doctrinal differences existed between the Covenanters (the Reformed Church) and the Secessionists (the Associate Church), so why did they not get together? As a matter of fact it took many years before the union process began, and the reason for this lies chiefly in two areas: support and communication.

The Scottish immigrants were few in number and widely scattered when they settled in America. They looked to the churches from which they came for pastors and for some financial support, so they could not afford to alienate their supporting congregations by a union with representatives from a rival group. Back in Scotland the Covenanters were still suspicious of the Seceders, and the Seceders were even more suspicious of the established church. So their adherents in the New World continued to perpetuate irrelevant differences, despite the fact that they all shared much more in common than they had dividing them.

In addition, the problem of communication undermined all attempts at cooperation. Without an adequate postal service, it took weeks, if not months, to get a message across the Atlantic and back. Even within the colonies, it was not easy to communicate from one settlement to another. So the American Presbyterians continued to be as fractured denominationally as they were scattered geographically.

The greatest need of the Presbyterian colonists was for pastoral leadership. Repeated appeals to Scotland for ministers brought little response. There were too few trained clergy to care for the churches at home, let alone to send to small congregations overseas. In addition, few pastors in Scotland, especially those with families, were willing to face the hazards of a frontier life thousands of miles from home. Clearly, the only solution to the dilemma of the American churches was to provide a domestic source of pastors in the New World that would enable them to fill the needs of the scattered congregations.

Congregational ministers were educated at Harvard (the Hollis Chair of Divinity was established in 1721) and at Yale (the Yale Chair of Divinity dated from 1755). Presbyterian ministers were trained at the College of New Jersey, later to be known as Princeton College. Beginning in 1784 Dutch Reformed ministers were prepared by Dr. John Henry Livingston at what came to be known as New Brunswick Theological Seminary. But neither Covenanters nor Seceders were willing to have their pastors tainted by an education outside their own fellowship.

Since the establishment of a full-scale theological seminary was out of the question, the next best thing would be to authorize a minister with some scholarly attainments to tutor candidates for the ministry on a private basis. This is what happened when the Second Associate Presbytery of New York chose the Reverend Robert Annan as a tutor; his first student was ordained in 1778. In that same year the First Associate Presbytery in Pennsylvania selected the Reverend John Smith, whose pastorate was in Octoraro, Lancaster County, to prepare candidates for the ministry through private tutoring.

Complicating the ecclesiastical picture at about this time was a union of the Reformed churches with the Associate churches to create the Associate Reformed Presbyterian Church. This union in 1782 looked like an answer to Presbyterian division, but it actually increased the number of different denominations. While all of the ministers and most of the members of the Reformed Church joined in the union, some of the members did not. Instead, they secured new ministers from the Covenanter Church in Scotland and so renewed the existence of the Reformed Church, which persists in the United States to the present day. There were also two Associate pastors and several congregations of that church who refused to enter the union. So now there were three denominations in place of two: the Reformed Presbyterian Church (Covenanters), the Associate Church (Seceders), and the Associate Reformed Church (the new union denomination).

Meanwhile, the outbreak of the Revolutionary War between Britain and her American colonies made it even more imperative that a local source of ministerial candidates be found. One of the Reformed Presbyterian ministers who joined in the Associate Reformed union was the Reverend Alexander Dobbin, a renowned Greek, Latin, and Hebrew scholar. He conducted an academy at his home in Gettysburg, Pennsylvania, from 1788 to 1799. This was the first classical school west of the Susquehanna River. While he had no formal appointment by an ecclesiastical court, he began training students in the theological disciplines, and twenty-five of his graduates were subsequently ordained to ministry in the church.

Associate Church Seminaries

The first theological seminary of a Presbyterian church established by the church for the exclusive purpose of training young men for the ministry was located at Service, Pennsylvania, not far from the modern city of Aliquippa. Today it is near a country crossroad, and at the time of its founding it was more isolated than it is today. Why did the Associate Church, the founding denomination, select a site so far removed from the center of church activity? Dr. John McNaugher, who wrote a history

Service Seminary building — 1894 photograph

of theological education in the United Presbyterian church, has suggested that it was because the leaders of the church sensed that the future of the church lay in the West.[1] It would be nice to think that the ecclesiastical fathers were blessed with such prophetic insight, but there is little evidence for this. The wagon trains over the mountains did not begin to roll until near the end of the eighteenth century. Pittsburgh was not surveyed until 1784, and two years later it could boast only about one hundred houses.

The much more likely reason for the location is that Service was where the one and only professor of the seminary had his church. The Reverend John Anderson was probably the finest biblical and theological scholar of the Associate Church. He had a good working library, and even more important, he indicated willingness to teach such candidates for ministry as the church would send him — this in addition to his pastoral

1. McNaugher, *The History of Theological Education in the United Presbyterian Church and Its Ancestries* (Pittsburgh: United Presbyterian Board of Publication, 1931), p. 11.

The Reverend John Anderson, Service Seminary's only professor

duties at the Service Church. So, despite the isolated location, Service was where the theological seminary began.

At first glance, John Anderson was a most improbable candidate for a seminary professor. Though his parents were of Scottish ancestry, he was born in 1748 at Brampton, England, just south of the Tweed River. He was an only child, and his father died when John was very young, so he was raised by his mother. After completing grammar school he was sent north and graduated from a Scottish university (probably the University of Glasgow), after which he studied theology at the Anti-Burgher Associate Divinity Hall. Even though he was an outstanding student, he was quite unprepossessing in appearance. Short and stocky (just over five feet in height) with a weak and quavering voice, he did not make a favorable impression on the churches where he candidated. After he was licensed to preach by his presbytery in 1774, he could not get a call to a church, so he took a position as corrector and editor of publishing firms in Edinburgh and Glasgow. In addition to his work there, he continued his studies of foreign languages and read prolifically. He also wrote religious and theological essays for church journals, so he got some recognition among the local clergy.

Meanwhile, the presbytery was getting impassioned appeals from the scattered Associate congregations in America for pastors. Since none of the ministers in the presbytery wanted to go, they appointed John Anderson to be their missionary overseas. Thus it was that John, accompanied by his aged mother, set sail in 1784 for the New World. It was not a propitious time. The Revolutionary War had just come to an end, and the new nation was faced with the problem of rebuilding a shattered economy. On the way over, John's mother died and was buried at sea. Furthermore, as the result of a severe storm, John lost most of his theological library.

Despite the fact that pastors were desperately needed for vacant churches, John could still not get a call. For four years he served as a traveling evangelist under the Associate Presbytery of Pennsylvania, and he was eventually ordained without a call in 1788 at Philadelphia. Four more years of wandering service led him beyond the Alleghenies, and at long last in 1792 he was installed as pastor of the congregation of Mill Creek and Harmon's Creek, the present location of Service. Two years later, on April 21, 1794, Rev. John Anderson was named professor of theology by the Associate Presbytery of Pennsylvania. Thus began Service Seminary, the first of a long line of seminaries that were forerunners of the Pittsburgh Theological Seminary of today.

It would be difficult to find much resemblance between the two institutions. Pittsburgh Theological Seminary is located on a spacious campus with many imposing buildings near the heart of a bustling metropolis. Service Seminary consisted of one building, the church manse initially, with one professor. The location was far from the heartland of either the denomination or the nation, "where roads were scarce and the neighbors distant."[2] Not long after the seminary was founded, John built

2. Brittain, unpublished dissertation, p. 43.

a modest two-story log cabin near his Mill Creek church where his students could live and where the lecture hall and the library could be located.

Yet for all its limitations, it was a full-fledged theological seminary boasting a resident professor, a building for recitation, and a library, plus a dormitory and a resident student body. Other seminaries began at earlier dates, but they did not have all the attributes of independence that Service had. For instance, New Brunswick Seminary of the Dutch Reformed Church dates from 1784, but when it was founded it had no building of its own, and for the first twenty-six years of its life it followed its professor, Dr. John Henry Livingston, from one location to another as the professor's pastorates changed.

The Service Seminary library consisted of the modest collection of books secured over the years by Anderson plus donations from other Associate Presbyterian pastors — in all about eight hundred volumes. The student body was likewise small in number — never more than nine at a time and usually five or six. There was no charge for tuition since the professor's salary was paid by the local congregation supplemented by the presbytery, in all $300 per year. Even so, the cost of room and board was often a financial hardship for students on the frontier, where money was always scarce. To help indigent students with their education the Associate Synod raised a Student Fund, which by 1816 had reached the sum of $1144.40. This was used by Professor Anderson to defray the cost of food and lodging for his young charges.

The curriculum of the seminary consisted of lectures on systematic theology and the Shorter Catechism as well as biblical studies in the original Greek and Hebrew. Latin was also required because the chief text on theology was the venerable *Medulla Theologiae* by the Dutch theologian Johannes Marck, written entirely in Latin. This was supplemented by an English text, *The Marrow of Modern Divinity,* by the Oxford professor Edward Fisher. Normally the students listened to lectures by John Anderson for four hours a day, four days a week. The rest of the time they studied in the library, reading theology, learning Greek and Hebrew, and also preparing sermons for delivery to the student body, with criticism by the professor. The students also accompanied Anderson on his pastoral calls, and they worshiped with the congregation during the Sunday services. Although there was only one professor, the more advanced students helped by tutoring the entering students, particularly in the biblical languages.

In addition to his arduous regimen of teaching, preaching, and pastoral visitation, John Anderson somehow found time to publish at least nine books of which we have knowledge. Even when riding on horseback, he also had a book along to read. In fact, he paid little attention to where the horse was going. The story is told, though it may be apocryphal, that on one occasion when he was going to a meeting of presbytery, he rode for several hours, reading intently all the way. When he finally looked up, he noticed that it was getting dark. Not recognizing where he was, he decided to seek shelter for the night. Then he saw a light in a cottage window. He went up to the house, knocked on the door, and began to ask for lodging, when he suddenly realized he was addressing his own wife at the door of his own home! His horse, not getting any directions, had spent the hours making a broad circuit, never getting more than half a mile from home.

Despite his absentmindedness, Anderson was elected moderator of the Synod in 1806. In 1819 he suddenly resigned his professorship because of old age. He was seventy-one years old at the time. He still continued his pastorate at Service, however, until his death in 1830 at the age of 82. (He is buried in the cemetery at Service.) When Anderson resigned as professor of theology, Service Seminary ceased to exist. Because no one in the church was willing at the time to take his place, the Synod decided to return to the apprentice system whereby candidates for ministry would study theology under the tutorship of the nearest minister. But there were many in the church who were dissatisfied with such an arrangement, and they urged the opening of a new seminary somewhere. In those days, the way to open a seminary was to find a scholarly pastor who was willing to take on the responsibility of teaching seminary students in addition to his duties as minister of a local congregation. Usually there was little, if any, additional compensation for this added work, so it is understandable that most of the prospective candidates for the position of professor of theology politely declined the honor.

Fortunately, however, the Associate Synod was able to secure a suitable candidate only one year after Service Seminary closed. In 1820 the Reverend Dr. John Banks of Philadelphia was appointed head of the Associate Seminary in Philadelphia. Born in Sterling, Scotland, John Banks had received his education in his homeland and was ordained to the pastoral ministry by the Sterling Associate Presbytery. For six years he served as pastor of a church near Edinburgh before emigrating to America in 1796. He served a number of Associate congregations in New York and Pennsylvania before being called to the Associate Church in Philadelphia. While there he opened a classical school for young men and ran the preparatory department of the University of Pennsylvania. He was a distinguished Hebraist. He had memorized most of the Hebrew Bible and even wrote in Hebrew. It was natural, then, that his colleagues in ministry selected him to lead the new seminary.

At the time of his selection Banks was receiving an annual stipend of $1000 from the University of Pennsylvania for his teaching responsibilities. Since he could not continue teaching at the university and also teach at the seminary (remember, he was also pastor of a local church!) he offered to resign his university position if the Synod would guarantee him $500 as professor of theology. At first the Synod demurred, but it finally agreed. Dr. Banks was also given $500 from his own congregation to purchase books for the seminary library. So the seminary was off to a promising start, and students began to register for courses.

In the general debate that ensued after the closing of Service Seminary, there was a consensus that the church needed a seminary to provide ministerial leadership for the growing church. There was also a consensus that the seminary should be located nearer to the heartland of the denomination. Some churchmen argued that since most of the Associate congregations were located near the eastern seaboard, that is where the seminary should be placed. Others, however, noted that the development of new churches came largely from the west, so it would be appropriate to locate a seminary near the growing edge of the expanding church. Of course, since the first consideration was to find a suitable professor, the location would be contingent on where the candidate's congregation was found. Dr. John Banks had agreed to head a seminary in Philadelphia, so the eastern churches could be served.

To the joy of the western churches, another candidate to head a seminary was the Reverend James Ramsay, pastor of the Associate congregation in Canonsburg, Pennsylvania, some miles south of Pittsburgh. Instead of deciding between the two, the Synod finally agreed to authorize both of them, one to serve each of the major sections of the church. The Eastern Hall, as it was called, would be located in Philadelphia and would be led by Dr. Banks. The Western Hall, led by James Ramsay, would reside in Canonsburg.

Unlike his colleague in the East, James Ramsay was born and bred in America. His parents were Covenanters who came from Scotland, but when the family moved from Lancaster County, where James was born, to Washington County farther west, they joined the Presbyterian Church, since no Reformed Presbyterian Church was located there. By the time James was a young man, his family had a dispute in their local church over the singing of Watts hymns instead of exclusive psalmody, so they left the Presbyterian Church and joined the Associate congregation at Service pastored by John Anderson. There James began his classical studies under his pastor's tutelage and then studied theology at Service Seminary. After ordination he was called to be pastor of the Canonsburg church, where he remained for the rest of his life.

When the Synod asked Ramsay to head up a western seminary, he at first refused. But later he relented when the Synod agreed to move the Service Seminary library to Canonsburg. The Synod formally appointed him professor of theology at the new seminary in 1821, and on December 1 of that year classes began, with five students in attendance. The remaining assets of Service Seminary were also transferred to Canonsburg. Classes were held in Ramsay's parsonage until 1829 when the growing student body made this arrangement impractical. Happily, Jefferson College, a small liberal arts college located in the same community, offered rooms for the seminary classes, so instruction could continue under more suitable circumstances.

In 1826 Dr. Banks died suddenly of apoplexy, as it was then called, and this spelled the end of the Philadelphia Seminary. During the six years that it was in operation a total of eleven students were educated there. Following the death of Dr. Banks, several attempts were made to locate someone who would lead that seminary, but without success. So the Synod finally decided that the church needed only one seminary after all. Thus in 1830 the library and assets of the Philadelphia Seminary were shipped west to Canonsburg.

As the student body at Canonsburg continued to grow, the space required at Jefferson College became more than the college could afford. In addition, the requirements of teaching the students were greater than one man could undertake. The Synod accordingly undertook an ambitious plan to expand the seminary. Jefferson College offered to give the Seminary some land adjacent to the college campus for a seminary building, and the Synod allocated $3,000, later increased to $6,000, to erect a building for the exclusive use of the seminary. It would provide classrooms, a library, and dormitory rooms to house students. In addition, it was decided to call a second professor to the seminary to serve full time rather than to add teaching duties to a local pastorate. The seminary course of study was set at four years, with classes being offered during five months of each year (November through March).

The new professor was the Reverend David Carson, who had graduated from Jefferson College in 1819. He was a student under Dr. Banks in Philadelphia, where he got a thorough grounding in biblical Hebrew. At the time of his call to the professorship he was serving as pastor of a church near Maryville, Tennessee. He was elected by the Synod to teach Hebrew and church history at the seminary beginning in 1834. David, his wife Jane, and their children made the long move from East Tennessee during the summer of 1834. But shortly after they arrived, David contracted a lung disease, probably tuberculosis, and died before classes began in the fall. The Synod allocated a year's salary of $300 to the bereaved family, now stranded far from their former home, and free housing was also provided for Mrs. Carson thereafter.

While the loss of Professor Carson was a shock to the seminary community, it was not unusual. Scarcely a year went by without the report of the death of a student. Almost nothing was known about the cause of disease in those days. Sanitary conditions were often lacking, and sickness was prevalent. Accordingly, life expectancy was short. All one could do was accept death as part of the providence of God and hope for the best.

Even though the seminary community was terribly disheartened by this turn of events, the precedent of a second professorship had been established, and a search was immediately undertaken to find a replacement. The selection finally came to the Reverend Thomas Beveridge, and a very happy selection it was. A son of the manse and a graduate of Union College in New York, Beveridge was another of John Anderson's students at the old Service Seminary. Prior to his call he had served churches in Ohio and Pennsylvania. When he took up his duties at the seminary in 1835, his annual salary was $300, and there were eighteen students enrolled. One of the great contributions that Thomas Beveridge gave to the seminary was continuity. He served as professor for thirty-six years. When the seminary was relocated from Canonsburg to Xenia, Ohio, he moved with it. This continuity also meant that when one professor died or retired the seminary did not disappear, as had happened at both Service and Philadelphia. Beveridge provided the continuity that allowed the seminary to evolve into the graduate school of theology that it is today.

With the new classroom/dormitory building and a second professor at the seminary, the future looked unusually bright. But there were still problems, and many of them had to do with money. Even though there was no charge for tuition, the costs of room, board, and books were more than many students could afford. Most of the student candidates came from homes where money was scarce. The Synod urged its congregations to provide grants for seminary students. Loans were of no help since many of the students already had debts from their college education, and the possibility of repayment from the very low salaries paid to ministers in those days was problematical at best. Finally, the Synod voted to "set up a comprehensive Education Fund to ease student progress."[3]

The Synod also became concerned about the spiritual nurture of the students. While education in the intellectual disciplines necessary for ministry is always a primary duty of a seminary, the Synod urged that the professors "tend well the spiritual condition of the students, acting as their preceptors, visiting their rooms like spiritual fathers, and strengthening their personal, private religion."[4] Unfortunately, there is no record of whether the seminary professors acted on this admonition.

Another concern of the students that engaged the Synod's attention was the prescribed length of the seminary course. Up to 1849 the course of study was set at four years, with a single five-month term each year. At the students' repeated request, a special committee of the Synod considered the matter and recommended a three-year course of study with two terms consisting of five months plus four months each year. The Synod approved this recommendation. In 1851 the course was changed again to one term of eight months each year instead of two terms totaling nine months.

In the Synod Minutes of 1832 there appeared a petition from "Titus Basfield, a man of colour, requesting aid in prosecuting his studies for the ministry."[5] It appeared that he owed $400 for the purchase of his freedom from slavery and needed support at the seminary. The favorable action of the Synod made the Associate Church one of the earliest denominations to admit an Afro-American to seminary training. He actually did not begin his studies at Canonsburg until 1839, but he did graduate in 1842 and subsequently served as pastor of an Associate Church for "coloured people" in Canada.

Another church issue that made itself felt in theological education was a concern for foreign missions. Of course, the church in America had

3. Minutes of the Associate Synod, 1839, p. 56.
4. Minutes of the Associate Synod, 1849, pp. 77-80.
5. Minutes of the Associate Synod, 1832, pp. 16, 13.

always been interested in missions, but usually this was associated with the expansion westward. But now a new dimension was added to this concern as European powers opened up colonies in Africa and vied for trade concessions in the Far East. In 1841 the Associate Synod received a memorial from the students at Canonsburg Seminary to begin a foreign mission enterprise. The students proposed the active participation of the church both by contributing funds and by supplying ministers to serve as missionaries. The suggestion was referred to the Committee on Foreign Missions of the Synod, which answered the student memorial affirmatively and proposed the selection of a mission station and a call for two ministers to go.[6]

Meanwhile, the student body at Canonsburg Seminary continued to grow. Between 1821 and 1838 the enrollment increased every year, beginning with five students and reaching twenty-four. By 1850 it rose to a resident student body of thirty-seven. This placed a considerable strain on the facilities of the seminary. Clearly they needed more classroom and dormitory space as well as more staff. There was no need for concern about over-production of ministers, because the advance westward was creating more churches than there were pastors to lead them.

In 1841 James Ramsay offered the Synod his resignation due to "age and infirmities." At first the Synod took no action, but then, reluctantly, in 1842 it accepted Ramsay's resignation and set about securing a replacement. The man selected was the Reverend James Martin, a graduate of Union College in New York and of the Philadelphia Seminary, where he studied under the legendary Professor Banks. He took over as professor of Hebrew and didactic and polemic theology in 1842, but four years later he died of a lung hemorrhage, what we would probably diagnose today as tuberculosis. James Martin's successor was the Reverend Abraham Anderson, who was serving as professor of languages at Jefferson College at the time. He was a colorful individual who had served under General Harrison in the War of 1812.

Once again the seminary community was saddened by a premature death when Anderson succumbed to illness in 1855, only eight years after joining the faculty there. Death struck not only the faculty; it was an ever-present hazard in the student body as well. Seminary records show that two students died in 1848 and two more in 1854. In fact, there is

6. Minutes of the Associate Synod, 1841, pp. 7, 37.

reason to believe that several more students died whose passing was unrecorded, so frequent was death in those days.

By 1850 the size of the student body was such that either a new building would have to be erected or the seminary would need to relocate. Once again, it was the students who took the lead by asking the Board of Managers to relocate. This came at the same time that the Board started plans for a new seminary building. The old building not only was too small but was also in need of considerable repair. While plans for rebuilding went on, the Synod debated the question of relocation. There were several reasons why this was an attractive option at the time. Canonsburg was located only a few miles from Pittsburgh, where the Associate Reformed Presbyterian Seminary was situated. Even though the Associate Church was a separate denomination, there was considerable passing back and forth of members and clergy between the two bodies. Further, the growth of the church was westward, and there was no seminary west of Pittsburgh. While the Synod was deferring action of the proposal for further study, a recommendation came in 1854 from the Presbytery of

Xenia Seminary, Xenia, Ohio (Associate, 1855-1858;
United Presbyterian Church of North America, 1858-1920)

Southern Indiana and Miami that the seminary be relocated in Xenia, Ohio, a community at the southwestern end of the state. Predictably, some students and most of the faculty did not want to move. But finally, the die was cast when the Synod voted 62 to 57 to relocate the seminary in Xenia.

Associate Reformed Seminaries

While the Associate Church was moving its seminaries from Service to Canonsburg to Xenia, with a brief stay in Philadelphia, its sister denomination, the Associate Reformed (Presbyterian) Church (ARP), was also active in sponsoring theological education. During the early years of the nineteenth century, the ARP Church faced the same problem as did the other Presbyterian bodies, namely, how to secure qualified ministers for their churches. Since the procuring of ministers from Scotland was becoming more and more difficult, the ARP Synod decided in 1801 to select a minister to go to Britain for the purpose of raising funds for a theological seminary in America. Their choice for this task was the Reverend John M. Mason, D.D., of New York City. Mason left New York on July 29, 1801, and was gone about fifteen months. During that time he raised nearly $3,000, a princely sum in those days. Most of the money went for the procuring and transporting of books. He was not only successful in fund-raising; he also secured five young pastors and one licentiate to accompany him back to the States.

Dr. Mason was an unusual man. His father had served as chaplain to George Washington during the Revolutionary War. As a lad, John graduated from Columbia College and then studied theology with his father and with John Henry Livingston of the Dutch Reformed Church. He then completed his education at the University of Edinburgh in Scotland. A superb preacher, he succeeded his father as pastor of the Cedar Street ARP Church in New York City. For five years he served as provost of Columbia College. He also edited and wrote for *The Christian Magazine,* the chief publication of his denomination. In later life he served for a time as president of Dickinson College in Pennsylvania. It was no surprise, then, that this was the man whom the Synod selected to be professor of theology in the new seminary. Classes were begun in 1805 in Dr. Mason's church building. The course of study would cover four years, with annual terms of seven months (November through June). When classes began, five students were admitted. This number gradually increased in subsequent years until it reached a maximum of twenty-eight students.

Several things were distinctive about the seminary from the start. For one, unlike most other Protestant seminaries, Mason's seminary did charge students for tuition. For members of the ARP Church, tuition was $24 per annum; for nonmembers the charge was $32. There was also a provision that no charge would be made for the indigent. How much money was raised from this source is not known since most seminary students (even now) regard themselves as indigent. Also distinctive was the emphasis on biblical studies rather than theology as central to the curriculum. Biblical studies, of course, meant study in the original languages of Scripture. The Synod resolved "that the scriptures themselves be the great system of study, and that what is called systematic theology be subordinate thereto."[7] Another provision of the Synod for the seminary is worth quoting at length:

> Every student shall begin and close the day with exercises of secret devotion; uniting to prayer the reading of a portion of God's word; and using as a help some books of impressive practical religion. In these exercises he is to read the scriptures, not as a critic, but as a *Christian;* as a saved sinner, who knows no other way of peace but that which belongs to him in common with the least of God's redeemed; and who lives by faith, for daily counsel, and strength, and consolation, upon that Saviour whom he is afterwards to preach to others.[8]

In short, the seminary was dedicated to preparing candidates not only intellectually for ministry but in experiential religion as well.

As with most seminaries, the question of finances was always a paramount concern at the Mason seminary. In theory, the chief expense — namely, the salary of the professor — was met by the congregation of which the professor was also the pastor. But this meant in effect that one congregation carried the whole financial burden of theological education for the whole denomination. Further, most of the students at the seminary needed additional financial support. Accordingly, as early as 1796 the ARP Synod voted to establish a Synod Fund to which each member of the

7. Minutes of the Associate Reformed Presbyterian Synod, 1805, p. 17.
8. Minutes of the Associate Reformed Presbyterian Synod, 1805, pp. 25-27.

church was asked to pay fifty cents a year. This fund was to defray part of the salary of the professor and also to help "pious youth who from poverty cannot comfortably and successfully pursue their studies."[9] Unfortunately, this fund was never subscribed sufficiently to pay Dr. Mason's salary, and since he had to give increasing time to instruction, his congregation became restive about supporting the seminary as well as the church.

When Dr. Mason requested help, the Synod directed that an assistant be appointed to teach a number of the classes. Elected to fill this post was the Reverend James Mathews, a member of the seminary's first graduating class. Mathews was called in 1809 to teach Greek and Hebrew, geography, chronology, and history. In addition he was to solicit funds for the seminary from ARP congregations! The last provision was a clear indication that there were no funds available to pay the new instructor. The most obvious solution to the problem was to secure a call as pastor to a local congregation, but this did not materialize at once since there were no vacant ARP pulpits in the vicinity. Finally, a call did come from the South Dutch Church, a congregation in the Dutch Reformed Church. But this created a new problem. In order to accept his call, Mathews had to join the Dutch Reformed Church. Could he serve as professor in the ARP seminary while he was a member of another denomination? The Synod, after lengthy debate, finally agreed that he could, but only if he repaid the ARP Church for all the aid he had received while he was a student at the seminary. The Scots Presbyterians had not lost their frugal instincts by transferring to the New World! Mathews taught at the seminary from 1809 to 1816, when the demands of his pastorate forced him to resign.

Enrollment at the seminary was spotty. From the original five students in 1805, the numbers gradually rose to twenty-eight in 1815. But almost half of these were from denominations other than the ARP Church. Many came from the Dutch Reformed and the Presbyterian churches. This made sense since all three denominations shared a similar theology, polity, and worship. Further, the Mason seminary was the only theological school of the Reformed tradition in New York City. But it also aggravated a basic ambivalence in the seminary policy. On the one hand, there was a strong demand of the Synod that the seminary emphasize in its teaching the distinctive features of the ARP Church in order to keep its graduates

9. Minutes of the Associate Reformed Presbyterian Synod, 1796.

true to the denomination. The Synod ruled that ARP seminary students must sign a commitment that, if they should leave the denomination, they would repay the seminary for any student aid received. On the other hand, however, it was important to attract students from other denominations in order to fill out the student body. These students paid a higher tuition than the ARP enrollees, and they did not require student aid from the ARP Church. So financially it was necessary to be ecumenical. There were also other areas where joint enterprise was advantageous, such as the cooperation with the Dutch Reformed and the Presbyterians in forming a "United Foreign Missionary Society."[10]

Meanwhile, there were forces at work that led the ARP Church to examine its modus vivendi. Dr. Mason suffered from recurrent bouts of illness, which along with advanced age made it clear that he could not serve much longer as head of the seminary. Further, close cooperation with the Presbyterian Church in a number of activities posed the question whether it was really necessary to maintain two separate denominations. In addition, the ARP denomination was undergoing growing pains as the western part of the church continued to grow while the eastern part remained static. In fact, the two parts were growing farther and farther apart. Finally, in 1821 the ARP General Synod agreed that the union of the Presbyterian Church and the ARP Church was "both desirable and agreeable." A joint committee of the two denominations had already been working for several years to draw up articles of union, which were then adopted by both bodies. These included a provision that the New York ARP seminary would merge with Princeton Seminary of the Presbyterian Church. What remained of the ARP seminary funds would be used to endow a chair of biblical literature at Princeton, and the New York Seminary library would be transferred to Princeton. With the completion of these arrangements, the Mason seminary in New York ceased to exist. During its sixteen years of operation (1805-21) it had educated ninety-six ministers.

When church unions take place, they rarely do so in a clear-cut manner. What usually happens is that in place of two denominations three are formed — the continuing remnants of the two existing bodies as well as the new union denomination. In the case of the ARP Church, however, it was even more complex than that. The supreme judicatory of the church was the General Synod, with four subordinate particular synods: New

10. Minutes of the Associate Reformed Presbyterian Synod, 1817, pp. 42-45.

York, Pennsylvania, Scioto, and the Carolinas. Even before Dr. Mason resigned from the New York Seminary, the General Synod began to break up. The Scioto Synod withdrew and formed itself into the independent Associate Reformed Synod of the West. Then the Synod of the Carolinas withdrew to form the Associate Reformed Synod of the South. What was left of the General Synod in 1822 voted by a scant majority to unite with the Presbyterian Church. The Synod of Pennsylvania immediately dissolved; its members either went over to the Presbyterian Church or joined the ARP Synod of the West. The Synod of New York largely went over to the Presbyterian Church, but a significant minority of thirteen ministers and twenty-five congregations refused to enter the union and reorganized as an independent Associate Reformed Synod of New York. Thus the General Synod ceased to exist.

The split of the ARP General Synod immediately posed a problem of theological education for the remaining parts. The ARP Synod of the West soon opened a new seminary in Pittsburgh. The continuing Synod of New York tried a stopgap measure of urging its presbyteries to send their candidates to some other approved seminary such as Princeton or New Brunswick or to place them under the tutelage of a competent minister of their own denomination. But this obviously could not last if the New York Synod was to maintain its own integrity. So in 1829 the Synod voted to reopen the New York Seminary, not in New York City where it had been previously located, but in Newburgh, New York. The choice of a new location, as one might expect, was determined by the choice of a professor, the Reverend Joseph McCarrell, who was pastor of the ARP congregation in Newburgh. The seminary began operation in October 1829, with three students enrolled.

Joseph McCarrell was a young man preparing for college when the War of 1812 broke out. Hearing that the British had attacked Washington, D.C., he enlisted, along with most of the youth in Shippensburg, Pennsylvania. He was sent to defend Baltimore, where he witnessed the bombardment of Fort McHenry. After the war, he graduated from Washington College and then studied theology under Dr. Mason in New York City. A precocious scholar from the start, he had read the whole Old Testament through in Hebrew before beginning seminary. He was an avid reader, and he wrote extensively on a wide variety of theological subjects. Little wonder, then, that his colleagues in ministry elected him to be the professor of theology in the resuscitated seminary at Newburgh. He served in that post for thirty years, much of the time alone. Something of a martinet, he insisted that all his students read the entire Old Testament in Hebrew and the New Testament in Greek before they were licensed to preach. His students recalled him as being a pedantic lecturer but solemn and impressive as a preacher.

One of the first things that McCarrell did upon taking up his professorial duties was to seek recovery of the New York Seminary library from Princeton. Twice the ARP Synod sent a letter to the Presbyterian General Assembly requesting return of the library, and it was refused each time. So the Synod brought a civil suit in the courts of New Jersey to force Princeton to surrender the library.[11] The court case dragged on for five years, but finally in 1837 the Court of Chancery of New Jersey decided in favor of the ARP claim. So 2,400 volumes plus $200 were returned to the Synod, and the books were settled in the Newburgh Seminary.

Up to that time seminary classes were held in the Newburgh church. But the arrival of the library made it imperative to secure a new building. With Synod approval, an appropriate structure was contracted and built, but only at the cost of a massive loan. The ensuing debt was to cloud the activities of the seminary for years to come. Repeated appeals to the church brought few results, and indeed it was not until 1851 that the debt was finally liquidated.

Meanwhile, the seminary was able to attract only a scattering of students. Total enrollment almost never exceeded ten in any one year, and in 1846 there were only two in attendance. Despite the low enrollment, another professor was added to the staff, the Reverend John Forsyth. Since he was already a pastor of the Newburgh Union Church, this did not entail additional expense. So Forsyth undertook the teaching of biblical literature and church history from 1837 until 1842, when he resigned to become professor of Latin at Princeton. In 1852 he returned to Newburgh to resume teaching there.

To jump somewhat ahead, the ARP Church had begun consultation with the Associate Church leading toward church union. The result was the incorporation in 1858 of both bodies into the United Presbyterian Church of North America. The union had immediate repercussions on theological education within the united denominations. The Associate Church had one seminary in Xenia, Ohio, which continued its operation much as before. The ARP Synod of the West had two seminaries at the

11. Minutes of the Associate Reformed Presbyterian Synod of New York, 1832, pp. 305-7.

time, one in Pittsburgh and the other in Oxford, Ohio. It was decided as a result of the merger to move the Oxford Seminary to Monmouth, Illinois, in order to serve better the western constituency of the denomination.

In 1855 the ARP Synod of New York, which had been an independent denomination, joined the ARP Synod of the West to form the General Synod of the West. But many of the eastern folk, particularly those of Newburgh Seminary, were not enamored of the idea of uniting with the Associate Church. Consequently, when that union took place, both Professors McCarrell and Forsyth, along with seven other ARP ministers, refused to join. The new United Presbyterian Synod of New York tried to get title to the Newburgh property, and when persuasion failed they sued in court. After protracted litigation, the Supreme Court of the State of New York ruled that the nine ministers constituted the continuing ARP denomination, so the court gave the property to them. It was a pyrrhic victory, however, because the seminary had ceased to function. All the professors could do was to create a Board of Trustees to administer the vacant property.

While these melancholy events were transpiring in the east, theological education in the western branch of the two churches was taking a different tack. The rapid growth of America westward during the first half of the nineteenth century put unexpected pressures on the church. Difficulty of communication, long distances, uncertain transportation, and the expense of travel brought divisions between the east and west in many Protestant denominations. The Presbyterians were not the least of those affected. Among the ARP congregations, this took the form of seeking a seminary closer to the western border, which at the time was western Pennsylvania. When the eastern branch of the church sought union with the Presbyterian Church, the ARP congregations of the west broke off and established an independent denomination, the ARP Synod of the West.

The next thing to do was to establish a seminary. Unlike all the other seminaries in our story, this one began as an ecumenical venture. The Western University of Pennsylvania, which was located in Pittsburgh, decided to inaugurate a theological department. The Reverend Dr. Black of the Reformed (Covenanter) Church and the Reverend Dr. Bruce of the Associate Church were to be professors. The former would teach church history, geography, and chronology while the latter taught Greek, Hebrew, and biblical criticism. The university indicated that the Rev. Dr.

Joseph Kerr of the ARP Church would be added to the staff to teach didactic and polemic theology if the ARP Synod would appoint him. The Synod promptly did so. Thus in 1826 began the first theological school in Pittsburgh, which was a direct antecedent of the Pittsburgh Theological Seminary of today.

So enthusiastic was Dr. Kerr for this project that he not only donated his first year's salary of $200 for the purchase of library books but also added $200 of his own money to the same cause so that the seminary library could begin with a respectable collection of books. Unhappily, Dr. Kerr lived only three more years; he died of a "bilious colic" in 1829. Seven students were enrolled in the first class of 1827, and they met initially in Dr. Kerr's church.

After the death of Dr. Kerr, the Synod appointed his replacement, the Reverend Mungo Dick, as professor pro tempore. He was a brilliant scholar. After graduating from Edinburgh University in Scotland, he came to the United States and joined the ARP Church. He was pastor of the ARP Church near Irwin, Pennsylvania, when he joined the seminary staff. In 1831 the committee that had been seeking a permanent successor to Dr. Kerr made its report. Their choice was the Reverend John Taylor Pressly, D.D., who was pastor of the ARP Church in Cedar Springs, South Carolina. After examining the candidate, the Synod unanimously elected him professor of theology at the seminary, and at the same time he was called to be pastor of the ARP congregation in Allegheny, across the river from Pittsburgh. Dr. Pressly had studied theology under Dr. Mason in New York. After being ordained in his home state of South Carolina, he had been appointed professor of theology in the Synod of the South, so he already had some seminary teaching experience when he was invited to join the Pittsburgh Seminary in 1832.

It was at about this time that the seminary ceased to be a theological department of the university and became an independent seminary under the control of the ARP Synod of the West. Classes now moved to Dr. Pressly's church in Allegheny, so the seminary became known thereafter as Allegheny Seminary. When Allegheny was finally incorporated into the city limits of Pittsburgh, the seminary changed its name back to Pittsburgh Seminary — but more about that later. Dr. Pressly served the seminary until his death in 1870.

Not everyone in the ARP Church, however, was pleased with the location of the seminary in Allegheny. Since classes were still held in the Allegheny ARP Church, the question of permanent location would not

*Allegheny Seminary, Allegheny, Pennsylvania (The First Associate Reformed
Presbyterian Church of Allegheny City, 1833-1855)*

be settled until a seminary building was erected. At the Synod of 1837
four locations were proposed: Alleghenytown in Pennsylvania, and New
Concord, Chillicothe, and Oxford, all in Ohio. By a close vote, Oxford
was chosen as the permanent site. But the decision threatened to split
the Synod, so final action was delayed until the following year.

When Synod met in 1838, the Ohio delegation brought with them
a full charter of incorporation from the Ohio legislature and a promise
of a lot for the seminary building in Oxford. There was even a building
already erected on it suitable for seminary classrooms, and space was also
available on the lot for a student dormitory. The Pittsburgh delegation
had little to offer except the fact that Dr. Pressly was there, and there was
some vague promise of financial support. Regardless, a vote to rescind
the action of the 1837 Synod was passed 48 to 33 with one abstention.
But this did not settle the issue. Passionate debate continued until a vote
was taken to rescind the rescission. This was passed 40 to 31. So they
were back to square one! Fortunately, the Presbyterian proclivity for
compromise finally prevailed, and it was decided to continue the seminary
at Allegheny for one more year and meanwhile to overture the presbyteries

within the Synod on the question of a permanent location for the seminary, the results of which were to be reported at the next Synod meeting.

Finally, at the 1839 meeting of Synod, the Gordian knot was cut. It was decided that two seminaries of the church would be established, one at Allegheny and the other at Oxford. The current seminary assets and library acquisitions would be divided equally between the two seminaries. To cap the matter, it was resolved that the Synod would be divided into two: the First Synod of the West (located in Pennsylvania) and the Second Synod of the West (located in Ohio).

When the furor had died down, Allegheny Seminary continued to operate much as it had done before. Additional funds were sought to replace books lost to Oxford Seminary. In 1843 it was reported that Dr. Pressly was ill much of the time, so additional help was needed for instruction. The pastor of the Second ARP Church in Pittsburgh was the Reverend James Dinwiddie, another product of the Mason seminary in New York. He was elected professor of biblical literature and sacred criticism in 1843, but three years later he suffered a "paralysis of the brain," what we would call a stroke, and had to retire. The number of students that year was twenty-eight. Three years later it had increased to thirty-eight; clearly additional staff was necessary.

The problem was not in securing qualified professorial candidates but in finding the resources to pay them. Almost none of the seminary professors during this period derived their whole income from teaching at the seminary. After the retirement of James Dinwiddie, his replacement was Dr. Alexander Downs Clark, a graduate of Allegheny Seminary and prior to that of Franklin College. In 1845 he had been elected president of his alma mater, Franklin, and two years later he became professor of biblical literature and criticism at Allegheny Seminary. For a time he spent the winters at the seminary and the summers at Franklin College, thus deriving from both a salary sufficient to live on. In 1861 he finally resigned from the college to accept a call to the Sixth ARP Church in Allegheny, but this meant that he still had to occupy a dual role as professor and pastor.

In 1851 the appointment of Dr. David R. Kerr as professor of church history and government brought the faculty of Allegheny Seminary to three. Dr. Kerr was the son of Dr. Joseph Kerr, the seminary's founder. At the time of his appointment he was editor of *The Preacher*, the church paper of the ARP denomination. He, too, continued a dual role as professor and writer after church union in 1858, when *The Preacher* became *The United Presbyterian*.

With three professors and more than thirty students, the next concern of the seminary was to find more adequate quarters. Happily, this was provided by a legacy from the estate of Mr. Thomas Hanna, a wealthy businessman who had served for a number of years as treasurer of the seminary. Following his death, much of his estate was deeded to the seminary to erect a new building, which was opened for use on November 11, 1856. It was a sturdy brick and stone structure with two classrooms, a chapel, and a library. It was a fitting contribution to the new denomination that came into being with the union of the ARP and Associate Churches in 1858 to form the United Presbyterian Church of North America.

Oxford Seminary, which was established as a result of dividing the ARP Church into two synods in 1839, began in a curious way. The Second Synod of the West purchased a one-acre lot for the use of the seminary. The local ARP congregation then agreed to relocate by building a new church for the use of both the congregation and the seminary. The two-story structure housed the seminary downstairs and the church sanctuary upstairs. The seminary and the congregation each paid half of the cost of erecting the building.

The first professor of Oxford Seminary was the Reverend Joseph Claybaugh, who was also pastor of the Oxford ARP Church. Even though he suffered from frequent ill health much of his life, he was a very energetic pastor, a good scholar, and a demanding instructor in the seminary classroom. His students also remembered him as a man of deep piety. He served as both pastor and professor for fifteen years. He succumbed to "scrofula," which we know as tuberculosis.

The trustees of Oxford Seminary seem, from their records, to have been always struggling with a shaky financial foundation. The erection of the church/seminary building left them with a sizable debt. Claybaugh's salary from the seminary was usually in arrears. Congregations within the Synod were urged and cajoled to contribute regularly to the seminary, not only to retire the debt and pay salary obligations, but also to assist in student aid. Unfortunately, times were hard and money was scarce. Dr. Claybaugh reported to the Synod in 1850 that some of the funds contributed to the Seminary were in counterfeit bills! The Synod with a straight face ordered him to destroy the false money.

When Dr. Claybaugh died in 1855, the Synod elected the Reverend Alexander Young to replace him. At the time, Young was pastor of the ARP congregation of St. Clairsville, Ohio. He had come to this country as a young boy from Glasgow, Scotland, and had graduated from Western University in Pittsburgh and from Allegheny Seminary. When he came to Oxford, like his predecessor he not only took up the duties of a seminary professor but was also called to be the pastor of the Oxford ARP Church.

The Synod continued to struggle with financial problems, so when in 1857 the trustees of Monmouth College in Illinois presented an offer to the Synod to have the Oxford Seminary transferred to Monmouth, it did not take the Ohioans long to make up their minds. With amazingly little dissent, the Second Synod agreed to "cheerfully comply with the desire expressed by the Synod of Illinois for the transfer of the Theological Seminary to Monmouth, Illinois."[12] The Second Synod of the West was allowed to retain a joint interest in the seminary, but the management of the institution would be committed to the Synod of Illinois. The trustees of the seminary transferred title to the land to the local congregation and sold their share of the building to cover salary arrears owed to the professor. A hundred students received their theological education from the Oxford Seminary.

One is led to ask why the Oxford site was changed so easily, particularly after the vigorous effort made to get it there in the first place. Several reasons are clear. The financial problems of the seminary finally convinced the churches of the Second Synod that they could not support a seminary alone. In addition, union with the Associate Church was already in the air, and the Associate Synod had a flourishing seminary at Xenia, Ohio. When union took place, clearly one of the seminaries would become redundant, and the Oxford Seminary was the latest and least viable of the two. Finally, the church continued to look westward for its future growth. Monmouth College had been founded in 1856, and as a beginning institution it could provide a continuing supply of ministerial candidates for the seminary.

With the union of 1858 the new United Presbyterian Church inherited four seminaries east of Indiana — Allegheny, Oxford, Xenia, and Newburgh. So the move to Monmouth made a good deal of sense. During the summer of 1858 the Oxford Seminary library of 3,000 books was shipped to Monmouth, where the new institution was named the United Presbyterian Seminary of the Northwest. Alexander Young accompanied the move and continued on as professor in the new seminary location.

12. Minutes of the Associate Reformed Presbyterian Second Synod of the West, 1857, p. 14.

He taught Greek and Hebrew along with systematic theology. Joining him on the faculty was the Reverend John Scott, who taught historical theology and church history. Since the seminary had no building of its own, classes were held in the First United Presbyterian Church of Monmouth. During the first term, eight students were enrolled, and during the next two years the number rose to seventeen and eighteen respectively. Because of the Civil War, however, the student body shrank back to nine.

Concluding Notes

Before continuing with the seminaries of the new United Presbyterian Church, we should pick up the story of the remaining Associate seminary in Xenia, Ohio. When the Associate Synod finally voted to relocate the Canonsburg Seminary to Ohio, the trustees of the seminary acted with alacrity. They secured an Act of Incorporation under Ohio law. They purchased a lot for the new school at a price of $1,500, and they made plans for erecting a two-story building (with a basement) to house the student body and classrooms. A contractor was secured, and at a cost of $6,598 the structure was erected. Thus by the fall of 1856 the seminary was ready for occupancy, and twenty-six students reported for the opening of the school year. The Board of Trustees reported to the 1857 Synod that the total cost of the new seminary building plus land and furnishings was $10,089.77, half of which was already paid, with the remainder covered by a bank loan. The following year, the year of church merger, the debt stood at $4,908.85, which was covered by a bank loan at ten percent interest. In that year the Board of the seminary was restructured under the United Presbyterian Second Synod of the West. The Synod not only proceeded to pay off the debt but also began an endowment fund.

It was clear to the church by this time that the only way to stabilize the finances of the seminary was to secure an endowment sufficient to accommodate the fluctuating donations of the church. Despite the scarcity of ready cash prevailing in the country at the end of the Civil War, the Endowment Committee of the seminary reported with joy in 1866 that $49,164 had been received and was invested in an endowment fund. Further, the payment of professors' salaries had been brought up-to-date, a tacit admission that this had not always been the case.

Having an endowment fund seemed to promise financial stability for the seminary, but this did not always follow. In our day endowments are invested in government bonds, bank securities that are covered by federal insurance, and other notes that are protected in one way or another from default. Such financial instruments, however, were not available at that time. Accordingly, most of the seminary funds were loaned either to church congregations or to individuals, some of whom never repaid their loans. Even banks were not exempt from foreclosure, with the loss of all their assets. The trustees of the seminary reported in 1873 that $3,733 of the endowment was listed as "doubtful" and $2,370 had been written off as "worthless." But on the whole, Xenia Seminary came to the union of 1858 with high hopes and with a sound program to serve the new church.

Bibliographical Material

Bibliographical material on the histories of the Associate, Associate Reformed, and United Presbyterian Seminaries is concentrated primarily in the Presbyterian Historical Association archives in Philadelphia and in the Barbour Library of Pittsburgh Theological Seminary. Primary sources include the minutes of the governing synods of the church, minutes of the boards of directors of the various seminaries, and the letters, articles, and books by various seminary professors.

Among secondary sources, I wish to acknowledge particular indebtedness to the unpublished Ph.D. dissertation of Raymond E. Brittain, "The History of the Associate, Associate Reformed, and United Presbyterian Seminaries in the United States," 1945, located in the Barbour Library.

Additional source material is found in the following:

Glasgow, W. M. *Cyclopedic Manual of the United Presbyterian Church of North America.* Pittsburgh: U. P. Board of Publication, 1903.

Harper, R. D. *The Church Memorial: Containing Important Facts and Reminiscences Connected with the Associate and Associate Reformed Churches Previous to their Union as the United Presbyterian Church of North America.* Columbus: Follett, Foster and Co., 1858.

Kelsey, H. A. *The United Presbyterian Directory: A Half-Century Survey 1903-1958.* Pittsburgh: The Pickwick Press, 1958.

CHAPTER FOUR

The United Presbyterian Seminaries

Wallace N. Jamison

In 1858 the long-awaited union of the Associate and the Associate Reformed Presbyterian (ARP) Churches finally took place. The new denomination, the United Presbyterian Church of North America, included among its assets four theological seminaries: Allegheny, Monmouth, Newburgh, and Xenia, which were to serve a constituency of 57,789 communicant members in 660 congregations. Of the four seminaries, one of them, Newburgh, was virtually moribund.

When the merger took place, the nine ministers of the ARP Church who refused to enter the union (among them were the two professors of the Newburgh Seminary) claimed that they held title to the Newburgh property because they represented the continuation of the ARP Church, which had held original ownership. The court battle that resolved the case in 1861 ruled that the ARP Synod maintained its identity and so legally held the seminary property. It was understood, however, that the synod-within-a-synod held the property (and the endowment) "for the use of the United Presbyterian Synod of New York."[1] Unfortunately, without students or professors, the building stood vacant. There were, however, a number of congregations in the West that wanted a seminary closer than Pittsburgh, so in 1864 the Synod of New York overtured the presbyteries and sessions within its bounds on the question, "Shall a Theo-

---

1. John McNaugher, *The History of Theological Education in the United Presbyterian Church and Its Ancestries* (Pittsburgh: United Presbyterian Board of Publication, 1931), pp. 35-36.

logical Seminary be revived and organized within the bounds of this Synod?"[2] The resulting vote was ambivalent at best. Two presbyteries were unanimously in favor, one was unanimously opposed, and the rest were split fairly evenly. The chief opposition, however, was not on the question of reopening the seminary but on the question of reopening in Newburgh. Unfortunately, there was no consensus on an alternate site, so Synod finally decided to reopen the seminary at Newburgh since the old building was still available there.

Newburgh Seminary

More difficult was the problem of securing staff. At length two professors were elected: the Reverend James Harper, D.D., of the Seventh United Presbyterian Church in New York City, and the Reverend J. B. Dales, D.D., of the Second United Presbyterian Church in Philadelphia. Dr. Harper was an immigrant from northern Ireland and was ordained in the Associate Church. He was an eminent theologian, historian, and exegete, and he proved to be an excellent teacher. John Blakely Dales came from the ARP Church and had been educated at Newburgh Seminary. He was a fine scholar and a voluminous writer, and at the time of his election he not only was pastor of the church in Philadelphia but was also editor of the *Christian Instructor*. While the two men selected were excellent choices, the problem was that they were located far from the seminary. Without any assets, the seminary could pay only a fraction of their salaries, so both professors were allowed to retain their pastorates, and the Synod agreed to provide pulpit supplies for their congregations while they were at the seminary.

Classes were begun in 1867 with nine students in attendance, but it was clear that running a seminary with all part-time instructors would not work. The next year Dr. Harper resigned his pastorate and moved to Newburgh to give full time to his seminary duties. The Synod promised him an annual salary of $2,000, which, unhappily, was usually in arrears. Dr. Dale retained his pastorate in Philadelphia because he did not think the future of the seminary was very bright. Every year he offered his resignation to the seminary directors, and each year they unanimously

2. Minutes of the U.P. Synod of New York, 1864, p. 136.

turned it down. Since frequent commuting was simply not possible, Dr. Dale took a train to Newburgh once a month, gave some non-stop lectures, and then scurried back to Philadelphia. While pedagogically this was a highly dubious arrangement, it was the best the seminary could do.

Recognizing that finances were the major problem confronting the seminary, the Board of Directors recommended that a capital drive be inaugurated to raise an endowment fund to support the two professors. A goal of $25,000 was set, which later was raised to $50,000. But the results were not promising. Pledges in the amount of $15,000 were received, but they would be paid only when the full $50,000 was subscribed. Further, only two students showed up for the opening of classes in 1869. Troubles continued to mount. Despite the fact that Dr. Dales did not take his salary, the salary of Dr. Harper was $700 in arrears. The treasurer reported that the seminary account was overdrawn to the extent of $853 and indebtedness had reached $1,553 by 1869.

Following increasingly insistent resignations from Dr. Dales, the Board finally agreed to release him in 1872 when a replacement could be found. Several attempts to secure another professor proved fruitless, but finally in 1873 the Reverend Robert Stewart, who was serving a church in Davenport, Iowa, agreed to teach exegetics and homiletics at the seminary. Regretfully, the ship was sinking rapidly. Student attendance continued to decline, and the financial state of the institution further eroded. Finally, on September 30, 1878, Professors Harper and Stewart both submitted their resignations to the Synod. Only two students had appeared for the fall term. To all intents and purposes, the seminary had ceased to function.

It is not difficult to detect what went wrong. The United Presbyterian Church was never very strong in the northeast sector of the country. The few congregations that survived were clustered in the New York City area and in New Jersey. Newburgh was simply too far from the base of support to thrive. Further, there were many strong seminaries of the Presbyterian and Reformed tradition close at hand where ministerial candidates could go. The fact that so many presbyteries in the East had strongly opposed reopening the Newburgh Seminary was a poor omen for the future. Reluctantly, New York Synod accepted the professorial resignations, and it was agreed that the funds and assets of the seminary would be transferred to the General Assembly if all the United Presbyterian seminaries were consolidated into one. Since this was not done, the trustees and directors continued to administer the property for two more decades. What little money remained after the seminary closed was used to pay the arrears in salary owed to the two professors. Harper was owed over $250, and Stewart was owed $1,850. Subsequently, Dr. Harper joined the faculty of Allegheny Seminary, and Dr. Stewart became editor of *The Evangelical Repository* for the year 1879-80. After that he went to Sialkot, India, where he taught in the seminary there.

To complete the story, the Newburgh Seminary building was sold to St. Luke's Hospital in Newburgh, and the proceeds became an endowment fund for theological education to be divided equally between Allegheny and Xenia Seminaries. The Newburgh library finally ended up at Allegheny.

Allegheny/Pittsburgh Seminary

Of the three remaining seminaries in the United Presbyterian Church, Allegheny was the oldest and also the largest. At the time of union the seminary had three full-time professors: John Taylor Pressly in the chair of theology, David Kerr in the chair of church history, and Alexander Clark in the chair of biblical languages and criticism. A fourth chair was created in 1874 when Alexander Young was called to be professor of practical theology. The election of John McNaugher as professor of New Testament literature and criticism created a fifth chair. For a six-year period (1920-1926) James Galloway Hunt occupied a sixth chair in missions and comparative religion. But this overstretched the finances of the seminary, so it reverted to five full-time professors, a faculty size that was maintained until 1930. The faculty was remarkably stable during this period. The three professors who were in the seminary at the time of union remained in office for thirty-nine, thirty-six, and thirty-seven years, respectively. Indeed, between 1850 and 1930 the majority left their positions only through death or retirement due to poor health. Since there was no Social Security system in operation then, retirement for any other reason was never considered.

Of the seventeen men who served on the faculty of Allegheny (later Pittsburgh) Seminary between 1858 and 1930, not many were eccentric or flamboyant characters. The chief criteria for appointment to a chair of theology seemed to be genuine piety, scholarly attainment, and a sober application to the teaching office. While a glint of humor was sometimes found in their pronouncements, both in dress and in demeanor they were expected to display to their students the same kind of sobriety that the church wanted in its pastors.

A good example of this was Joseph Tate Cooper, who succeeded Dr. Pressly in the chair of theology. An easterner by birth, his first pastorate was in Philadelphia. But he also served as a missionary in an organizing parish in California. He published widely, serving by turns as editor of *The Evangelical Repository* and as coeditor of *The Christian Instructor.* He taught at the seminary for sixteen years but was forced to retire at the age of seventy-three because of severe ill health. At his retirement the Board named him professor emeritus and granted him full salary for life. This generous gesture is less impressive when we learn that he died three months later, in 1886.

One of the more colorful professors was Oliver J. Thatcher, a classical scholar who graduated from Union Theological Seminary in New York, took graduate study at the Universities of Berlin and Marburg in Germany, and attended the American School of Classical Studies in Athens, Greece. All of this was before his ordination by the United Presbyterian Church. He was immediately called to be instructor in church history at Allegheny Seminary, and two years later he was elected professor. He lasted only two years longer, resigning his chair under the pretext of aversion to the climate of Pittsburgh! He then became professor of medieval history at the University of Chicago. More likely than weather, his liberal background probably made him less than congenial to his brethren in the church.

He was succeeded by John A. Wilson, whose impeccable credentials included an education at exclusively United Presbyterian schools and a succession of pastorates in United Presbyterian churches. He did have one unusual record in his background, however. Before going to seminary he studied law, and after admission to the bar he practiced law for a couple of years in New Castle, Pennsylvania.

By far the most influential of the professors at Allegheny was the Reverend John McNaugher, D.D., LL.D., Litt.D. A graduate of Westminster College, Pennsylvania, and Xenia Seminary, he did one year of graduate study at the Universities of Edinburgh and Glasgow in Scotland. After a one-year pastorate in Ohio, he was called to Allegheny Seminary, where in 1886 he was installed in the chair of New Testament literature and criticism. He was to occupy that chair for an amazing fifty-seven years. In 1909 he became president of the seminary and served in that capacity until his retirement in 1943. During that time he also served a term as president of the World Alliance of Reformed Churches, as chairman of the commission on the new confessional statement of the church, and once as moderator of the General Assembly. He also found time in his busy schedule to edit no less than seven hymnals for the church. His somewhat starchy manner earned him the affectionate nickname "the Pope" among his brethren. There is no question, however, that he placed an indelible stamp on the worship and theology of the United Presbyterian Church.

At the time of church union in 1858, the Allegheny Seminary was as solvent as any seminary in the new denomination. But this is not saying very much, because all of these institutions were dependent almost entirely on the donations of their constituent congregations for survival. Unlike colleges and universities, which can rely at least in part on tuition payments from students to pay their bills, seminaries made no charge for tuition at all. Even worse, most of their students needed financial assistance just for room, board, and books, and the seminaries were expected to provide some of the help. The Board of the Allegheny Seminary reported to the First United Presbyterian Synod of the West in 1864 that debt was piling up just to pay the professors' salaries and that increased funding by the church was necessary if the seminary was to survive. The Board indicated that if each member of the church paid seven cents per year, solvency would be assured, but only half of this amount was ever raised.

The only solution for fiscal stability was to create an endowment fund. Accordingly, the Synod set about seeking funds for an endowment and set a goal of $30,000. But war taxes and the poor economy of the nation made such a collection very difficult. By 1866 only $16,297 had been raised. The agents of the Synod reported that some potential donors refused to give until all the seminaries of the church had been consolidated into one institution. Others expressed dissatisfaction with the course of seminary training. In 1871 the usable part of the endowment had shrunk to $12,882. But then the tide began to turn, and in 1872 the total had risen to $28,790. In 1874 the nation had begun to emerge from the postwar depression, and the Board was able to report to the Synod that the seminary debt had been retired, salaries had been increased, and there was even a modest balance in the Seminary Fund. From then on the endowment grew steadily. Much of the credit for this is due to the efforts of a certain Mr. Ure, who volunteered his time to canvass the church for generous donations to the endowment. By 1880 the endowment reached

$61,800. Ten years later it was over $130,000. In 1900 it was nearly $240,000, and it kept climbing steadily after that.

But while the funding for the seminary improved, the enrollment in the student body fluctuated widely. In 1869 there were thirty-two students in attendance. The number increased to forty-nine in 1872, but by 1878 it had dropped to twenty-six. Thereafter it grew slowly until 1890 when it reached fifty-seven and peaked at eighty-nine in 1897.

The growing size of the student body placed an increasingly heavy burden on the seminary building. Additional living space was clearly in order. In 1875 the Board reported that it had been offered a lot next to the seminary on which to erect a new dormitory. It took five years to raise the funds and sign a contract for the building, to be named "Hanna Hall" in honor of the principal donor, James P. Hanna. When completed it would boast thirty-two suites of rooms sufficient to accommodate fifty students. The total cost of the building and furnishings was $16,426. Before the new structure was begun, however, there were complaints in the church that the seminary was in a poor location of the city and should consider relocation. A committee of the Board was named in 1892 to look into the matter, but it was unable to come to any agreement. It suggested that a greatly enlarged committee including members of the faculty and trustees be given the task of researching the project. In 1894 at a specially called meeting of the Board it was decided to move the seminary to a new location "where it could find more ample accommodation."[3] The Committee on Removal was asked to survey the possible sites and prepare plans and estimates for the Board. Meanwhile the trustees were to put the present property up for sale.

But then a reaction set in. At the regular meeting of the Board in the same year it was voted to retain the present site, to purchase adjacent land for expansion, and to raze the old building and replace it with a new and more commodious structure. The following year an even more modest plan was adopted whereby the old building would be remodeled into additional dormitory space and a new structure would be erected to house classrooms, a library, and a chapel. The new building was begun in 1898 and was completed a year later. It was a sturdy five-story structure containing four lecture halls, a chapel, a library with reading room attached, a gymnasium, and additional dormitory rooms — twenty-three single rooms, eighteen double rooms, and seventeen triple rooms —

3. Minutes of the First U.P. Synod of the West, 1894, pp. 138-40.

designed to house over one hundred students. The total contract without furnishings came to $82,000.

In 1893 the faculty dealt with an entirely new problem. In 1890 for the first time a young woman had enrolled in the seminary. Now she had completed the prescribed courses and was ready to graduate. The exercises, however, included students reading their theses from the pulpit, and it was not deemed proper for a woman to do this. The faculty agreed to give her the diploma, but a man would read her thesis for her. When she refused to accept this compromise, the dilemma was solved by simply eliminating the reading of theses at commencement! So Lee Alma Starr became the first woman to graduate from an antecedent of Pittsburgh Theological Seminary. She was ordained and became a minister in the Methodist-Protestant denomination, which accepted women as clergy.[4]

About this time the question of seminary governance became a controversial issue in the church. From the beginning of seminary education, the synods had been responsible for the governance and support of the institutions within their bounds. There were some churchmen, however, who were convinced that the General Assembly should have the controlling voice in running the seminaries. This, they claimed, would lead to more uniform education for the church's ministry and would provide more equitable support for all the seminaries. Predictably, every such suggestion in this direction was met with stout opposition on the part of the synods. Finally, in 1894 the General Assembly sent down two overtures to the presbyteries: "Shall the Assembly have veto powers over the election of Theological Professors?" and "Shall the Assembly have power to remove any Professor for unsoundness of faith?" In 1895 the presbyteries approved both overtures with clear majorities, so they became part of the constitutional law of the church. Thus while the synods retained a controlling voice in managing the seminaries, the election of new professors was not complete until the General Assembly gave its approval.[5]

In 1912 two more modest changes occurred at the Allegheny Seminary. The first was a change in name. Because the city of Allegheny was merged with the city of Pittsburgh in that year to form the greater city of Pittsburgh, the seminary voted to change its name to the Pittsburgh Theological Seminary of the United Presbyterian Church, a title it retained until

4. A lengthy account was carried by *The Pittsburgh Press,* July 31, 1939, p. 19, several years after her death.

5. Minutes of the First U.P. Synod of the West, 1895, pp. 191-94.

1930.[6] Second, the seminary received authorization and began to offer the Bachelor of Divinity (B.D.) degree to its graduates. Before that time graduates had only received certificates of completion to be presented to their presbyteries for ordination. Two years later the faculty announced a cooperative program with the University of Pittsburgh to permit a seminary student to earn the Master of Arts degree in two years. Then in 1921 the seminary discontinued the B.D. degree in favor of the Bachelor of Theology (Th.B.) degree, to be awarded to students who had the Bachelor of Arts or its equivalent and who completed the prescribed seminary course. Two years later the seminary was given the right to confer the Master of Theology (Th.M.) degree to those who qualified for it.

No one would suspect from reading the annual reports of the seminary to the First Synod that there was another Presbyterian seminary in Pittsburgh at the same time. But then in 1916 a small ray of ecumenicity broke through the smog of the city. It was reported to the Board that Pittsburgh Seminary and Western Seminary had combined to offer a joint course in missions. And in the same year Western Seminary offered to make available to Pittsburgh Seminary students its series of lectures under the Severance Foundation. It was a brief foretaste of greater things to come. We also learn that in 1923 the two seminaries combined to celebrate the fiftieth anniversary of American participation in the work of Bible translation. As if this broadening educational horizon were not enough, in the same year Pittsburgh Seminary granted the Th.B. degree to its first woman graduate, Mary Emelinne Pitt. This, however, was of course long before the church was willing to ordain a woman to the ministry of word and sacrament.

Monmouth Seminary

We noted earlier that at the time of church union in 1858 the seminary in Oxford, Ohio, was moved to Monmouth, Illinois. The rationale for the move rested on the conviction that church growth lay primarily in the west. The state of Ohio could be served adequately by the United Presbyterian seminary in Oxford, but the churches of Indiana, Illinois, and Iowa had no close source of ministerial training. Further, a new United

6. Minutes of the First U.P. Synod of the West, 1912, pp. 747ff.

Presbyterian college had recently been founded in Monmouth, and both college and community there welcomed the idea of relocating the Oxford Seminary in the same town. Though it was officially named the United Presbyterian Seminary of the Northwest, it was always popularly called the Monmouth Seminary.

Dr. Alexander Young, who had served as professor of Hebrew and Greek at Oxford, supervised the transfer of the seminary library, some 3,000 books, and he moved along with it. He became professor of systematic theology in the reconstituted school. During the first few years in Monmouth, classes met in the First United Presbyterian Church. The opening class in 1859 numbered eight students. In the next three years the enrollment increased from ten to seventeen to eighteen. But the manpower demands of the Civil War brought the number down to nine in 1863. Then, as the war wound down, discharged veterans began to fill up the classes again. Among the eighteen students who enrolled in 1864 there were two captains and a colonel from the Union Army.

In addition to Dr. Young, the seminary was also served at this time by Dr. John Scott, a colorful Scotsman who came to this country as an immigrant in 1818. For ten years he served as a stonecutter, building locks for canals in Pennsylvania and Ohio. When work on the canals declined, he became a lumberjack in the cypress swamps of the lower Mississippi River. It was as a mature man, then, that he was called to the ministry. After studying at Franklin College and Canonsburg Seminary, he was ordained as a missionary in Trinidad. The climate, however, did not agree with him, so he returned to the United States, and it was while serving as a pastor in Henderson, Illinois, that he was called to be professor of historical theology and church history. Unfortunately, he continued to be plagued by recurrent periods of ill health, and several times he offered to resign, but each time the resignation was turned down by the directors.

In 1864 a third professor, Dr. Andrew Morrow Black, was added to the faculty as professor of biblical literature. Dr. Scott continued to teach part-time as his health permitted. At the time of his appointment, Dr. Black was already serving on the faculty of Monmouth College, and before that he had been a professor at Muskingum College, Westminster College, and Franklin College, so he was already a veteran academic when he joined the seminary.

Despite a good faculty and a slowly expanding student body, the seminary had trouble right from the start. It was the same problem all the other seminaries experienced at one time or another: poor financial support from the church. With no student tuitions on which to rely and no endowment, the seminary was totally dependent on the erratic contributions of the congregations within the bounds of the Illinois and Iowa Synods. The church members were predominantly farmers, and while business prospered after the Civil War, the farm community was frequently destitute. Payment to the professors fell further and further behind. By 1866 the Board reported that all professors were more than a year's salary in arrears. A plan to found a "Claybaugh Professorship" at $10,000 endowment was proposed to the synods, and an appeal was made for funds, but not nearly enough was collected to provide financial stability. In 1870 the trustees reported that the seminary indebtedness stood at $3,245.

While financial straits were foremost in the directors' minds, it was not the only reason the seminary faced dissolution. It had never had a building of its own. Like a penniless stepchild, it had to carry on its classes in the Sunday school rooms of local churches or in classrooms at Monmouth College. Without a home to call its own, the seminary was never able to develop the image of a viable, going concern. Perhaps because of this, its student body remained small and unimpressive. While other institutions expanded with the growing population, the seminary even shrank in enrollment.

Finally, at a specially called meeting on June 20, 1870, the directors resolved to hand over the seminary to the General Assembly as the Assembly itself had suggested in its annual meeting a few weeks earlier. The faculty even agreed to resign en masse so that the Assembly could select its own faculty. But nothing was done, and by 1872 the debt stood at $4,250 and continued to rise. Unfortunately, the General Assembly had no special funds with which to bail out the Monmouth enterprise. In desperation, the directors met on November 10, 1874, in Monmouth and voted to consolidate their seminary with the seminary in Xenia, Ohio. The debt of $4,339 was paid off from the modest endowment Monmouth had received through a few legacies and bequests. The balance of the endowment and the library were transferred to Xenia, and Monmouth Seminary ceased to exist. Professors Black and Young resigned, and Dr. Scott was voted a pension of $500 per year for the rest of his life. During its sixteen years of service to the church, Monmouth Seminary graduated about 116 students.

Xenia Seminary

This left the United Presbyterian Church with two functioning seminaries: Allegheny Seminary, which had come out of the old Associate Reformed Church, and Xenia Seminary, which was a daughter of the Associate Church. As has already been noted, Xenia Seminary had moved from Canonsburg just before the church union of 1858. At the time of union twenty students were enrolled at the seminary. The faculty consisted of two full-time professors: the venerable Thomas Beveridge, who had already taught twenty years while the seminary was at Canonsburg, and the Reverend Samuel Wilson, who was pastor of the Associate Church in Xenia. His father, William Wilson, had been the first student to study under John Anderson at the Service Seminary. Samuel Wilson taught systematic theology, and Dr. Beveridge was officially professor of church history and polity. Actually the two of them covered all the theological disciplines, including Greek and Hebrew exegesis, assisted by other local clergy who taught individual courses on a part-time basis. The seminary was housed in a two-story building containing the library and classrooms on the first floor and dormitory rooms for students on the second floor. Shortly after the seminary relocated, a third professor, the Reverend Joseph Clokey, was secured to teach pastoral theology.

The student population of the seminary varied dramatically from year to year. In 1866 thirty-seven students were enrolled. Two years later enrollment dropped to twelve. No reason is given in the seminary records for the drop, but it may have been due in part to the poor health of the faculty, two of whom were well advanced in years. About this time the whole faculty was replaced. When Dr. Beveridge retired in 1871, Jackson B. McMichael, pastor of the Sugar Creek Church, took his place in the chair of church polity. William Moorhead was elected to teach Greek exegesis and biblical literature. William Bruce (son-in-law of Dr. Beveridge) was chosen to teach church history and biblical criticism. His formal installation in his chair marked the first time at the seminary that a new faculty member began his term with an installation service.

Even more important for the success of the seminary in this period was the closing of Monmouth Seminary and the consolidation of its library and assets with the Xenia school. Though none of the Monmouth faculty moved to Xenia, a number of the students did. Hence the rise in the student enrollment during that period. To accommodate the larger number of students, a fourth professor, Dr. James Carson, who was pastor of the Second Church in Xenia, was secured to teach pastoral theology and homiletics. Another professor to teach biblical literature and apologetics was sought by the Board. Despite the expanded faculty and the enlarged library, however, the student body expanded only moderately. In 1873 there were nineteen students. After consolidation that number jumped to thirty in 1875. But thereafter the total number of students remained fairly consistently in the twenties.

Changes continued to take place in the faculty. Dr. McMichael resigned in 1878 to take the presidency of Monmouth College, and his place was taken by Dr. James Harper, who had been on the faculty of the Newburgh Seminary prior to its closing. Meanwhile Dr. David MacDill, a professor at Monmouth College, accepted a call to Xenia Seminary in 1885 to teach apologetics, homiletics, and church history. Another colorful professor was Wilbert Webster White, who was armed with a Ph.D. from Yale. He came to Xenia from the presidency of Tarkio College and taught Hebrew and Old Testament literature from 1889 to 1894. He resigned to join the Moody Bible Institute in Chicago and from there went on to become president of the Bible Teachers Training School in New York City, later called Biblical Seminary. Following the resignation of Dr. White, the seminary called John Douds Irons, a Civil War veteran who had participated as a foot soldier in twenty-one battles and was at the front when Lee surrendered. Before coming to the seminary, he had taught at Westminster College in Pennsylvania and then had been president of Muskingum College.

In 1879 the seminary moved into a larger and better building equipped to accommodate forty to fifty students. The sum of $6,500 required to effect the transfer was raised entirely within the bounds of Xenia Presbytery, but this did not supply furnishings for the rooms. The other presbyteries within the controlling synods were asked to provide $50 apiece to cover the cost of the furnishings. While not all the presbyteries filled their quotas, furnishings were provided. Even so, it was not until 1900 that electric lights were installed in all the rooms, and it was 1901 before interior bathrooms with flush toilets were available. In 1903 plans were made to erect a new library and classroom building beside the old structure, which was then to be converted entirely into dormitory rooms. The new building was completed in 1905 and was named "Anderson Hall" in honor of John Anderson, the founder of Service Seminary.

Despite the fact that student enrollment gradually increased, the finances of the seminary experienced disconcerting fluctuations. In 1880 the endowment income, on which the seminary depended to pay most of its bills, had decreased sharply. Income was only $2,900, while expenses were $4,000. Faculty salaries once again were in arrears, and no funds were available for the library. But only four years later, thanks in large measure to the Quarter Centennial Fund raised by the denomination, the endowment was increased to $68,737, which yielded an income of $5,000 annually. This was sufficient to meet all seminary obligations and leave a modest cash balance. Unhappily, endowments were subject to bank failures and periods of depression, so that the endowment itself fluctuated a great deal. For instance, in 1885 the endowment was valued at $73,668, but in 1889 it had dropped to $65,000. By 1897 it had reached $121,924 thanks to a bequest of $33,000 from the Speer estate. But of this sum, $5,488 was in uncollectable notes. The church, however, did encourage its members to include the seminary in their wills, and as a result of such bequests the Xenia endowment rose by several thousand dollars each year. By 1918 it had reached $210,135.

At the turn of the century the faculty consisted of William Gallogly Moorhead, professor of Greek exegesis and New Testament literature (and also serving as president); John Douds Irons, professor of Hebrew exegesis and Old Testament literature; Joseph Kyle in the chair of theology; and Jesse Johnson, former president of Muskingum College, professor of church history and apologetics. John Elliott Wishart replaced Dr. Irons in 1905, and in 1908 J. Hunter Webster was elected professor of Greek exegesis and New Testament literature. Dr. Moorhead retired in 1914 after serving the seminary for forty-one years.

Also in 1908, the seminary added Melvin Grove Kyle as a part-time lecturer in biblical archaeology. Thus began an interest in archaeology that has persisted in Xenia's successor seminaries to the present time.[7] Dr. Kyle was an ardent archaeologist. He excavated the reputed sites of Sodom and Gomorrah in 1924 and Kiriath-Sepher in 1926-28, and he was also notable for the numerous books on biblical archaeology that he published and for the artifacts that he brought home from his digs, artifacts that provided the start for a seminary Bible Lands museum. He also served as the editor of the well-known journal *Bibliotheca Sacra*. In 1915 Dr. Kyle was elected to the full-time position of Newburgh Professor of Biblical Theology and Archaeology.

7. See Chapter 10, "Archaeology and the James L. Kelso Bible Lands Museum," pp. 237-62.

On the surface, the position of Xenia Seminary within the United Presbyterian Church seemed secure. Student enrollment was stabilized between twenty-five and thirty-five each year. The faculty of four full-time professors was approved by the church as competent and able instructors. The facilities of the seminary were adequate for its purposes, and the endowment continued gradually to increase. But a sizable number of voices within the church held that two seminaries were more than a denomination of a quarter of a million communicant members needed to provide an adequate supply of ministers. Indeed, at the General Assembly of 1918 a recommendation was made that the two seminaries of the church unite. It was pointed out that while the enrollment at Xenia between 1892 and 1898 had averaged forty-eight students, by 1913 it had dropped to twenty-seven, and the highest thereafter was thirty-two. Apparently no one thought to consider the effect of World War I on enrollment, but the decline was enough to cast doubt on the efficiency of maintaining two seminaries. President McNaugher of Pittsburgh Seminary[8] wrote to the officers of the First Synod of the West offering to cooperate in any way beneficial to the church. He warned that the dislocations of the war might reduce seminary enrollments, but if such were the case Pittsburgh Seminary would place some of its faculty in pastoral positions until the crisis passed. Second Synod, on the other hand, suspecting that in the event of a merger it would be Xenia that would have to go, strongly opposed the idea of merger. Their fears were well founded. In 1919 the First Synod formally voted 91 to 16 to advise a union of the two seminaries to be located in Pittsburgh under the direct control of the General Assembly.

Predictably, the Xenia faculty and Board were solidly against union with Pittsburgh Seminary, particularly when it appeared that the union would be little more than the swallowing up of Xenia by Pittsburgh. On the other hand, while the Xenia people were opposed to union, they were not averse to relocation. The faculty and Board held many meetings on the subject without consensus, and then suddenly the New World Movement of the church offered $400,000 to the seminary contingent upon its moving to St. Louis, Missouri. The New World Movement, it should be noted, was an ambitious drive on the part of the church following the

---

8. In 1914 the charter and name of the Seminary were changed to "Pittsburgh Theological Seminary" to reflect the merger of Allegheny and Pittsburgh, which had taken place several years before.

end of the World War to promote missions both within the United States and abroad.

The proposal seemed to carry considerable merit. For one thing, Xenia was far from any great population center, and St. Louis would provide such a center. In addition, while the student body at Xenia was small, a better location would likely attract more students. Further, the westward movement of population indicated the wisdom of a relocation westward. Thus Pittsburgh Seminary could continue to handle the needs of the east while St. Louis would provide for the needs of the west. It was pointed out that St. Louis was a hub for transportation all over the Midwest. It also provided a large metropolitan area and the cooperation of a major educational institution, Washington University. With the financial backing of the New World Movement, the future looked promising indeed. Accordingly, on April 28, 1920, Second Synod took action endorsing the move to St. Louis. To satisfy the nostalgic interests of the remaining opponents to relocation, the school would retain its old name, Xenia Seminary.

Among the most immediate needs of the seminary upon its move to St. Louis was adequate housing. Fortunately, a building was available that, with minor alterations, could provide classroom space, a location for the library, and rooms for the students. But the New World Movement was able to provide only $22,000 in 1921, so the seminary liquidated its endowment to secure the $105,000 needed to purchase the building. Professors Kyle, Wishart, Webster, and Johnson made the move to the new location, but this created an additional financial burden. Not only was there considerable expense in transporting the household goods of the professors, but their salaries had to be increased substantially to meet the higher cost of living in a metropolitan area. Despite these premonitions of trouble, the seminary got down to work with high hopes. The associations with Washington University were cordial, and the resources of the university library and faculty were a welcome addition to the seminary program. The presence of the seminary was also a great support to the United Presbyterian churches located in Illinois and Missouri.

Unfortunately, however, these churches were too few and too small to provide a strong support for the seminary. With the coming of world peace in 1918, the Midwest soon relapsed into a period of economic depression. This centered chiefly in the farm communities, where most of the United Presbyterian churches were located. The high price of grain during the war years had encouraged many farmers to enlarge their holdings by purchasing additional acres on credit. This in turn raised the price of farm land. But when the war ended, the price of grain plummeted, which left the farmers less and less able to meet the mortgage payments on their farms. It need hardly be noted that this had a disastrous effect on church income. The economic gloom of the Midwest deepened with each passing year until the stock market collapse in 1929 threw the entire nation into a colossal depression. Despite careful economies and intense fund-raising attempts, the seminary expenses exceeded income every year from the time Xenia Seminary moved to St. Louis. In 1921, the year of the transfer from Ohio, the deficit was $13,000. The following year it dropped to $12,600. By 1926, however, the total deficit had reached $82,454. Meanwhile, the payments from the New World Movement funds had declined, so that instead of replacing the endowment that had been expended to pay for the seminary building, these funds barely kept up with the deficits. By 1929 the New World Movement payments stopped, and the accumulated deficit had reached $102,357. Then the stock market crash in the fall made additional sources of funding for the seminary increasingly problematical.

Despite these gloomy predictions, additional faculty members were added to the staff. Robert McNary Karr, a graduate of Monmouth College and Allegheny Seminary, was elected professor of systematic theology and homiletics in 1922. The following year, when Dr. Wishart resigned to go to San Francisco Theological Seminary, James Leon Kelso was elected professor of Hebrew and Old Testament literature. Like Melvin Grove Kyle before him, Dr. Kelso was an avid archaeologist; he participated in the excavations of Tell Beit Mirsim and at Bethel. He was a member of the American Oriental Society and the Archaeological Institute of America. He was also a contributing editor of *Bibliotheca Sacra,* and as such he was arguably the best-known nationally of the whole Xenia Seminary staff. In a procedure that would be highly suspect today, Dr. Kelso was awarded the Th.D. degree in 1927 from Xenia Seminary while he was still teaching there. In 1924 George Boone McCreary was elected professor of the philosophy of religion and of applied Christianity. A graduate of Muskingum College, he studied at Allegheny Seminary and at the University of Chicago. He also received a Ph.D. degree from Grove City College. Before coming to Xenia he had already served on the faculties of Epworth University in Oklahoma, Sterling College in Kansas, and Hope College in Michigan.

To One United Seminary

Although there was a capable faculty, a good location, fine facilities, and an enrollment double what it had been in Ohio, it was clear by 1929 that Xenia Seminary in St. Louis was never going to become solvent. The only alternative was merger with Pittsburgh Seminary, a procedure that Xenia had gone to St. Louis to avoid! Despite the often bitter opposition to this proposal in the past, the negotiations for consolidation were remarkably cordial. Six representatives of Xenia Seminary and six from Pittsburgh Seminary met in Indianapolis to propose a merger agreement. After lengthy discussion, the following points of procedure were accepted by the whole committee: (1) The united seminary would meet in the Pittsburgh Seminary building until a more suitable site in the Pittsburgh area could be found. (2) The new seminary, to be named the Pittsburgh-Xenia Theological Seminary, would be under the direct control of a board selected by the General Assembly rather than by one or more synods. (3) The combined boards of the uniting seminaries would select eight professors from the two uniting faculties, four from each, to be the faculty of the newly merged seminary. (4) Professors not selected for the uniting seminary faculty would be designated "professor emeritus" with an annual income of $2,000 each for life. (5) Dr. McNaugher of Pittsburgh Seminary would be designated president of the merged seminary. (6) Each seminary board would name five members to work out any additional union details. Dr. Karr of Xenia Seminary was asked to prepare a statement covering the program of expansion and the scope and purpose of the new seminary. This final merger agreement was then presented to the First and Second Synods for approval, and when it was ratified the combined committee of ten set to work on the final details of merger.

The Pittsburgh-Xenia Seminary began its life as a union institution of the church in 1930. Faculty members from Pittsburgh Seminary included John McNaugher, who was appointed president and professor of New Testament literature and exegesis; Robert Montgomery, who occupied the chair of Old Testament literature and exegesis; David McGill, who was professor of church history and government; and William Wilson, who served as professor of pastoral theology and homiletics. Faculty members from Xenia Seminary included Robert Karr, who taught systematic and biblical theology; James L. Kelso, who was professor of Semitics and biblical archaeology; George Boone McCreary, who occupied the chair of philosophy of religion and religious education;

Pittsburgh-Xenia Seminary, North Avenue, Pittsburgh (1912-1954)

and John Webster, who was professor of New Testament language and literature.

Three professors from the former seminary faculties were retired "emeriti." Melvin Grove Kyle had served Xenia Seminary for twenty-two years and was its last president. Jesse Johnson had taught church history there for twenty-eight years. The only faculty member of Pittsburgh Seminary to retire was James Doig Rankin, who had taught systematic theology since 1914.

Few things are more difficult than the merging of academic institutions on anything like an equal basis. Usually the nuptials carry all the enthusiasm of a shotgun wedding, and they are often attended by rancor and bitterness from their constituents, which may well last for decades. In this case, however, the merger of Xenia and Pittsburgh produced remarkably little gall and wormwood. While the two institutions were roughly equal in faculty, student enrollment, and facilities, they were far from equal economically. Pittsburgh could boast a respectable endowment, a stable income, and a succession of balanced budgets. Xenia, on the other hand, was economically prostrate. Its endowment had been dissipated in purchasing the seminary building in St. Louis. The New World Movement pledge was never fully paid, and what little came in was used to cover the annual deficits that the seminary experienced. The only asset that Xenia had was its building, which it had to sell in the depth of the depression at a small fraction of what it had paid for it in 1921. Not only did Xenia lose its financial base in moving to St. Louis, but it lost most of its constituency as well. Whereas in Ohio it was surrounded by a large circle of United Presbyterian churches and strong presbytery support, in Missouri the United Presbyterian churches were few and prevailingly small in size. So there was relatively little support for the seminary and, concomitantly, little outcry when it left. At the same time there was not much gloating in Pittsburgh. The financial state of the country made it clear that the whole church was headed for hard times, and the Pittsburgh enclave welcomed the additional support from the whole denomination in promoting the merged and sole surviving seminary of the church.

In another sense, the merger also underlined a fact that was not always apparent up to that time: the United Presbyterian Church was finally united. The two constituent bodies that joined in 1858 had retained their two seminaries. Pittsburgh was the Associate Reformed seminary, while Xenia carried on the tradition of the Associate Church. By 1930 not many church members knew what those specific traditions entailed, but nonetheless they did continue different strains in the history of the church. The merger of the seminaries in 1930 finally completed the process begun in 1858, and the church became demonstrably one. In addition, the hardships of the times also contributed to a relatively amicable marriage. In this spirit the combined seminary set about its task of educating its future ministry with more attention to what lay ahead than to what lay behind.

CHAPTER FIVE

Pittsburgh-Xenia Seminary

Robert L. Kelley, Jr.

If an institution can be viewed as the lengthened shadow of its chief executive officer, then the thirty-year history of Pittsburgh-Xenia Seminary can be appreciated by following the course of leadership provided by its three stalwart presidents: John McNaugher, George A. Long, and Addison H. Leitch.

The McNaugher Presidency (1930-43)

Along with forty-four years of experience as a teacher of New Testament, Dr. John McNaugher brought to his administrative task twenty-one years of service as president of Allegheny/Pittsburgh Seminary. Furthermore, he had just completed a year as Moderator of the General Assembly of the United Presbyterian Church, an honor befitting his manifold contributions to the life and work of this branch of Christ's church. His selection to lead the newly established and united seminary, Pittsburgh-Xenia, was highly applauded. Hence, at age seventy-two, amid difficult economic times in the nation, he assumed the reins of the now one and only seminary of his beloved denomination. Simultaneously, he continued his professorial responsibilities without a single sabbatical. His retirement in 1943 brought to a climax fifty-seven years of seminary service, thirty-four years featured as the titular leader. The last thirteen of those professorial and presidential years were at Pittsburgh-Xenia.

*John McNaugher, Allegheny, Pittsburgh, and Pittsburgh-Xenia
Seminaries (Professor, 1886-1943; President, 1909-1943)*

During the final school year (1929-30) of the still separate but soon
to be united seminaries, 133 students were involved, of whom 71 were
doing graduate work. As a positive indicator of the promising future in
store for the consolidated seminary, Dr. McNaugher, in just two months,
conducted an intensive and highly successful financial compaign in the
Pittsburgh district. At its conclusion he was able to report to the 1930

General Assembly a total of $187,000 in pledges, with eighty percent of that amount already paid.

The theological training of United Presbyterian candidates for ministry was at last under one roof when Pittsburgh-Xenia Seminary opened its doors for classes on September 17, 1930. An expanded and diversified curriculum led to the Bachelor of Theology (Th.B.) degree. In addition to the recently doubled library, a Bible Lands Museum was in evidence as a valuable educational resource.[1] No tuition or rental fees were charged, and kitchen and dining facilities in the seminary provided board at cost. Advanced study was also available for a Master of Theology (Th.M.) degree. Total enrollment in the new school for that first year numbered 114 students, 54 of whom were in the graduate division. Comprising the 60 undergraduates were 22 seniors, 14 middlers, 18 juniors, and 6 part-time students.

October 9, 1930, was the day set aside for institutionally celebrating the recent merger. Events began in heavy rain with a parade of forty automobiles (under the guidance of four city motorcycle policemen) wending its way from the seminary on Pittsburgh's North Side to the site of Service Seminary in Beaver County, where the rain obligingly ceased. There were stops (and speeches) at the grave of Dr. John Anderson, then at Canonsburg, after which lunch was served at the Chartiers Church. Afternoon visits followed to the old seminary building and the log academy established by John McMillan, and to the Hill Church, where Dr. McMillan lies buried. The "pilgrims" then returned to Pittsburgh. A catered dinner was served, and the great day of remembrance and prospect was climaxed with a grand meeting at the Sixth United Presbyterian Church. More speeches followed, including a historical address by President McNaugher. Greetings were conveyed in person and by letter from the colleges of the denomination as well as from more than forty other educational institutions. The merged seminary was off and running.

The roll call of full-time faculty in Pittsburgh-Xenia's three decades includes the names of twenty-one men and two women. Dr. McNaugher was one of the initial group of eight professors (four from Pittsburgh, four from Xenia), and during his presidency there were three early losses: Dr. Robert N. Montgomery to become the president of Tarkio College; Drs.

---

1. It was initially furnished by Dr. Melvin Grove Kyle (renowned archaeologist and recently retired president of Xenia Seminary) and later supplemented from excavations conducted by Dr. James L. Kelso of the faculty. See Chapter 10, pp. 251, 258-62.

D. F. McGill and John H. Webster to death. Later, in 1940, came the retirement of Dr. W. R. Wilson. Two additions to the faculty (nominated to the eleven synods by the Board of Directors and their election then confirmed by the General Assembly) were Dr. Albert H. Baldinger in 1931 and Dr. Clarence J. Williamson in 1932, both coming from the pastorate. In fact, the majority of those who would be elected to the faculty of Pittsburgh-Xenia throughout its history came from the pastoral rather than the purely academic field. Accordingly, there was ever present on the seminary scene, in companionship and competent instruction, the practical component so desirable and so necessary for ministerial preparation.

During the first five years under Dr. McNaugher the Pittsburgh-Xenia graduating classes numbered twenty-eight, eighteen, fifteen, twenty-five, and nineteen, respectively. While these were unprecedentedly hard years for the denomination financially, the school was praised regularly for its sound and responsible handling of fiscal matters, and surprisingly its programs and services experienced minimal curtailment. Hence Dr. Baldinger, one of the newer faculty members, could write glowingly of the seminary's status in 1935:

> The Pittsburgh and Xenia seminaries were united five years ago. The wisdom of this merger is no longer in question. The united seminary is serving the interests of the church quite as effectively as was ever possible with two institutions. The traditions of both seminaries have been conserved in the union, the standards of theological education have been maintained, the demands of the church for a trained ministry are being adequately met, and the work is being done at considerably less cost than was formerly possible.[2]

May 1937 marked the completion of fifty years of service by Dr. McNaugher as a seminary professor. A testimonial dinner, scheduled during the course of commencement activities at Pittsburgh-Xenia, was attended by 650 persons and highlighted the celebration of his semi-centennial. The General Assembly, through its Committee on Theological Seminaries, took grateful note of his outstanding leadership and particularly rejoiced that Dr. McNaugher had played such a large part in the training of the majority of ministers currently active in the United Presbyterian Church.

2. *The United Presbyterian,* May 23, 1935, p. 33.

Although Pittsburgh-Xenia in 1936 had submitted its credentials for accreditation to the American Association of Theological Schools immediately after that organization had been formed, it was not until three years later that such status was favorably granted. The Association delayed the school's admission because the library did not yet contain the required minimum number of volumes. At the time of the merger Xenia had 18,000 books and Pittsburgh 12,000. In the ensuing years, President McNaugher remedied the deficiency by increased acquisitions, and accreditation promptly followed. Happily, Dr. McNaugher could report to the Board of Directors at their 1939 spring meeting that the United Presbyterian "School of the Prophets" was now classed as a first-rank seminary.

The concluding years of Dr. McNaugher's presidency, and the opening ones of Dr. Long's, were administered within the context of the country's involvement in World War II. Much institutional energy was consumed in communicating and negotiating with respect to the draft status of pretheological students and seminarians, establishing a chaplaincy training program as part of the Navy's V-12 education program, and consequently adjusting the seminary course of studies so that the curriculum of six semesters could be covered in two rather than three years. In order that the faculty might have some breathing space in the accelerated schedule, Dr. McNaugher turned to the neighboring Western Theological Seminary of the Presbyterian Church, as he had done several times previously, in order to share the teaching load among the two staffs. Therefore classes were conducted in both North Side schools for the Pittsburgh-Xenia and Western students under wartime exigencies in a "semi-union" plan of cooperation — perhaps as a foretaste of the future.

President McNaugher tendered his resignation to the Board on May 4, 1942, and requested that it become effective May 31, 1943. The directors regretfully accepted his resignation. They took steps to fill the vacancy by a twofold nomination to the synods: Dr. George A. Long to be president as well as to hold the chair of English Bible, and Dr. Theophilus M. Taylor to be professor of New Testament literature and exegesis. If elected, both men would have the advantage of a year's preparatory study before assuming their tasks, and this was the case. A special committee was also named by the Board to arrange for a suitable recognition of Dr. McNaugher's lengthy and fruitful service. Dr. McNaugher's response to the latter proposal, however, was to express his conviction that any such testimonial event should be deferred because the wartime circumstances made such a celebration improper and untimely.

The last commencement over which Dr. McNaugher presided took place on May 13, 1943. Many in the audience that evening came, as they had done year after year at graduation time, to hear yet another classic address delivered by the president of the seminary. Once more they were inspired as he spoke on the theme "For Such a Time as This." Thirteen of these valedictories in which "Mr. United Presbyterian" set forth passionately and eloquently the message and ministry of the church have been preserved in a book entitled *Quit You Like Men*.

In deference to Dr. McNaugher's wishes there was no testimonial banquet on his behalf that May. Nevertheless, with grateful appreciation for his extraordinary leadership and service, the directors presented him with a "beautifully embossed copy of appropriate resolutions." They then proceeded to take two further actions: Dr. McNaugher was designated president emeritus, and the New Testament chair was henceforth to bear the name "The John McNaugher Chair of New Testament Literature and Exegesis."

For many a United Presbyterian, Dr. McNaugher epitomized the intellectual life of the church. He was a devout, thoroughly painstaking, and brilliant scholar, whose masterly mind and prolific pen humbled even those who were his colleagues and friends. Yet when those who sat under him shared remembrances of their relationships to him, they were just as apt to recall the times when he insisted on their wearing hats outside the building, dressing in white and not colored shirts, and preferably remaining single while being seminarians. Likewise a faculty colleague vividly remembered Dr. McNaugher's denunciation of bedroom slippers as a work of the devil and the symbols of a lazy mind.

Following retirement Dr. McNaugher was by no means inactive. He continued to work on manuscripts for publication, he supervised the historical records of the denomination, he served as an advisor on the Revised Standard Version of the New Testament, and he accepted invitations for guest preaching and speaking.

Dr. McNaugher died on December 11, 1947, some four and a half years after he retired and just nineteen days shy of his ninetieth birthday. Dr. Taylor, the initial occupant of the McNaugher Chair, in writing the faculty's tribute to its former president and teaching colleague, noted that "A Prince and a Great Man Is Fallen."[3] *The Pittsburgh Press* in a December 12th editorial on the relationship of Dr. McNaugher to the United Pres-

---

3. Cf. 2 Samuel 3:38, the words of David on the death of Abner.

byterian denomination, stated: "No man since the Church was founded in 1858 has had a more influential part in directing the destinies of the church and no other leader has approached his record of uninterrupted service since his ordination to the ministry in 1885." Much the same appraisal can be voiced with respect to the relationship of Dr. McNaugher to Pittsburgh-Xenia Seminary during his presidential tenure. For the United Presbyterian Church and its seminary, he was the right man in the right place at the right time.

The Long Presidency (1943-55)

Dr. George A. Long, the second of Pittsburgh-Xenia's presidents, came to that office and to his faculty position following thirty years in the pastorate, first at Second Church, then at Homewood, Pittsburgh. During his twenty-two years in the latter parish he baptized 426 babies, conducted communicants' classes with a total membership of 390, received 1,306 members (753 of them by profession of faith), and preached 1,851 sermons in his own pulpit and 783 elsewhere. Yet he was no stranger to the affairs and activities of the seminary. Few men knew the administrative side of the school as well as Dr. Long did. He was a member of the original committee of ten charged with overseeing the consolidation of the two schools into one institution. When this task was accomplished, he was elected a Pittsburgh-Xenia director and tirelessly served as secretary of the Board until he was selected to be Dr. McNaugher's successor.

Historically, 1944 marked the observance of the 150th anniversary of the seminary's founding through its Xenia ancestry, and the new president took full advantage of the opportunity to publicize the work of the school in the courts of the church and in wider theological circles. Articles were prepared and appeared from time to time in the church papers, and a place was provided in most of the synod programs as well as at General Assembly for this recognition. Moreover, on June 8 and 9, in conjunction with Western Seminary, Pittsburgh-Xenia hosted and Dr. Long addressed the Biennial Meeting of the American Association of Theological Schools. More than 100 seminaries were represented by the 120 delegates in attendance.

A trio of programmatic accomplishments can be attributed to Dr. Long's initiative during the first five years of his leadership. First, in response to the growing needs of those engaged in the regular ministry as well as many returning chaplains, the graduate department was once more opened, with course work offered in any of four fields leading to the Master of Theology (Th.M.) degree. Second, along the lines of "refresher" courses and what we would now designate as "continuing education" opportunities, two week-long summer institutes of theology were regularly scheduled to take place on the campus of the various church colleges. These popular institutes were staffed principally by seminary faculty, but they were augumented annually by church and theological leaders of considerable reputation. Third, in 1947 a much-needed department of religious education was inaugurated under the direction of Florence M. Lewis, newly selected as the first female professor and dean of women in the school's history. This newest of academic programs was designed to provide training on the graduate level for women preparing to become directors of Christian education, church secretaries, parish workers, or missionaries, and it led to the Master of Religious Education (M.R.E.) degree. The department was begun as a bold adventure, open to part-time as well as full-time students, but within half a decade it became one of only eight programs given full accreditation by the American Association of Schools of Religious Education. By 1955 Pittsburgh-Xenia had granted nineteen degrees to those satisfactorily completing the two-year curriculum. All three of these programs, once introduced or reintroduced (as was the graduate school), continued to play vital roles in the training, equipping, and updating of leaders for the United Presbyterian Church and many other denominations throughout the remaining years of the seminary's existence.

One of the foremost challenges Dr. Long faced during his presidency was that of rebuilding the faculty. In 1942 the Board had taken action establishing seventy as the age for mandatory retirement. What the new ruling meant was that by 1950 all but Drs. Kelso and Taylor would be lost to the teaching force. To Dr. Long's credit, by that date significant replacements had been secured in the persons of Addison H. Leitch, Florence M. Lewis, H. Ray Shear, Gordon E. Jackson, and John H. Gerstner. In the first half of the next decade, Bessie M. Burrows and I joined the staff as full-time faculty members. In addition, several part-time instructors were utilized, and Howard M. Jamieson, Jr., was nominated to become professor of English Bible in Dr. Long's place. Thus by 1955 the ranks of Pittsburgh-Xenia's faculty had been both replenished and enlarged.

The crowning achievement of Dr. Long's tenure at the administrative helm was the relocation of the seminary from 616 West North Avenue on the North Side to 616 North Highland Avenue in the East Liberty district of Pittsburgh. Relocation had been an expressed intention as far back as the 1930 plan of seminary consolidation.[4] Five years later, church history professor Williamson, writing in *The United Presbyterian,* saw fit to remind readers of this commitment: "A dream in the hopes of the faculty and the board foresees the seminary moved to another part of the city, when finances return to normal, where there may be more of a scholastic and less commercial atmosphere than in the surroundings of the present building."[5] Dreams, however, often take considerable time to materialize. How true this was in the case of a new location for Pittsburgh-Xenia! But in due time, thanks to the astute leadership of Dr. Long, this particular dream did become a glorious reality.

Beginning with the 1947-48 school year, enrollment at the seminary grew substantially so that at the time of Dr. Long's retirement the size of the student body had more than tripled during his term of office. The steadily mounting numbers in record-breaking proportions put extreme pressure on a physical plant whose main building had been constructed in 1899 and was designed to house eighty to ninety single students. Despite a succession of major improvements over the years, as the 1940s came to a close it had become increasingly evident that the present facilities had been repaired and patched to very near their limit. It came as no surprise, therefore, that the Committee on Theological Seminaries, upon receiving a memorial from the Pittsburgh-Xenia Board, concurred in making the following request of the 1950 General Assembly: "The urgency of relocation and new building is apparent to anyone who is familiar with the present situation of the seminary. Your committee would urge that the Church, with all possible speed and diligence, provide adequate facilities for the theological training of its leadership."[6] The time for action had arrived.

The Assembly responded positively by appointing a committee of fifteen and mandating it to devise ways and means to raise one million dollars for the purpose of relocating the seminary at a site to be selected

4. This had also been considered during the period of the antecedent Allegheny Seminary. See p. 114.
5. *United Presbyterian,* editorial, May 2, 1935.
6. *General Assembly Minutes, 1950,* p. 813.

by its Board. As proof that the project had widespread appeal to the grass
roots of United Presbyterianism and not just at its top echelon, within
one year congregations and individuals had wholeheartedly subscribed
over $1,019,000 to finance the relocation project. Never before had the
church pledged so much in so short a time to any of its institutions. In
July of 1951, Dr. James T. Vorhis, a pastor in Coraopolis, Pennsylvania,
and a member of the Board, accepted the position of vice president at
the seminary to be Dr. Long's right-hand man in the development and
business management of the new campus. Miss Mildred Cowan, secretary
to the president, continued to process payments and pledges as seminary
treasurer. Also that same summer an architect was employed to prepare
the plans and specifications for the projected new buildings.

The all-important question of where to rebuild the seminary was
not hastily decided. After a thorough study of eleven prospective sites in
the Pittsburgh area, a new location finally was chosen when the highly
desirable Lockhart-Mason property in East Liberty became available. This
beautiful ten-acre site was ideally situated close to several strong United
Presbyterian congregations and not far from the University of Pittsburgh.

Pittsburgh-Xenia Seminary, Pressley Chapel

Long Administration Building

For many years Charles Lockhart had been a trustee of the Sixth United Presbyterian Church, a generous supporter of Allegheny Seminary, and the largest contributor to the erection of the existing seminary building in 1899. In March of 1951 the twelve heirs of his son-in-law, Henry Lee Mason, Jr., gave the family estate on North Highland Avenue, directly across from Peabody High School, to the seminary for the purpose of its relocation. Pittsburgh-Xenia had found a new home.

The dedication of the campus and the accompanying ground-breaking ceremonies for two new buildings, an administration complex and a dormitory for single men, occurred in connection with the opening of the fall term in September 1952. A target date for occupancy was set for two years hence. That goal was met with the move from the North Side to East Liberty in the summer months of 1954. During a week of dedication events in September, more than 2,000 persons visited and saw for themselves Pittsburgh-Xenia's new quarters.

McCune Chapel in the Long Building. When the Hicks Chapel was built
in 1970, this became a lounge for lectures, receptions, faculty and
board meetings, student use, and worship.

Dr. Long's last year as president (1954-55) was the seminary's first
year on the East Liberty campus. A greathearted and devoted man of
foresight and wisdom, he had persisted on behalf of the institution until
the long-cherished dream of a relocated seminary had actualized. No
wonder that he was properly and widely acclaimed for being an efficient
administrator who combined largeness of vision with care for the smallest
detail. It seemed that something of himself had gone into each brick and
stone of the new seminary. Though modestly he would have been the first
to share credit with a host of others, it was most fitting that the main
administration building should be named after him and known as such
ever since. It contained classrooms, the McCune Chapel, library, museum,
offices, reception area, and social hall. Significantly, its three-story dormitory companion piece has preserved for posterity the name of the il-
lustrious first president by being designated McNaugher Memorial Hall.
Two buildings, two presidents, one seminary, and one grateful church!

The Leitch Presidency (1955-59)

While Dr. Long came to the presidential office from the pastorate, Addison Leitch rose from within the ranks of the faculty to this position, as did Dr. McNaugher, and proved equally capable in the face of its constant challenges and demands. Like his predecessors he also was a graduate of one of the United Presbyterian colleges. In contrast, however, his years of service before coming to the seminary as a teacher had largely been in the church's academic institutions: Assiut College in Egypt, Pikeville College in Kentucky, and Grove City College in Pennsylvania. His post-seminary studies as the Jamison Scholar of the Pittsburgh-Xenia class of 1936 took him abroad to Cambridge University, from which he earned his Ph.D. degree. Called under Dr. Long to be on the faculty of his alma mater in 1946, he initially taught in the area of the philosophy of religion and religious education. When Dr. Karr retired in 1949, Dr. Leitch was transferred to the chair of systematic and biblical theology. That same year, along with his teaching tasks, he was appointed to the newly created office of dean, a position he held until he was elected to be Pittsburgh-Xenia's third and last president.

Upon the occasion of his formal installation in November of 1955, Dr. Leitch paused at the outset of his inaugural address to pay tribute to the two men who had provided the seminary with such strong presidential leadership during the preceding twenty-five years. Dr. McNaugher always "set the tone" of the seminary and the church. Dr. Long would always be remembered as the one who in twelve years "brought us into a new era." Now it remained for President Leitch to maintain and enrich the school's proud tradition, preserve and build upon the goodwill currently enjoyed between seminary and church, further strengthen the faculty in response to growing curricular needs and peak enrollment, and see to it that a much-needed married students' apartment dormitory finally was funded and constructed. All of these responsibilities he was able to meet successfully within the comparatively short span of his presidency.

Four new faces were added to the full-time faculty roster during the Leitch years. First came Howard M. Jamieson, Jr., in 1955 from the pastorate of Third United Presbyterian Church in Pittsburgh to teach Bible. Two years later, John M. Bald, pastor of the Highland Community United Presbyterian Church since 1945, took up responsibilities in theology and ethics. In 1958 Malcolm S. Alexander, eight years a practicing attorney before seminary and thereafter twice pastor of West Coast congregations, assumed duties in pastoral theology and as director of field education. And Harold E. Scott, pastor at Santa Ana, California, came to teach homiletics when Dr. Shear retired in 1959.[7] Throughout its history, Pittsburgh-Xenia consistently affirmed its commitment to be a theological school with one dominating purpose: to prepare students for the pulpit and the pastorate. The records show that the majority of its graduates went forth to the pastoral ministry. The four men who were the last to join its faculty were no exception: they were all products of the school itself and brought to their teaching task an aggregate of more than forty-five years of "hands on" pastoral experience. They averaged forty-one years of age. Together with other faculty colleagues, they made up the "Leitch Team," which continued to enhance the school's reputation and service record until the time of consolidation with Western Theological Seminary to become Pittsburgh Theological Seminary.

The colleagues who shared the teaching task with Dr. Leitch, the students who were privileged to sit under him, and the countless persons who heard him as a popular speaker in a variety of settings will forever remember his sharp mind and keen wit. He was truly one of those winsome individuals whom it was a sheer delight to quote. "When you take notes," he remarked, "the pencil writes at both ends: on the paper and in your mind." "The hardest way to learn anything is to read an easy book." When a student once asked him, "How much Greek does the average minister use?" his ready response was, "That's what makes him average." When asked for a candid appraisal of a certain pastor, he said: "He's the world's champion lightweight." Nor did he ever object to being quoted, as he so frequently was, for as he himself said facetiously, "It isn't plagiarism if you forget where you got it."[8]

Under President Leitch the final phase of Pittsburgh-Xenia's building campaign was brought to fruition. Before the seminary's relocation, the denomination had faced the necessity of relocating the seminary for more than a decade. The first concrete step in that direction was taken in 1945 when an allotment of $400,000 was made in the budget of the Worldwide Christian Advance Fund. Next, the 1950 General Assembly authorized the raising of one million dollars. It was soon evident, however, that rapidly rising building and labor costs would require an additional

7. In 1978 Dr. Scott left the faculty to become the Executive of Pittsburgh Presbytery.

8. Thanks to Rev. Dr. Richard K. Kennedy for some of these recollections.

amount. The General Assembly of 1953 approved the extension of the campaign to include another half million dollars to finish the task.

As originally planned, the relocation project was to consist of four units: a main school and administration building, a dormitory for single men, a dormitory for women in the department of Christian education, and a married couples' dormitory. When Dr. Leitch assumed the presidency in the fall of 1955, the first three units had been completed and in use for a year. While the Long and McNaugher buildings were entirely new, a women's dormitory was obtained by remodeling an existing brick structure on the campus. Only the married students' dormitory remained to be built.

The number of married students coming to seminary had steadily grown to the extent that shortly after the midpoint of the twentieth century the majority of seminarians fell into that category. Pittsburgh-Xenia was typical of the larger seminary scene. Whereas in 1945 it had only thirteen married students, five years later there were sixty-four, and by 1955 there were ninety-eight. Housing for married students was a necessity.

Under Dr. Long and then under Dr. Leitch, the seminary continued to receive pledges and gifts toward the campus home for married couples. The prevailing sentiment in the church seemed to be: "It ought to be done, it can be done, and it will be done." Early in 1956 Dr. Leitch's leadership in such stewardship efforts resulted in the largest single cash contribution ever made to the seminary up to that time: Miss Mary and Dr. Jennie Prentiss, sisters in the First United Presbyterian Church, Steubenville, Ohio, gave $200,000. This generous gift changed the whole financial picture and made possible the ground-breaking ceremonies on September 10, 1956, for the final relocation unit. Dr. James Kelso, senior member of the faculty, affectionately known as "Mr. Dig" for his renowned archaeological endeavors, turned the first shovelful of earth. A year later, the married students' apartment building was in service. It was named Fulton Memorial Hall, after the late General Chairman of the Relocation and Completion Fund Campaigns, Samuel A. Fulton. With its official dedication on November 16, 1957, the "unfinished seminary" had at long last been completed. By commencement the following May, President Leitch was able to report that Pittsburgh-Xenia had become free of debt on all its buildings and was the grateful caretaker of a plant whose estimated worth was three and a half million dollars.

The year 1958-59 was a momentous time for both denomination

and seminary. Following the historic union in 1958 of the United Presbyterian Church of North America and the Presbyterian Church, U.S.A., Pittsburgh-Xenia and Western were now sister seminaries of the United Presbyterian Church in the U.S.A. Thus they began to explore ways to fulfill their responsibility to provide a trained ministry for more than 600,000 United Presbyterians within two hundred miles of Pittsburgh, and to share in developing leaders to carry on the ecumenical mission of the church. A special survey committee of nationally known educators, chaired by Dr. Herman N. Morse, was requested by both schools to study the resources and potential for theological education in the Pittsburgh area and to report its findings to their Boards of Directors. In May of 1959 the directors voted in accord with the report of the study committee that there should be established one consolidated seminary to be located at the site of the North Highland campus of Pittsburgh-Xenia Seminary.

It was at this time that Dr. Leitch submitted his resignation as president. Because he had expressed strong opposition to the consolidation, he felt that he could no longer serve effectively in an administrative position. The Board granted him a year's sabbatical leave, and he agreed to return as professor of theology in the new school.

The 1959-60 academic year featured a number of shared efforts, though classes continued to be conducted both in North Side and in East Liberty, and the year culminated in a common commencement. Special lectures were co-sponsored. Professors for electives were exchanged. Communion was celebrated. A faculty retreat was held. Faculty discussions on matters of common concern took place. Joint committees on library and curriculum functioned and reported. On December 9, 1959, the formal charter of consolidation was granted by the Commonwealth of Pennsylvania to Pittsburgh Theological Seminary. Thus it was a year of transition and intensified preparation for the emergence of a single, unified, theological enterprise in a key geographical and ecclesiastical location.

Merger had brought Pittsburgh-Xenia into existence, and merger brought its three decades of faithful service to a conclusion. Good roots, deeply planted and carefully nourished, had yielded much fruit. Once more, a new chapter in United Presbyterian theological education was ready to unfold in Pittsburgh.

CHAPTER SIX

Western Seminary

Howard Eshbaugh and James Arthur Walther

A Presbyterian Seminary in the West

In the years after the General Assembly established a seminary at Princeton, there was debate as to whether there should be more than one seminary. In 1819 Francis Herron, pastor of Pittsburgh's First Presbyterian Church, and James Graham were appointed a committee by Redstone Presbytery[1] "to enquire into the propriety and practicability of forming an education society for the education of poor and pious youth for the Gospel ministry." At the meeting a year later it was found "expedient and practicable," and an Education Society was formed "auxiliary to Board of Education under the care of the Genl. Assembly."[2] This, then, led to action by the Assembly.

In 1825 the General Assembly voted that it was "expedient forthwith to establish a theological seminary in the west." It was to be called the Western Theological Seminary. A commission (which included elder Andrew Jackson from Nashville) was named, but it never made a final recommendation.

---

1. Redstone included most of the Pennsylvania frontier of which Fort Pitt was the focal point. On October 15, 1822, the minutes of Redstone Presbytery note that "so much of the bounds of this [Presbytery] as lies North & West of the rivers Ohio & Aleghany, was attached by the Synod of Pittsburgh, at their last meeting, to the [Presbytery] of Ohio." *Minutes of the Presbytery of Redstone, of the Presbyterian Church in the U.S.A.* (Cincinnati: Elm Street Printing Company, 1878), p. 327.

2. *Minutes of the Presbytery of Redstone*, pp. 301, 305-6.

There was much political maneuvering, and at least thirteen sites were proposed. They included Charleston, Indiana, Meadville and Allegheny in Pennsylvania, and ten towns in Ohio — Chillicothe, Cincinnati, Decatur, Georgetown, Lebanon, New Richmond, Ripley, Springfield, Walnut Hill, and West Union. Inducements were offered to influence location in the various towns. The first vote, by less than half of the board, was split between West Union and Allegheny.

The final choice at the Assembly of 1827 was between Walnut Hill (now a part of Cincinnati) and Allegheny (located across the river from Pittsburgh). The former offered three plots of land worth $6,000. Allegheny pledged $21,000 in cash installments plus eighteen acres from the Allegheny Commons, valued at about $20,000. The moderator of the Assembly was Francis Herron, and he gave a stirring endorsement of Allegheny. The Assembly chose that site — by two votes. The strength of the Presbyterians in this area and the sizable financial considerations offered by the town made the selection a wise one.[3]

If Dr. Herron of First Church was influential in bringing the seminary to Pittsburgh, the key person in launching the seminary was Elisha Pope Swift, a descendant of John Eliot (usually regarded as the first missionary in America). Swift had come from Delaware in the fall of 1819 to be pastor of Second Church, Pittsburgh. He brought new life into that congregation, but he also showed great zeal for education. He helped Pittsburgh Academy after it became the Western University of Pennsylvania (1819) — the antecedent of the University of Pittsburgh (1908). There Dr. Swift taught "moral science and evidences of Christianity" for some five years. So his vision was to make the new seminary more than just a training school.

The General Assembly of 1827 chose Jacob Jones Janeway of Philadelphia as the first professor for Western Seminary. He was pastor of the largest church in the denomination. At first he declined. The process of organizing the seminary, however, was under way, and the teaching task was to begin in the fall of 1827. The Board of Directors decided that, in order to provide as far as was practicable for the reception and instruction of students and to commence the operations of the institution, Elisha Swift and Joseph Stockton, pastor of the Allegheny Church, should perform the teaching duties until General Assembly's appointment should

---

3. Since all of the Ohio locations were in the western half of the state, eight of them in or near Cincinnati, that region offered no support for the new seminary. Eventually Lane Seminary was founded at Walnut Hill.

Elisha Pope Swift, instructor at Western Seminary;
founder of the Western Foreign Missionary Society

be resolved. During the fall and winter terms Swift instructed four students in the session room of First Church, Pittsburgh. In the following summer term Stockton was the teacher.[4]

Dr. Swift used much of his time to canvass Presbyterian churches in Pennsylvania and Ohio to raise money for the young seminary. It is a mistake to imagine that in those days when educational institutions were

4. Streets in Pittsburgh today bear the names Herron and Stockton.

laying their foundations the people were willing to offer substantial support. On the contrary, the seminary weathered the early years simply because a few people, mostly ministers, perceived its importance to the church and lived sacrificially in order that it might grow. On October 6, 1830, Redstone Presbytery "Resolved that the Members of P b y [Presbytery] use their best endeavours to have the 2d Installment of the subscription in behalf of the Western Theol. Seminary collected, & forwarded to the Treasurer with as little delay as possible."[5]

Dr. Janeway finally accepted the Assembly's appointment and was inducted on October 17, 1828. His son Thomas came with him to serve as instructor in Hebrew. After only a year Dr. Janeway presented his resignation to the 1829 General Assembly. The reasons for his leaving are probably manifold. He had just five students but had expected many more. The rent for adequate housing seemed exorbitant. It was said that Mrs. Janeway preferred the more sophisticated life-style of Philadelphia and that their servant did not like Alleghenytown. Perhaps Dr. Janeway lacked the western pioneer spirit.

The Earliest Years

In 1829 the General Assembly chose Luther Halsey to lead the faculty. He was then professor of natural philosophy at Princeton College and was a minister of great erudition and eloquence. To assist him the Board of Directors called John Williamson Nevin, an instructor in theology at Princeton Theological Seminary. Western's third year began with two able teachers and fifteen students. By later standards the three-year course of study was somewhat limited in scope, but it was carefully directed toward a clearly defined purpose.

The six students who began their studies in the fall of 1829 were called the biblical class. The Reverend Mr. Nevin who taught them wrote about the course:

A thorough foundation [is] to be laid in the study and interpretation of the Holy Scripture, which is the basis of all sound theological knowledge. It is our wish that every student who finishes an entire course in the Seminary

5. *Minutes of the Presbytery of Redstone,* p. 408.

shall have critically read the whole New Testament in Greek and most of the Hebrew Scriptures besides being well grounded in Jewish and Christian antiquities and the canons of criticism.[6]

They read twenty-three chapters of Genesis in Hebrew, and 1 and 2 Corinthians and Hebrews in Greek. They also studied the first two parts of Jahn's *Archaeology* and reviewed sacred geography.

The middler class of four students was known as the theological class. They devoted most of the year to the Presbyterian Confession of Faith and other Presbyterian standards. The senior class of five was designated the ecclesiastical class. Their study lay in the fields of church history and church government. All students were assigned hours for lectures and for recitation. There was also supervised study, and each student was required to engage in some healthful exercise.

The first graduating class was truly "Western." Although only one member was born west of Allegheny, every member died west of the city. Of the first fifty graduates of the seminary, only four died east of the Allegheny mountains.

From the earliest days until 1959 all students were required to sign a Matriculation Pledge Book. The words of the pledge were these:

> Deeply impressed with a sense of the need of improving in knowledge, prudence and piety in my preparation for the gospel ministry, I solemnly promise in reliance on divine grace, that I will faithfully and diligently attend to all the instructions of this Seminary, and that I will conscientiously and vigilantly observe all the rules and regulations specified in the plan for its instruction and government, so far as the same relates to students, and that I will obey all the lawful requisitions and readily yield to all the Professors and Directors of the Seminary while I shall continue a member of it.

First Physical Facilities

Dr. Herron was the first president of the Board of Directors. At once the Board set about planning for a group of seminary buildings. The principal building was to be of cut stone, four stories in height, and flanked by

6. In the Matriculation Pledge Book of Western Theological Seminary, now in the Pittsburgh Seminary archives.

other buildings, including homes for the professors. It would stand in the center at the top of the hill in Allegheny overlooking the city of Pittsburgh and the point where the Allegheny and Monongahela rivers meet to form the Ohio.[7]

Local Presbyterians subscribed $12,000, but little other money had been raised when building began in 1829. The main building plan was revised. Only one building was to be built, of brick rather than stone, and it would not be as large as first proposed. It was now sixty by fifty feet, with fifty-foot wings for living quarters, a chapel, and a library room. The building was occupied unfinished in the spring of 1831, for room to house twenty students was needed. Dr. Swift called this location "the mount of sacred science." The building was later described thus:

> its appointments and accommodations . . . were not such as to en-
> courage luxurious habits, or to unfit young men for the practice of
> self-denial in the ministry. The ascent from the street was laborious,
> the furniture meagre, the walls bare, the descent in either direction
> dangerous for those not accustomed to stand in slippery places, the
> outlook from the windows less exhilarating than might have been
> expected, in view of the cloud of smoke which made it difficult at times
> even to trace the outline of the hills, or to discern the meeting of the
> rivers.[8]

The Faculty and Other Developments

That same year, 1831, marked a milestone in the missionary outreach of the church. The Synod of Pittsburgh had tried to get the General Assembly to organize a foreign missions board, and when that failed they proceeded to establish the Western Foreign Missionary Society. The key leader in this effort was Elisha Swift. A plaque on the wall outside the president's office in today's seminary administration building memorializes this event. Nearly a century later at the Centennial Convocation of Western Seminary, Robert E. Speer declared that behind both the seminary and the Western Foreign Missionary Society "lay a great principle and a great

---

7. The hill was later known as "Monument Hill." Buildings of the Allegheny Community College now stand there.

8. William H. Jeffers, *Occasional Addresses and Sermons by the late Reverend Samuel J. Wilson* (New York: Dodd, Mead, & Co., 1895), p. 15.

personality. The principle was that the work of Foreign Missions is not an optional interest to be left by the Church to individuals and voluntary associations. Our fathers here conceived instead that the missionary obligation is the obligation of the Church in her essential character and that every member of the Church is committed to this obligation." He quoted Elisha Swift: "On what appointment do pastors and elders sit in the house of God and hold the keys of the Kingdom of Heaven, but that which commissions them to go and disciple all nations?"[9]

Dr. Halsey resigned in 1836. Perhaps he was daunted by the financial condition of the school. That same year Dr. David Elliot began a teaching career at Western that extended to 1874. At one time or another, he taught almost every branch of the theological curriculum.

One of the unsung fathers of Western Seminary was Alan Ditchfield Campbell. He was ordained in the Associate Reformed Church but later joined Redstone Presbytery of the Presbyterian Church. From 1820 to 1827 he was pastor of the First Presbyterian Church of Nashville. There he formed a deep friendship with Andrew Jackson.[10] He was appointed a director of the seminary about the same time he moved back to western Pennsylvania. He served Fourth Church, Pittsburgh, for a time, but soon resigned to become "general agent" of the seminary. Thus he was the first of a long list of staff persons, most of whose names are remembered only in the records contemporary with their service.

In 1828 Campbell went to England and Scotland and collected 2,000 volumes to be the base of a theological library. Dr. Swift referred to these books as "a valuable collection of choice and appropriate works."[11] Without his indefatigable labor in support of the seminary it is doubtful whether the school would have survived its early financial problems. For a time he also served as instructor in church government and discipline.

In 1840 he terminated his official relationship with the seminary and became pastor of the Second Presbyterian Church of Allegheny. He continued, however, to be an advocate for the seminary. He wrote a history

9. The address is printed in full in *The Bulletin of the Western Theological Seminary* 20, 3 (April 1928): 62-80 (the quotations are on pp. 65-66). This issue of the *Bulletin* also contains other historical chapters. For further narrative about Western's graduates on overseas mission fields, see Chapter Nine, "Pittsburgh Theological Seminary in World Mission," pp. 207-36 below.

10. It was said that when Campbell was not praising Western Seminary he was praising President Jackson for his Christian loyalty and character.

11. See W. W. McKinney, ed., *The Presbyterian Valley* (Pittsburgh, 1958), p. 369.

of the seminary entitled "The Founding and Early History of the Western Theological Seminary."[12] He is buried in Allegheny Cemetery.[13]

The year 1840 also marked the resignation of Dr. Nevin. He went to the German Reformed Church, where he became a proponent of the Mercersburg theology. To replace him the seminary called Lewis Warner Green, a native of Kentucky. He had studied law and medicine before he took his theological training at Princeton Seminary. He taught until 1847.

In 1842 Alexander T. McGill became professor of ecclesiastical history and church government. He had studied law and had graduated from Jefferson College and the Canonsburg Seminary. He served until 1854.

Difficulties

Three problems beset the school in the 1840s. In the first place, the financial outlook was dark. Professors often were not paid; sometimes the arrears reached a year's salary. Dr. Nevin wrote to Alan Campbell: "My salary was never paid when due, and I got no interest on arrearages, but was glad to get the principal as I could by piecemeal when it suits the churches to replenish our lean treasury."[14] Salaries owed to the professors were just part of the seminary's heavy debt.

A second problem concerned the property on which the seminary was located. In 1827 a grant from the city of Allegheny to the seminary had been confirmed by the Legislature of Pennsylvania. It included eighteen acres. In 1842 some Allegheny citizens managed to file a suit to recover the property. The matter dragged on until late in 1849, when an agreement was finally reached. The seminary retained one acre, and the city of Allegheny assumed a token permanent debt to the seminary.[15]

The third difficulty came from a theological schism in the Presby-

12. See *The Bulletin of the Western Theological Seminary* 20, 1 (October 1927). The account covers 130 pages — evidence of how abbreviated the present chapter must be.

13. He became chaplain of the Home Guards in 1861. He marched in a parade on July 4 that year and never recovered from that fatigue.

14. McKinney, ed., *Presbyterian Valley*, p. 373.

15. Pittsburgh continued this agreement when Allegheny became a part of that city. The city made a token yearly payment until the Seminary moved from that location in 1959.

terian Church. Until 1837 Presbyterianism had come nearest to being a national church. Professor Elliott was the moderator of the General Assembly that year. He and conservative colleagues decided that four synods and one other presbytery were not following pure polity and doctrine. They had the votes to sever those bodies — 533 churches and over 100,000 members. The following year, when commissioners of those bodies were refused seats at the Assembly, the denomination split into Old School and New School, each claiming to be the legal heir of the General Assembly.

The courts ruled that the Old School was the legal Presbyterian Church and so held Princeton and Western Seminaries. The division continued until 1869. Of course the controversy affected the financial condition of the seminary adversely. Nevertheless, there were hopeful signs. The student body increased to about fifty annually. The library was growing. Dr. Herron continued as president of the Board until 1860, and Dr. Swift was its secretary until 1865.

Dark Days

In the decade before the Civil War student enrollment reached 150. The financial burden, however, was staggering. The agreement to abandon the city's property meant that funds had to be raised for a new building. On January 23, 1854, fire destroyed the old building, which was still being occupied. Some good books from the library were saved, but the students lost everything. Since the building was on a high hill overlooking the city, the fire was widely viewed, and it was said that "the preacher factory was on fire" — a statement that reflected "the growing industrialism of the community."[16] The seminary had only $5,000 of insurance.

School continued in space provided by the First Church of Allegheny and the Second Church of Pittsburgh. But now monies began to come in from the churches. Property was purchased at the corner of Ridge and Irwin Avenues (the latter now Brighton Road), a location occupied until the consolidation of 1959. Within a year a new building was occupied debt-free. Soon four houses were built for professors, and in 1859 a

---

16. F. D. McCloy, "The Mount of Sacred Science," in McKinney, ed., *The Presbyterian Valley*, p. 372.

Western Seminary (Presbyterian U.S.A.), Pittsburgh, Seminary Hall
(burned in 1854)

student dormitory, Beatty Hall,[17] was ready. Three years later a library building was built.

One bright spot in this decade was the coming of Melancthon W. Jacobus as professor of Oriental and biblical literature and exegesis. His outstanding service extended from 1851 until 1876. He was also pastor of Old Fifth Church, Pittsburgh, until 1872. Such dual service was regularly an economic necessity for the professors.

In 1855 the seminary for the first time called an alumnus to the faculty. Samuel J. Wilson came from Second Church, Wheeling, as in-

17. Named for Mrs. Charles Beatty, of Steubenville, Ohio, who contributed $10,000. She and her husband had founded the Steubenville Female Academy.

structor in church history. In 1857 he was promoted to professor, and he continued teaching until 1883.

Wartime Shadows

This is no place to rehearse the tribulations of the Presbyterian churches in the years leading up to the Civil War.[18] Slavery had been a factor, though not the principal one, in the Old School–New School division. Persons from both sides who took a strong abolitionist stand left the jurisdiction of both schools and formed "Free" presbyteries and eventually the Free Presbyterian Church in America. One leader was Joseph Gordon, a graduate of Western Seminary. Other detailed information about the seminary and the conflict is scarce.

Churches in the North did not really speak boldly against slavery until after the churches in the South had withdrawn. In 1858 New School Presbyterians divided over the slavery issue. When the Old School did likewise in 1861, the two southern groups joined to form the Presbyterian Church in the United States. Although Western Seminary generally had Old School leaders, it did not experience difficult disputes. The split in the North was ended in 1869, at which time Professor Jacobus was moderator of the Assembly.

In 1854 William S. Plumer was called as professor of pastoral theology. He also served as pastor of Central Church of Allegheny. The church grew, but when he refused to take a stand against slavery he was forced to resign in 1862. Meanwhile, a new congregation had formed to protest Dr. Plumer's position. It was called North Church of Allegheny and was just around the corner from the seminary.

In 1864 Western called Archibald Alexander Hodge, a son of Charles Hodge, to replace Dr. Plumer.[19] He also served the North Church

---

18. A summary may be read in E. B. Welsh's essay "Wrestling with Human Values: The Slavery Years," in *They Seek a Country,* ed. G. J. Slosser (New York: Macmillan, 1955), pp. 210-33.

19. Charles Hodge was the author of the three-volume *Systematic Theology,* which was used at Western for many years around the turn of the century. Robert H. Nichols says of Hodge: "his thought was profoundly Biblical, governed by a high doctrine of verbal inspiration and infallibility; and he steadfastly maintained that his theology was only the teaching of the Bible" (in *Dictionary of American Biography* [New York: Charles Scribner's Sons, 1932], vol. 9, p. 98b).

after 1866. In 1877 he went to teach at his alma mater, Princeton Seminary.

Faculty in the Late Nineteenth Century

Space will not allow mention of all the teachers who came to the seminary in the ensuing years. A complete list of all professors inaugurated in Western, in the other antecedent seminaries, and in Pittsburgh Seminary appears in an appendix at the end of this volume (see pp. 267-71). Several names, however, call for attention.

Benjamin B. Warfield came in 1878 and taught New Testament until he was called to Princeton in 1887. Robert Dick Wilson came in 1885 and taught Old Testament until 1900, when he, too, went to Princeton. W. H. Jeffers also taught Old Testament for thirty-seven years, beginning in 1877.

One of the most influential professors in the history of Western Seminary was Matthew Brown Riddle. His father, David Riddle, was pastor of Pittsburgh's Third Presbyterian Church and was one of the few ministers in Pittsburgh to join the New School. He managed his minority position with grace and avoided bitter controversy. Matthew bore the name of his mother's forebear, Matthew Brown, who had been president of Jefferson College.

Dr. Riddle joined the seminary faculty in 1887 and served until 1916. In later years Professor McCloy described him as "a personality of sheer incandescence . . . an exciting, fearless, and compassionate teacher. . . . The meticulous concern for truth; the spontaneous, natural challenge of all hypocrisy and tyranny; the candid, simple trust in God brought into the life of the Seminary a new concept of the Christian life and a new understanding of authority."[20] He carried the affectionate nickname "Bunkie," which was "a colloquial term for mate or fellow."[21] He was deaf and used a fan-shaped audiphone, which he held between his teeth. He walked the aisles among his students and on occasion could intimidate them with his face-to-face questioning.

Dr. Riddle is perhaps best known for his service on the American

20. In McKinney, ed., *Presbyterian Valley*, p. 376.
21. James A. Kelso, *Western Watch* 1, 1 (1 January 1950): 7.

Western Seminary, faculty group (front row, Schaff, Christie, Kelso, Breed, Snowden)

Revision Committee, which produced the American Standard Version of the Bible in 1901. His scholarship made a major contribution to the New Testament revision. He was one of six American contributors to *The Illustrated Bible Treasury,* writing the "Introduction to the New Testament" and the articles on Matthew, Mark, Luke, John, and the General Epistles.[22] He was passionately prejudiced in favor of Tischendorf's Greek Testament and vigorously challenged any student who used Westcott and Hort. He is reported to have pleaded with his students to "learn a little Greek for Christ's sake."[23]

It is safe to say that his influence extended well beyond his life. One of his students, James A. Kelso, studied in Europe and then beginning in 1897 taught Old Testament at Western. He became president in 1908. The theological controversies during much of that period found Western

22. Twenty-seven British writers and one Canadian contributed to *The Illustrated Bible Treasury,* ed. William Wright (New York: Thomas Nelson & Sons, 1896). B. B. Warfield wrote a well-balanced article on "Revelation."

23. J. A. Kelso, *Western Watch* 1, 1 (1 January 1950): 7.

maintaining a careful course that avoided the extremes of fundamentalism and liberalism that plagued the church. After Dr. Kelso, Dr. Riddle's nephew Henry became president of the seminary.

Robert Christie taught theology from 1891 to 1923. David Riddle Breed, who was pastor of First Church, Pittsburgh, began in 1898 to teach preaching and continued on the faculty for thirty-three years. In 1911 he published a textbook on homiletics, *Preparing to Preach*.[24]

Into the Twentieth Century

In the nineteenth century, leadership in Western Seminary was the responsibility of the senior professor. In 1903 Dr. David Gregg was called to become president and was inaugurated the following year. He retired in 1908, and James A. Kelso became president. He continued in that office, in addition to teaching, until 1943, a total of forty-six years.

Beginning in 1903 David S. Schaff taught church history. He was the son of Philip Schaff and so was in the great tradition of Johannes Neander. David Schaff taught until 1926. The Schaff Lectures are named in his honor. In 1906 David E. Cully began a teaching and administrative career at Western that lasted forty-two years. Old Testament was his field. Few schools could boast of such a team as Kelso and Culley. William R. Farmer taught New Testament and homiletics for thirty-two years.

This brings us to one of the most remarkable teachers in Western's history, James H. Snowden. We must be satisfied here with merely skimming his life and thought. However, a 240-page book entitled *The Incomparable Snowden,* written by six persons who were close to him during his life, provides much more information. It is filled with quotations and anecdotes from his career.[25]

Snowden was a product of western Pennsylvania. He completed the four-year course at Washington and Jefferson College in three years and graduated as valedictorian. Then he distinguished himself at Western Seminary and graduated in 1878. He was very adept at debating. In the winter

24. Breed, *Preparing to Preach* (New York: Hodder & Stoughton, George H. Doran Co., 1911).

25. *The Incomparable Snowden,* ed. W. W. McKinney (Pittsburgh: Davis & Ward, 1961).

of 1878 he wrote a sixty-page letter to Professor S. N. Kellogg at the seminary explaining how he differed from his teacher in his views on millennialism, a subject that was to become very important forty years later.

Snowden served churches at Huron, Ohio, and at Sharon, Pennsylvania, and then in 1886 he was called to Second Church, Washington, Pennsylvania (now Church of the Covenant). There he had a distinguished pastorate lasting twenty-five years. He was a great preacher. His evangelistic zeal brought over six hundred members by profession of faith. He was also a devoted pastor. He rode a bicycle on many of his pastoral calls. He was active in college affairs and taught political economy and ethics. He ministered to many students. He could play the piano and organ and occasionally wrote hymns. At his last service at Second Church a hymn he wrote for the occasion was sung:

> God of our fathers, who didst lead
> Their feet in thine own ways,
> Thou hast led us with loving care
> Through all these happy days. . . .

In October 1893, he began to write a weekly exposition of the International Sunday School lessons for *The Presbyterian Messenger,* a Pittsburgh-based journal. In 1898 this paper was merged with an older rival, *The Presbyterian Banner,* and Dr. Snowden became the editor. The *Banner* had a profound effect on western Pennsylvania Presbyterianism until Dr. Snowden's death in 1936. Beginning in 1921 he wrote annually *Snowden's Sunday School Lessons,* sixteen volumes published by Macmillan Publishing Company.

In 1911 he was called to both McCormick Seminary in Chicago and Western Seminary. He chose to go to his alma mater. There his philosophical acumen, his thirst for truth, and his practical concern for the church brought a fresh direction to the study of theology in the school. Instead of Charles Hodge's work, he had his students read Strong's *Systematic Theology* — but he paid tribute to A. A. Hodge, under whom he had studied at Western, as "the greatest teacher he ever had in his seminary course and probably the only man of genius he was ever personally under."[26]

He wrote four books while at Washington and, in addition to the

26. Quoted in McKinney, ed., *The Incomparable Snowden,* p. 137.

Sunday school lessons, nineteen more books at the seminary — thirty-nine books in thirty-four years. He set forth his theological agenda in *The World a Spiritual System — An Outline of Metaphysics* (1910). This "philosophy of theistic Idealism . . . apparently remained as the unchanged expression of his thinking both as pastor and professor."[27] At his death an unfinished manuscript was found that perhaps was intended to be a sequel.

His penchant for debating and his philosophical and scientific turn of mind led to an event that must always be recounted when Snowden's life is reviewed. Clarence Darrow had smeared William Jennings Bryan and the Bible in the Scopes "Monkey Trial," and although he lost the case, Darrow decided to issue a challenge to debate anyone who would defend religion. In his seventy-sixth year "Jimmy" Snowden agreed to meet him in Carnegie Music Hall, Pittsburgh, on the question "Is Man a Machine?" Evolution was a hot topic on college campuses, and the press gave the event dramatic fervor.

The full details of the debate are well worth reading in Snowden's biography. In short, the professor turned the weapons of scholarship and sarcasm upon the lawyer. Darrow apparently lost control of himself, especially when Snowden offered to take the opposite side of the question in another debate. Darrow's remark to Snowden after the event is classic: "The reverend doctor is a very learned gentleman." Darrow abandoned his plans to debate further.

In the 1920s the Presbyterian Church was wracked by the modernist-fundamentalist controversy with attendant millenarian contention. In *Old Faith and New Knowledge,* Dr. Snowden wrote:

> I am a "conservative" in the sense that I try to see and seize upon and keep all the truth and good I have inherited and that I have obtained in my own experience. . . . I am a "liberal" in the sense that I claim and exercise the liberty of doing my own thinking and of keeping pace with all the widening thoughts of men. . . . I am a "fundamentalist" in the sense that I hold to the real fundamentals of theistic philosophy and evangelical Christianity. . . . I am a "modernist" in the true sense that I try to bring all my knowledge up to date and unify my total experience.[28]

27. D. R. Guthrie, "The Philosophical Theologian," in McKinney, ed., *The Incomparable Snowden,* p. 207.

28. Snowden, *Old Faith and New Knowledge* (New York: Harper and Brothers, 1928), p. 26.

In 1919 he wrote *The Coming of the Lord: Will It Be Premillennial?* and *Is the World Growing Better?* He was really an "amillennialist" and an incurable optimist.

Snowden decried the acrimony that produced factionalism. He probably did more than any other theologian to bring the Presbyterian denomination to accept and use the results of scientific inquiry and keep Presbyterian churches united during the controversies of his time. He and other members of the Western faculty helped the seminary avoid extremism. "No Presbyterian church in Pittsburgh withdrew from the denomination in the nationwide strife. Western Seminary, in its faculty and students and alumni, calmly walked the middle road."[29]

For many years it was the custom for professors to have their portraits painted and hung on seminary walls. Many of these are still on display today. Others whose faces have been forgotten and whose names are listed only in musty archives made contributions to the seminary in their day and in their own ways.

New Buildings and New Faces

The years just before the first World War brought important changes to the seminary facilities. In 1912 the students' residence on Ridge Avenue was replaced with a large Y-shaped building, a design that meant there were no inside rooms. It retained the name "Memorial Hall," which had commemorated the reunion of Old School and New School Presbyterians. The building had an English Collegiate tower.

In 1916 two buildings were dedicated on the other side of Ridge Avenue. Herron Hall contained administration offices and classrooms. It had an even finer English Collegiate tower. These towers inspired lines in the seminary alma mater: "Thy towers are stately sentinels, all vigilant for truth." Behind Herron was Swift Hall, which contained a chapel, classrooms, and the library, designed for 165,000 volumes. These buildings formed the front and back of a projected quadrangle, and the court between them was a fine lawn.

Lowrie Hall, west of Memorial Hall, was remodeled from the former

29. McCloy, "The Mount of Sacred Science," p. 377.

library. It was named for John C. Lowrie,[30] the first Western graduate to go to the overseas mission field. He founded Presbyterian Missions in North India. The original purpose of Lowrie Hall's seven apartments was to house missionaries on furlough. Later it also served faculty and married students.

Gaius Jackson Slosser began a notable term of service in 1928, teaching ecclesiastical history and history of doctrine. He was an internationally known leader in the ecumenical movement and participated in the early councils at Lausanne and Edinburgh. His *Christian Unity, Its History and Challenge in All Communions, in All Lands* was the first major history of ecumenism in the modern church.[31] He was also renowned among the students for a twenty-six-foot-long chart of church history. Dr. Slosser had been ordained in the Methodist Episcopal Church, and he taught Methodist doctrine and polity to Methodist students who attended Western. Pittsburgh Theological Seminary has continued to the present day to make such instruction available.[32]

In 1936 John Wick Bowman came to teach New Testament. He had served the church in the Punjab in India. In 1944 he moved to California to teach at the San Francisco Theological Seminary. He was the author of a number of important books.

Also in 1936 William F. Orr began a teaching career that spanned thirty-eight years. He taught systematic theology until 1957, when he became professor of New Testament literature and exegesis. During the early years of World War II the students gave much time to debate about participation in the war and about pacificism.[33] Drs. Bowman and Orr led some lively debates, with the former leaning toward pacifism and the latter stressing that Hitler must be stopped.

In Dr. Orr's long career his principal focus was teaching. He was also famous for his participation in young people's summer conferences (six in one year!) and later for his lectures on marriage and sex problems.

---

30. For more on Lowrie, see pp. 217-21.

31. Slosser, *Christian Unity, Its History and Challenge in All Communions, in All Lands* (New York: E. P. Dutton, 1929), 425 pages. There are introductions by Archbishop William Temple and Principal Alfred E. Garvie. Slosser sometimes referred to the book as "my very own volume," and students jokingly called it the "MVOV."

32. In 1990 there were over forty United Methodists studying at Pittsburgh Seminary.

33. In 1939 students were required to register for the draft. A special classification, 4-D, was available to theological students and ministers.

In 1990 a large group of his former students published *He Came Here and Loved Us: A Festschrift in Honor of William F. Orr.*[34] In this book Fred M. Rogers remembers: "When I asked him what his hopes are for the Christian Church, he invariably answers, 'I want Christians to be the body of Christ, not just representatives of some religion.'"[35]

A New Era

James A. Kelso played a unique role in the history of the seminary. At the time of his retirement he was referred to as "Dean of all Seminary Presidents in the Presbyterian Church." When he died in 1954, a Board minute took note of his sixty-year association with Western and bore this tribute: "Through the years when our seminaries were hapless stepchildren of the Church, when the demands of theological education lay lightly on its conscience, and when four of our historic seminaries either closed their doors or sacrificed their identity, Dr. Kelso . . . brought Western Seminary safely through."

This time also marked the beginning of a new era in Western's history. It was to be a relatively short time, for fifteen years later Western and its neighbor from across West Park would become one school. War and the postwar period brought new and unique problems. Practical and theological questions faced the students. In early 1943 seventeen alumni went into military chaplaincy, and the list reached fifty-seven before the end of the war. Dr. Culley wrote an article entitled "The Seminary in War Time," and he also became an air raid warden in his community.

The Presidency of Henry A. Riddle

It was also a time of opportunity. Henry A. ("Hal") Riddle came to the presidency in 1944 after thirty-five years in the pastorate. He was a

34. *He Came Here and Loved Us,* ed. Robert C. Curry, Thomas J. Kelso, and Charlene Stoner Maue. Privately published by the William F. Orr Festschrift Foundation, Inc., 112 W. Ninth St., Watsontown, PA 17777.

35. *He Came Here and Loved Us,* p. 26.

grandson of Matthew Brown, who was president of Jefferson College from 1822 to 1845 and a member of the seminary's first Board of Directors. In May 1944, Dr. Culley wrote in *Western Towers,* an occasional student-faculty publication, about "A New President and a New Day at Western."

Dr. Riddle's administration was marked by his pastoral concern for the whole seminary community. A Board minute notes that the students referred to him as "Pastor." Dr. Orr recalled him as "a complete Christian." On one occasion Dr. Riddle quoted Woodrow Wilson: "Too many ministers have as their chief motive to *do* something, when it should be to *be* something."

At this time Hugh Thompson Kerr, distinguished pastor of Pittsburgh's Shadyside Church, was president of the Board of Trustees. He also directed a department of homiletics at the seminary aided by several area pastors,[36] and later he was guest professor of homiletics. He was author of an alma mater entitled "O Western, Mother of Us All," which was sung with some regularity at seminary functions.[37]

The faculty in this period was strengthened. A German refugee, Paul Leo, came as a guest instructor and taught both church history and New Testament courses. Jarvis Cotton, who had been a guest lecturer in homiletics, joined the faculty in 1944 and later became vice president of the administration and director of field service and extension. F. Dixon McCloy, who had been a graduate teaching fellow, became instructor in biblical languages in 1944. In the next twenty-three years he served as professor, dean, and librarian. The Archives Room in the Barbour Library is named in his honor. Also in 1944 J. Carter Swaim became professor of New Testament literature and exegesis.

In 1945 Walter R. Clyde was called from Dubuque Seminary and became professor of Christian education and missions. He served for thirty-one years. David Noel Freedman came as an assistant professor of Old Testament in 1948. He received $4,000 a year and housing. Three years later he became professor of Hebrew and Old Testament literature and was soon among the best-known scholars and writers in his field. Ralph Turnbull became professor of homiletics in 1949. Howard Ralston was instructor in music at both Western and Pittsburgh-Xenia.

36. Two of these, Stuart Nye Hutchison and W. Paul Ludwig, would later act as interim presidents of the Seminary.

37. Many of Dr. Kerr's papers and sermons were placed in Pittsburgh Seminary's archives in 1990 through the kindness of his sons, Professor Hugh T. Kerr, Jr., and Dr. Donald C. Kerr.

Generations of alumni remember Frank Sams, who was custodian and everyone's friend for many years. It is a pity that these pages cannot include the names of all the faithful people who served the seminary in inconspicuous ways — one of Frank's duties was driving Dr. Kelso. Western students used to have a rousing song that included the line, "and here's a toast to Maggie Reed, who makes the blamed thing run" — Miss Reed was Dr. Kelso's secretary. Perhaps we should begin this list with Mrs. John Anderson, who doubtless mothered the first students in the frontier school.

During this period several graduate degrees were offered. A Master of Theology degree was given for a year of study beyond the Bachelor of Sacred Theology (S.T.B.). In 1949 a Doctor of Theology degree was authorized. During the next decade only one student completed this degree, Yun Kuk (David) Kim, who became a distinguished pastor and scholar both in his native Korea and in this country. A Master of Arts in Religious Education was instituted with the University of Pittsburgh, and students could also get advanced standing toward the Ph.D. at the university. Extension courses were offered at Canton, Ohio.

On January 1, 1950, the first issue of *Western Watch* was published.[38] This small journal appeared four times a year from 1950 through 1959. The name was derived from Habakkuk 2:1. It regularly contained articles by faculty, students, and guest writers as well as alumni news and reports about seminary affairs.

In the spring of 1950 Dr. Riddle suddenly proposed that he intended to resign on the eighth of June because of "ill health of a nervous nature." The Board noted his "rare and devoted service, his valuable spiritual guidance,"[39] and tried to dissuade him by offering a sabbatical leave. A month later, however, the resignation was accepted. The next year Dr. Riddle was guest professor in pastoral theology.

Dr. Stuart Nye Hutchison, pastor of the East Liberty Presbyterian Church and president of the Board of Directors, became president pro tempore of the seminary and served for a year. Observance of the 125th anniversary of the seminary was limited to the commencement address in May 1951 because of "the conditions in the world."[40]

---

38. Some wags suggested that the name was connected with the Western Pennsylvania Horological Institute, which was located across Ridge Avenue from the Seminary.

39. Board Minutes, 5 April 1950, p. 86.

40. Board Minutes, 27 March 1951.

Clifford E. Barbour, Western Seminary (President, 1951-1959);
Pittsburgh Seminary (Acting President, 1959-1962)

The Presidency of Clifford E. Barbour

A new president was chosen quickly. Rev. Clifford E. Barbour, Ph.D., pastor of the Second Presbyterian Church of Knoxville, Tennessee, was inaugurated on November 11, 1951, in the East Liberty Presbyterian Church. His inaugural address was entitled "The Church's Ministry in a Tragic Time." In it he declared, "The only solution to the world's tragic needs is Christ and His Gospel."[41]

One of the first events of his administration was the acquisition of a new building. The Board proposed to purchase the former home of B. F. Jones, Jr., of Jones & Laughlin Steel Company, located between Memorial Hall and the corner of Ridge Avenue and Brighton Road, if it could be acquired for no more than $75,000. Fortunately the owner, Pennsylvania Transformer Company, presented the building to the sem-

41. *Western Watch* 3, 1 (1 January 1952): 6.

Western Seminary, aerial view (Swift Hall, Herron Hall, lower left; Jones Building at intersection; Memorial Hall [Y-shaped] and Lowrie Hall [hidden] behind)

inary as a gift on June 14, 1952. It quickly became the administrative center of the seminary. That fall for the first time each member of the faculty had his own office.

In May 1952, a reorganization of the seminary was approved that was known as the "New Plan." Official relationships were clarified. Questions to new professors, somewhat parallel to ordination vows, were required, and professors' powers and duties were spelled out. Curricular details were addressed. Personal religion was stressed. Instructed by the staff, the students were "to cultivate godliness, as an essential qualification for the ministry"; they were to "become an exemplar of the Lord Jesus Christ."[42]

There had been some thought of relocating the seminary, but in the

42. Board Minutes, 13 May 1952, pp. 145-49.

fall of 1952 the Board voted to remain at the Ridge Avenue location. Dr. Hutchison reported on the progress of a three-way church union that was being studied. It involved the United Presbyterian Church of North America (UPCNA, with its Pittsburgh-Xenia Seminary "across the park") and the Presbyterian Church in the United States (the so-called "Southern Church").

With the decision to stay in the same location, the Board in June 1953 engaged architects to plan for completion of the quadrangle at 731 Ridge Avenue. A chapel would fill the west side. Significant gifts from Lewis and Wenman Hicks were to go for this project. The same year, the Hicks family gave a carillon, which was installed in the Herron Hall tower.[43]

Faculty

At that same Board meeting President Barbour stated that the faculty were persons "who are primarily teachers." Some faculty members had other skills that the church utilized. In 1954 Dr. Turnbull went to the First Presbyterian Church of Seattle. Dr. Swaim became Director of the Department of the English Bible of the National Council of Churches. The same year, other teachers came to the faculty. James Walther began teaching New Testament and Sidney Hills Old Testament. In 1955 Robert C. Johnson came to teach systematic theology. In 1957 Elwyn A. Smith began to teach church history, and Walter E. Wiest came from the Board of Education to teach philosophy of religion. William Nicholson at various times taught Greek, homiletics, and pastoral theology. For three years George Arthur Frantz was guest professor of preaching.

Students

In the spring of 1947 the Student Presbytery was instructed to cooperate with the corresponding body of the Pittsburgh-Xenia Seminary in "as many things as possible." Annual football and basketball games were

43. The carillon, identical to the one at the Arlington National Cemetery, was given in memory of Wenman A. Hicks, who died in 1953. The carillon is now in the tower of the Hicks Chapel of Pittsburgh Seminary.

played with fierce enthusiasm, but it was observed unofficially that some-times these games set ecumenism back significantly.[44] Exchange of faculty and joint lectures were more constructive.

In the fall of 1949, Western had 105 students, 71 of them Presby-terian. There were 49 military veterans in the number. In the spring of 1951, charges for room and board were raised to $330 a year, and it was noted that all available student space was being used. A Student Wives Club was organized.[45]

In the late 1950s, the student body reached an all-time high of 145 students. Eight men and a manager were given work scholarships to devote ten hours a week to the choir. They sang in chapel services and accom-panied professors on speaking occasions in area churches.

It is a pity that oral traditions about student life tend to die with the passing of student generations. Social events with extravagant parodies, such as "Memorial Madcaps," were not uncommon. One could record but not document water battles to celebrate the ending of ordination examinations. A story from the 1950s tells how one professor refused to cancel class for the first televised World Series. By way of concession he provided a small Crosley radio and announced that he would alternate ten minutes of lecture with ten minutes of the baseball game. At one point, with Mantle facing Koufax and the call at three and two, the professor turned off the radio just as Mantle swung. . . . But student life was never unbalanced. A solemn day of prayer was regularly observed.

One tradition survived the consolidation. Students found in a storage room a large, framed portrait of an unnamed professor. They gave him a complete identity: "Atkins Flegley, D.D.S., 1794-1787," and all sorts of stories were invented about his character and exploits. His portrait has hung at various times and spots in the seminary halls among the portraits of other professors. There has even been a serious suggestion that an annual Atkins Flegley lectureship be inaugurated.

44. In 1952, after Western defeated Pittsburgh-Xenia, Wilbur Christy, the team captain, claimed that the Western Wildcats team was "the first in the nation to complete its season undefeated and untied."

45. Its successor in Pittsburgh Seminary is now known as "Spice" (plural of spouse?).

Toward Union

When the three-way plan of union failed, the Presbyterian Church in the U.S.A. (PCUSA) and the UPCNA kept plans for union alive. In 1958 this plan came to fruition.[46] A Western Seminary brochure produced at the time was entitled "Great Forces Moving," but Dr. Barbour warned that "an advancing army must not move too fast." There were many, many details to be worked out, and all the road would not be smooth. But as the brochure declared, "All the Departments at Western Seminary are bound by a common concern for the Word of God." So the foundation for the future was firm.

In summary, in 133 years Western Seminary produced some 3,000 graduates, over two hundred of whom served on mission fields. Fifty professors were inaugurated, and many other persons taught for various periods of time without inaugural recognition.

46. For an account of the union of the seminaries, see pp. 132, 159-60.

CHAPTER SEVEN

Pittsburgh: Where the Streams Meet

James Arthur Walther

The Birth of Pittsburgh Theological Seminary

"1 + 1 = 1" — this was the title of a large brochure published at the time Western and Pittsburgh-Xenia Seminaries came together. The records are careful to point out that the new seminary was not a "merger" but a "consolidation." This was intended to mean that the old schools lost their individual identity in the new institution. This was, as the brochure's subtitle put it, "The Mathematics of a Dream."

The Special Committee had rejected three alternatives to the consolidation: (1) "That the two Seminaries continue to operate in Pittsburgh as separate institutions"; (2) "That the two Seminaries continue to operate as separate institutions, one in Pittsburgh and the other elsewhere"; (3) "That a form of merger or confederation of the two Seminaries be effected, not involving unified operation but with a clear distinction of educational function between them."[1] At one stage a rumor had it that Western would be moved to Denver. Some had hoped that, if the concept of a "theological university" could be brought to reality, each school might continue a unique existence. Not everyone was happy with the consolidation. Sentiment and loyalty are durable.

The *Articles of Consolidation and Joint Plan of Consolidation* stated: "The purpose or purposes of the new corporation are that of conducting a

---

1. *Report of Special Committee on the Study of Presbyterian Theological Education in the Pittsburgh Area* (located in the seminary archives), pp. 3, 4.

theological seminary which shall be solely devoted to the education of suitable persons for the work of the Christian ministry and for other fields of Christian service." And so it came to pass. The seminary Boards acted on the Report of the Special Committee on May 8, 1959; the Special Committee on Consolidation acted on May 19; and the General Assembly approved the action on May 22. The new school was a reality on paper. It operated on the separate campuses in the 1959-60 academic year, and unified operation on one campus began in the fall of 1960. Dr. Barbour wrote that the leaders of the new school would need "the continuing leading of Almighty God, that His way may be made known among men, and the saving grace of Christ preached among all peoples."[2]

The Special Committee recommended that the school be established on the Pittsburgh-Xenia campus in East Liberty. Possible highway relocation made the future of the Western campus on the North Side uncertain. The buildings in East Liberty were new, and there seemed to be reasonable opportunity to expand that campus to meet growing needs. The location is attractive in that it is precisely on the border between East Liberty, where there are commercial facilities, and Highland Park, which is a fine (though aging) residential district. It is also literally within sight of the University of Pittsburgh, and Carnegie-Mellon University and Chatham College are both nearby.

The assets of the two schools totaled $7,300,000. Western had building-fund monies of $440,000, which the Committee on Theological Education of the General Assembly would release. There was an endowment with a book value of $3,602,836. The joint operating budget for 1960-61 was $795,651.36. A financial compaign for $4,910,000 was immediately planned.

Thirty-six directors were appointed, with balanced representation from the predecessor institutions and equal distribution between clergy and laity. Records showed that there were 2,064 alumni of the two schools. A new Alumni Association was organized in the chapel of the East Liberty Presbyterian Church on May 17, 1960.

The combined faculties numbered twenty-three, plus three librarians. The student body in 1960 was projected to be 382. The combined libraries would contain 102,693 books plus journals and other resources. The Special Committee recommended that immediate attention be given to securing additional dormitory space and dining room facilities. A new

2. Barbour, in *Western Watch* 10, 2 (15 May 1959): 2.

library building would also be necessary, with room to house at least 200,000 volumes. Utilities and parking space were also needed.

Developments in the next three decades happened at a rate far more accelerated than was the case in the earlier periods of seminary history. Published records are extensive. In the McCloy Archives Room of the library many of the materials may be studied, and there are additional archival resources in other library areas. *Panorama,* initially edited by Robert Kelley, began publication at once, and it has carried and disseminated news of the seminary at regular intervals during each year. *Perspective,* which I edited for a number of years and which was later edited by David Buttrick, contained records of academic activity. The annual *Catalogue* has increasingly reflected diverse aspects and details of seminary life. Accordingly, this chapter of our history must be a very condensed summary.

Faculty

The heart of a school is its faculty. Pittsburgh Seminary began rich in this regard. There were ten full professors, the numbers divided equally between the two former schools. There were eleven associate professors and two assistant professors. Howard Ralston, assistant professor of church music, was unique in that he had been on both faculties at the time of the consolidation. Besides the twenty-three teachers from the two schools, there were seven professors emeriti: Baldinger, Culley, Karr, Long, Riddle, Shear, and Slosser. One instructor and seven guest instructors rounded out the teaching faculty the first year.

The faculty was organized in three divisions: biblical; history and theology; and church and ministry. At the outset these divisions met regularly, and a representative from each division met with the other divisions. Thus there was a unique thrust toward a unified curriculum and teaching strategy. After a few years, however, this arrangement became cumbersome. The divisions continued to exist in the descriptive structure, but the faculty functioned mostly in subject task groups.

Initially, the biblical division was notably strong, with nine teachers, soon growing to twelve. For a number of years this was a principal inducement for students outside the geographical area to come to Pittsburgh. As the needs of curriculum diversified, the balance among the divisions changed. The faculty in the 1990s is weighted in the church and ministry division.

To write in detail about the able teachers who have been on the faculty since 1959 would require a separate volume. Some of those who came through the consolidation finished their careers elsewhere. Dr. Leitch resigned soon after consolidation and taught at Tarkio College. Theophilus Taylor in 1962 left to become Secretary to the General Council of the General Assembly. In 1964 Dr. Freedman moved to San Francisco Seminary, and Dr. Grohman went to Knoxville College. Elwyn Smith went to Temple University in 1966. In 1968 Robert Johnson became Dean of Yale Divinity School. Four new teachers came to the faculty during this time: J. Gordon Chamberlin in Christian education in 1960, and Gayraud S. Wilmore in social ethics, Arlan P. Dohrenburg in speech, and David G. Buttrick in church and ministry in 1961.[3]

Administration

The decision as to who should head the new school was difficult. It was agreed that a president would be sought outside the consolidating schools. To oversee the immediate complicated tasks of beginning the new institution, Dr. Barbour became vice president and acting president, the appointment to terminate at the end of the 1961-62 academic year. This seemed to be a good compromise since he was already of retirement age. He served wisely and energetically. One of his last messages to the seminary urged faithfulness to the vision God gives: "Whatever he saith unto you, do it" was his biblical text.

Gordon Jackson, professor of Christian education, became acting dean. Before the unified campus opened, he was appointed dean for a three-year term, and his professorship was changed to pastoral care and counseling. Howard Jamieson became acting dean of students, and Bessie Burrows served as acting registrar; both of these also had teaching duties. The Reverend James T. Vorhis was appointed business manager and John C. Bramer, Jr., treasurer. Dr. W. Bruce Wilson was president of the Board of Directors, and Dr. Frederick B. Speakman was vice president. Henry Herchenroether was appointed counsel; he has served continuously until the present.

---

3. A "Historical Roll of Professors" is given in an appendix at the end of this volume; see pp. 267-71.

Courses of Study and Students

For the fall of 1960 it was necessary to prepare three concurrent curricula, two for the students of each of the consolidating schools and one for those entering the new institution. This tour de force was accomplished by the genius of Professor Freedman, and the teaching that year went with little difficulty.

In March 1961, Dr. Barbour called attention to Article II.2 in the seminary's constitution:

> the Seminary shall provide instruction in the knowledge of the Word of God, contained in the Scriptures of the Old and New Testaments, the only infallible rule of faith and practice, and of the doctrine, order and institutes of worship taught in the Scriptures, and summarily exhibited in the Constitution of the United Presbyterian Church in the United States of America; and shall impart to its students the various disciplines by which they may be properly prepared for service in the work of the Church; and shall cultivate in them spiritual gifts and the life of true godliness; all to the end that there may be trained a succession of able, faithful, and devoted ministers of the gospel and other Christian workers.[4]

Not everything was easy that first year. The faculty had to learn to work with new colleagues, but this was quickly and willingly accomplished. There were tensions in the student body, as might have been expected; their sense of the flow of events was not as deep as that shared by the faculty and the Board. On May 4, 1961, the faculty adopted a resolution that is worth quoting at length:

> The Faculty of the Seminary is sensitive to the tensions which have existed in several areas during the past school year and which have impinged upon our life and work in the school. We desire the Board of Directors to know that such tensions have not grown up within the Faculty. The differences that have arisen among us have been mostly of the healthy sort that develop in the normal course of communication among men of conviction.
>
> Indeed, many happy incidents have made us clearly conscious that the Spirit of God has moved among us during the year. Pressures from

4. Barbour, in *Pittsburgh Perspective* 2, 1 (March 1961): 2.

problems in the Church, strains from multiplied responsibilities for the development of the academic program, and unusual demands upon our time have not unsettled us; and we attribute this encouraging estate to the grace of God.

We express our satisfaction at every manifestation of sympathetic like-mindedness among members of the Board, and we bespeak their diligence that our labors together may continue to thrive under God's blessing.[5]

Physical Plant

One recommendation of the Special Committee was acted upon at once. Office space for the expanded faculty was arranged, and the Ridge Avenue campus was not used after May 1960. Seventeen student rooms in McNaugher Hall were taken to accommodate faculty, but work began at once on a new dormitory for single men.

Instead of a ground-breaking ceremony for the new building, a large tree was to be felled. Men dressed as John Anderson and John McMillan would wield ceremonial axes, and a truck would help to pull down the tree, which would previously be cut partway through. Unfortunately, when the preparatory cut was made, the tree fell, for it was decayed at its heart — a circumstance that naturally prompted homiletical illustrations. But a ceremony was enacted, and Fisher Hall[6] was ready for use by the fall of 1961.

An addition was built at the eastern end of McNaugher Hall that provided a large dining room. The dining areas could now accommodate not only the enlarged student body — and their families upon occasion — but various gatherings at the seminary. The annual alumni banquets have been held there.

Efforts were immediately undertaken to secure some of the properties adjacent to the seminary grounds. Soon an existing apartment building across St. Marie Street (the northern boundary of the original property) was purchased and became The Highlander, with apartments for married students. Other property was acquired extending to Stanton

5. Quoted in *Pittsburgh Perspective* 2, 2 (June 1961): 2, 10.
6. George Fisher had been a generous member of Western's Board of Trustees.

Pittsburgh Seminary, 1959. Dr. Barbour with participants dressed as John Anderson and John McMillan at a tree-chopping ceremony marking the site of Fisher Hall. The partially cut tree fell untimely before the ceremony began.

Avenue, the next east-west thoroughfare. On this property after 1966 two more apartment buildings were built and named for Anderson and McMillan. In addition, some individual lots with houses in the original block were bought, but the seminary does not yet possess the entire block of property.

The seminary has been fortunate in being welcomed to the facilities of the East Liberty Presbyterian Church. Its large Gothic sanctuary has often been taxed to seat the throngs at the commencement programs of the seminary. Usually the commencement speaker has been someone of note, and many friends outside the seminary family attend.

Library

In June and July of 1960 the Western Seminary library was moved to the East Liberty campus. This was a Herculean task, and many volunteers helped. Although the available space was known to be inadequate, it was important for the combined library resources to be available as soon as

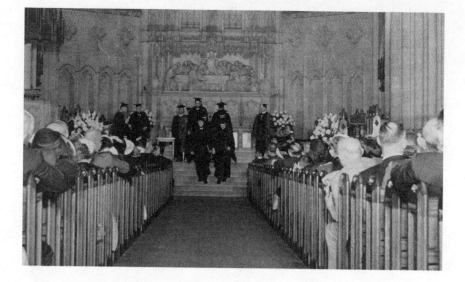

Seminary Commencement, East Liberty Presbyterian Church

possible. Dr. James Irvine was in charge of this move.[7] A new library building would not be ready until four years later.

The Seal of the Seminary

A faculty committee was appointed to draft a seal for the new school. They planned and submitted a design that was drawn by Professor Taylor, and it was adopted on May 6, 1961. Later several different logos were used on stationery and other material, but this is the official seal.[8]

The circle that circumscribes the seal represents the world and embraces the name and founding date of the seminary. Within this is a trefoil, symbolic of the Holy Trinity and trinitarian theology. In the top lobe of the trefoil is a ship, an ancient symbol of the church, with a Latin cross on the sail. (This symbol came from the seal of Western Seminary.) In the right lobe is a stylized representation of the Anderson cabin, where

7. Dr. Irvine later moved to Princeton Seminary.

8. The seal appears as the frontispiece to this volume. An official interpretation of the seal appeared in *Pittsburgh Perspective* 2, 3 (September 1961): 4-5.

Seal of Western Seminary   *Seal of Pittsburgh-Xenia Seminary*

the seminary began. (This detail is from the Pittsburgh-Xenia seal.) In the left lobe is the bicentennial symbol of the city of Pittsburgh, which includes a triangle, where two rivers meet to form a third, and a stylized, growing tree.

Thus the symbols in the seal represent the close relationship between the church, the seminary, and the community and point to their histories and functions. Within the encompassing circles are two further symbols. On the left is a celtic cross, which has rich associations in the history of Christianity in Western Europe and the British Isles. On the right is a stylized burning bush, which is found in the seal of the Church of Scotland and in a number of other seals of historic Reformed churches.[9]

The Presidency of Donald G. Miller

Donald G. Miller arrived on the scene in the spring of 1962 after a distinguished career in the Presbyterian Church in the U.S. He is a New Testament scholar, and he taught at Union Theological Seminary in Rich-

---

9. A number of these seals are set in the frieze around the Long Building wing that originally housed McCune Chapel. There is also a display of reproductions of some of these seals in the Barbour Library.

mond. One of his first pronouncements to his new colleagues was this: "Others have labored, and [we] have entered into their labor."[10] He was inaugurated April 18, 1963.

As president, Dr. Miller had a fine feel for history. During his presidency the seminary made several pilgrimages to the site of the old Service Seminary. He wrote about recovering a "sense of the past" and its importance. James Vorhis discovered that George Swetnam, a feature writer for *The Pittsburgh Press* and an ordained United Presbyterian minister,[11] had written a history of theological education in western Pennsylvania. The University of Pittsburgh had decided not to print it, and permission was given for it to appear in *Pittsburgh Perspective*. Vorhis and the editor revised the piece to bring it up to date, and it appeared under the title "Star in the West."[12]

A number of readers responded to the Swetnam history, and several provided additional information and corrections. Gaius Slosser wrote from retirement, among other matters insisting that the history of the seminary should be traced to the Canonsburg Academy in 1785. To quote Slosser himself:

> the 1785 date and line is unbroken while the 1794 date has a break of at least two years when there was neither teacher nor students, neither locale nor trustees. John McMillan's institutional creation was in 1825 transferred as to students, continuous instruction, and trustees, as individuals, not as bodies.[13]

10. John 4:38. See *Pittsburgh Perspective* 3, 2 (June 1962): 2. With this issue the journal's circulation reached 9,000.

11. Dr. Swetnam served for a number of years as Stated Supply at the Service United Presbyterian Church. The church is near the granite marker on the site of Service Seminary, and John Anderson is buried in the adjacent cemetery.

12. Swetnam, "Star in the West," *Pittsburgh Perspective* 4, 4 (December 1963): 4-39.

13. *Pittsburgh Perspective* 5, 1 (March 1964): 4. The Barbour Library has a typed monograph by Dr. Slosser, in which he argues his point in some detail. See also *Western Watch* 4, 1 (January 1953): 4, 11. Dr. Guthrie has told me that he agrees in general with this position. The matter turns both on how one understands continuity and on how one defines a seminary.

Faculty

The faculty was strengthened during Dr. Miller's administration. George H. Kehm came in 1962 as instructor in theology. Today he occupies the James H. Snowden Chair of Theology. In 1963 Dietrich Ritschl was called as professor of the history of biblical interpretation and doctrine. He taught until 1970, when he left for a post in Germany. Markus Barth came as professor of New Testament. In 1973 he returned to Switzerland, where he occupied a chair in the University of Basel.[14] Edward Farley came as associate professor of systematic theology. He left Pittsburgh in 1969 and has since had a notable career at Vanderbilt University. Lynn B. Hinds was instructor in speech until 1972. Iain G. Wilson became professor of homiletics; he stayed until 1968, when he went to a pastorate in Baltimore.

In 1964 Douglas R. A. Hare joined the faculty to teach New Testament, and in 1965 Donald E. Gowan and Jared J. Jackson began teaching Old Testament. Both are today professors, and Gowan occupies the Robert C. Holland Chair of Old Testament. In 1966 H. Eberhard von Waldow came as a visiting professor of Old Testament, and the following year he began a distinguished tenure. Also in 1966 Dikran Y. Hadidian became librarian and professor of bibliography; he retired in 1985. Peter Fribley was an instructor in homiletics until 1970.

In 1967 Robert S. Paul came to the seminary as professor of modern church history. He served until 1977, when he went to Austin Theological Seminary. Ford Lewis Battles became professor of church history and history of doctrine. In 1978 he went to the Center for Calvin Studies in Grand Rapids. In 1968 Paul W. Lapp became professor of Old Testament and archaeology. He died in a drowning accident in 1970 while on an archaeological expedition in Cyprus.[15] Neil R. Paylor, who had been a guest instructor in a program of advanced pastoral studies, became an assistant professor in church and ministry (1968). He returned to private counseling in 1982. In 1969 Robert M. Ezzell came to teach homiletics and New Testament, and Ronald H. Stone, a Niebuhr scholar, was associate professor of ethics.

14. The following year there was an exhibition of materials in honor of Professor Karl Barth, Markus Barth's father. The desk upon which he wrote the *Church Dogmatics* is on permanent display in the Barbour Library, a gift of the Barth family.

15. For more on Lapp, see Chapter Ten, "Archaeology and the James L. Kelso Bible Lands Museum," pp. 255-56 below.

An impressive list of guest professors and instructors came to the seminary during the 1960s. A recital of the names is beyond the scope of this chapter, but among them may be mentioned Roland E. Murphy, O. Carm, and Fred M. Rogers ("Mister Rogers"), an alumnus who was for a year a teaching fellow in church and ministry. There was also a regular program of guest lecturers, whose names would read like a Who's Who of the theological world. In the academic year 1968-69 there were sixteen guest professors and twenty-two special lecturers.

Barbour Library

One of the most important landmarks of Dr. Miller's presidency was the completion of the new library. It was dedicated on September 21, 1964, in a memorable service held on what is now the patio between the library and the Long Building. Dr. Martin Niemöller gave the address.[16] The full story of the library is the subject of Chapter Eight in this volume (see pp. 181-205).

Schaff Lectures

In the fall of 1965 the first of a distinguished annual series of lectures was given by Professor C. F. D. Moule of Cambridge University on the subject "The Basic Meaning of the New Testament." The lectureship was endowed in honor of David S. Schaff, professor of church history at Western Seminary from 1903 to 1926. Besides the lectures at the seminary, the lecturer presents a lecture at the First Presbyterian Church of Youngstown, Ohio.

A stipulation of these lectures is that they lead to publication. Dr. Moule's lectures became *The Phenomenon of the New Testament*.[17] The second series was presented in 1966 by Paul Ricoeur. The list of lecturers is impressive, and many of the published books have been widely acclaimed.

16. The text of the address is printed in *Pittsburgh Perspective* 5, 4 (December 1964): 4-9.
17. Moule, *The Phenomenon of the New Testament: An Inquiry into the Implication of Certain Features of the New Testament,* Studies in Biblical Theology, Second Series, 1 (London: SCM Press Ltd.; Naperville, IL: Allenson, 1967).

Pittsburgh Seminary, aerial view
(Fulton Hall, left; Hicks Chapel; Long Administration Building, center front;
Barbour Library, center rear; McNaugher Hall and dining rooms, right)

Hicks Chapel

In the spring of 1970 a second notable building was added "at the center of the campus," as the catalog of that year described it. The McCune Chapel in the Long Administration Building was adequate for daily worship, but it could no longer accommodate special occasions. The Hicks family had marked gifts to Western Seminary for a new chapel, and after the consolidation they added significantly to this fund. A large Georgian edifice[18] was constructed, with a noble spire surmounted by a golden weathercock, a traditional symbol warning against denial of the Lord.

The building also contains a large, theater-like auditorium and a variety of offices that have been utilized for continuing education and other special projects. The foyer of the auditorium is a popular meeting place after daily chapel services and on other occasions.

18. Dr. Miller is reported to have said, upon first entering the building, "Georgian, pure Georgian."

Lewis W. Hicks Family Memorial Chapel

One of the first special events held in the new chapel was a "Festival of the Gospels," which brought together some seventy notable scholars for a broad discussion of topics related to the Gospels. Many of the addresses were published in a special issue of *Pittsburgh Perspective*.[19]

The chapel room in the Long Building was refurnished as a beau-

19. *Pittsburgh Perspective* 9, 1 and 2 (1970, 1971), totaling some 635 pages.

tifully appointed lounge and became a center of official and social gatherings. During the fuel emergencies in the early 1970s, the Hicks Chapel was closed during the winter months, and chapel services were again held in this chapel-become-lounge.

The room beneath it became an informal center of student social life. It was popularly known as the "Hungry-I." Here the Alumni/ae Association conducts its annual "Phonathon," which has brought financial support from about half of the graduates, a remarkable percentage.

Music

The three-manual Schantz organ in the Hicks Chapel, which has a positive division and thirty-nine stops, was dedicated with a concert by Professor Robert Baker, Dean of Union Seminary's School of Sacred Music. The two-manual Schantz organ from McCune Chapel is now in the new auditorium, where it is often used on special occasions and for practice by student musicians.

In 1964 Roy R. Snowden, M.D., and his wife presented the seminary with funds for annual concerts in memory of Dr. Snowden's father, Professor James Snowden. The first concert was given by opera star Frances Yeend in the McCune Chapel. A succession of notable musicians

Pittsburgh Seminary, first meeting of the Board of Directors, December 30, 1959

were featured annually. The first concert in the Hicks Chapel auditorium was by the Carnegie-Mellon String Quartet. Mrs. Snowden continued the concerts after her husband's death until 1975.

Professor Ralston led choirs at both antecedent seminaries. Occasionally, the choir went on tour. In the new school he led a mixed choir, which sang on special occasions and gave public concerts. Today these concerts are gala events in the fall and spring.

A Time of Transition

The academic year 1969-70 marked the 175th year of the seminary. In the fall of 1969 the anniversary was celebrated at old Service Church. Dr. Wallace Jamison, then professor of church history and president of New Brunswick Theological Seminary, delivered the address.[20]

Dr. Miller resigned in the fall of 1970 to become the pastor of the Laurinburg, North Carolina, Presbyterian Church. He had led the way from the consolidation years through the years when the seminary was solidifying its identity. Professor Jamieson became interim president. Professor Bald was the interim dean, and the office of dean was rotated among faculty members.

The period of the Vietnam conflict became a difficult time in academia. There was widespread unrest in student bodies. This of course affected the seminary. Authority was strongly challenged — and the challenge was sometimes accommodated. The seminary catalog for 1970-71 states:

> Pittsburgh Seminary has a curriculum which gives each student freedom to plan his studies in light of his own background and his own aims. The curriculum is a free elective plan. No courses are required, with the exception of Greek and Hebrew which are essential tools for theological work. Furthermore, there are no formal prerequisites, for this could be merely another way of regimenting studies. Each student is free to study what he needs to study when he wants to study it.

20. New Brunswick Seminary, founded in 1785, is the only seminary in the Reformed tradition in America older than Pittsburgh's antecedent Service Seminary.

Even such a statement was open to challenge, for the percentage of women in the student body was growing, and "inclusive language" was soon requisite.

The Presidency of William H. Kadel

The search for a new president came to a quick and fortunate conclusion with a call to William H. Kadel, who had graduated from Pittsburgh Seminary in 1938. He came after a career as a pastor, as the first president of Florida Presbyterian (now Eckerd) College in Florida, and as an administrator in the Presbyterian Church in the U.S. The year 1971 was declared an Inaugural Year, with special convocations.

It was not an easy time. With the unrest at the end of the 1960s came a drop in financial resources. Fund-raising was an important task of the new president. The students irreverently dubbed the president "Dollar Bill" and caricatured him in their unofficial publication as a Superman, come to save the seminary.

The Vietnam fallout was not over. Graffiti appeared on the front wall of the chapel sanctuary. Dr. Kadel's leadership was severely challenged, but time and patience finally prevailed. In 1975 a new curriculum was adopted, with requirements in all the major areas of theological study. At the same time the academic year was changed from the traditional two semesters to three terms during the year.

Faculty

During the Kadel years a number of teachers joined the faculty. John W. Nelson and Arthur C. Cochrane came in 1971 to teach systematic theology. John S. Walker taught black church history for a year. David T. Shannon was called from Bucknell University to the deanship in 1972. He served until 1979, and then the deanship reverted to faculty rotation. M. Harjie Likens began to teach in church and ministry (1973). Samuel K. Roberts was the first teacher called to teach sociology of religion. He was succeeded by Gonzalo Castillo-Cardenas, who is now associate professor of church and society and Third World studies.

In 1977 Ulrich W. Mauser became the Errett M. Grable Professor

of New Testament and later served several terms as dean. Marjorie Su-
chocki became associate professor of theology. Dr. Orr retired in May
1974 but continued to teach occasional courses for a number of years.
Charles B. Partee began teaching church history, and in 1980 he temporarily occupied the W. Don McClure Chair of World Mission and
Evangelism. The William F. Orr Chair in New Testament was inaugurated
in 1978, with Dr. Hare as the first occupant.[21]

Many persons have served in administrative offices; the list is too
long to give in full. Several have gone on from Pittsburgh to important
posts in the denomination — for example, William Phillippe, Frank
Hainer, and Joseph Small. Richard J. Rapp was director of the doctor of
ministry program and of continuing education. After his death, his wife
Jeanette became director of continuing education and special events.
George Tutwiler has for more than a decade been organist and choirmaster
and also lecturer in church music and United Methodist studies.

Academic Programs and Lectures

Before the consolidation, both seminaries had working relationships with
other institutions of higher learning in Pittsburgh. These were extended.
Pittsburgh Seminary is a member of the Pittsburgh Council on Higher
Education, which allows cross-registration with nine other schools when
courses are appropriate. Joint degree programs have been offered with
the University of Pittsburgh, among them Master of Divinity (M.Div.),
Master of Social Work, and Doctor of Philosophy.

In the fall of 1972 Pittsburgh Seminary joined a small but rapidly
growing number of seminaries offering the Doctor of Ministry degree. At
first it was designed to include an in-sequence track in which students
added a year to their M.Div. curriculum and an in-ministry track for those
who had previously completed the Master of Divinity degree. Eventually
the in-sequence program was discontinued.

The first graduates of the program completed their work in 1974,
and there are now more than three hundred graduates. Three distinct
focuses are available: the parish focus, the Reformed focus, and the
pastoral care focus. For a period of time a satellite program was maintained

---

21. Another named chair, the Hugh Thompson Kerr Chair of Pastoral Theology,
was held by Gordon E. Jackson.

at Eckerd College, St. Petersburg, Florida. John E. Mehl became director in 1985 and is also lecturer in church and ministry.

Many distinguished persons visited the campus in this period under several lectureships. In addition to the Schaff Lectures there are the Elliott Lectures, inaugurated at Western Seminary in 1871 in honor of Professor David Elliott. The Kelso Lectures, named for Professor James Leon Kelso, are usually given in connection with Martin Luther King Day.

A Time of Transition

In the fall of 1978 President Kadel announced his retirement. Dr. W. Paul Ludwig, a 1934 alumnus and chairperson of the Board of Directors, became interim president. He served from January to June 1979. Dr. Ronald V. Wells then became interim president and served until February 1981.

During this period Richard J. Oman joined the faculty. He came from several distinguished pastorates and graduate studies. He is now Howard C. Scharfe Professor of Homiletics. Nancy Lapp became the curator of the Bible Lands Museum and later also lecturer in archaeology and Hebrew. Rabbi Philip Sigal became lecturer in New Testament.

The Presidency of Carnegie Samuel Calian

In the fall of 1981 Dr. Carnegie Samuel Calian came from Dubuque Seminary, where he was professor of theology, to be president and professor of theology at Pittsburgh. Like Dr. Miller, he has been proud of his role as a teaching president. He has also continued to write, publishing several important books in addition to articles.

Endowments

Probably Dr. Calian's most visible achievement has been in the area of endowments. The endowment of the seminary has increased nearly six-fold. A significant amount of this has gone into the funding of endowed faculty chairs. The standard set for such a chair by the Board is $1,000,000. No chair was fully endowed when Dr. Calian arrived.

Now there are eight endowed chairs, and others are nearing completion. Besides those mentioned earlier, there are the Hugh Thompson Kerr Chair in Pastoral Theology; the John Witherspoon Chair of Christian Ethics, occupied by Ronald H. Stone; and the Director of the Library, held by Stephen D. Crocco.

Other endowment funds have strengthened the doctor of ministry and the continuing education programs. Lectureships have also been

Carnegie Samuel Calian, President 1981-

undergirded, including the new J. Hubert Henderson Conference on Church and Ministry and the W. Don McClure Lectureship on Evangelism and World Mission.

Faculty

Appointments in Dr. Calian's years include Andrew Purves in pastoral theology and spirituality; Ronald H. Cram, who taught Christian education from 1983 to 1985; John E. Wilson, Jr., who teaches modern European and American church history; Susan Nelson, who teaches theology; Byron H. Jackson, who now occupies the Louise and Perry Dick Chair in Christian Education; Martha A. Robbins, who teaches pastoral care and psychology; and Keith F. Nickle, who is professor of New Testament studies.

Under the president's leadership a Metro-Urban Ministry Institute was begun. Its first director is Ronald E. Peters, who also occupies a faculty position in urban ministry.

Programs

The continuing education program has grown significantly. In 1981 a few hundred people attended the events. Now around 3,000 participants attend 35 to 40 events each year.

The Center for Business, Religion, and the Professions was begun in 1988. Under the direction of a succession of notable lay professionals, the program brings together a variety of concerned leaders to study quality-of-life issues.

Dr. Calian initiated a program of distinguished pastors and laypersons in residence, which exposes students to many models of Christian ministry and witness. Another program brings visiting professors from abroad on a regular basis to teach for a term.

Administration, Finances, and Facilities

The various administrative offices have been expanded and staffed. The registrar, the director of the doctor of ministry program, and the director of continuing education and special events have become full-time positions. Other tasks that were performed by professors now have part-time directors: placement for seniors and alumni, financial aid, and pastoral counselor to the seminary community. The library staff has been expanded. The seminary catalog for 1991-93 listed fifty persons in various staff positions.

The business system has been credibly reorganized, and administrative operations are being computerized. Computer facilities for faculty and students have been expanded and updated.

Classrooms have been remodeled and equipped with modern communications facilities. A speech studio has been developed. Accessibility for physically challenged persons has been achieved through installation of elevators and ramps. Maintenance has been improved in needed areas. The natural beauty of the grounds has been preserved.

*   *   *

I will conclude with a statement by Dr. Calian that summarizes his feelings about Pittsburgh Theological Seminary today:

> All in all, I thank God for allowing me to have this leadership experience which has been an exciting challenge. . . . Together, the staff, faculty and administration are all key players in moving the Seminary forward to fulfill our mission in preparing men and women for ministry.[22]

22. Letter to the author, April 13, 1992.

CHAPTER EIGHT

The Library

Stephen D. Crocco

A chapter on the history of the library provides an opportunity to highlight important events and persons in the Seminary's past that might not otherwise be remembered. It also calls attention to several outstanding collections now housed in the Clifford E. Barbour Library. The story is difficult to tell, however, because it is as complex as the history of the Seminary's antecedent institutions. The upheavals of moving, merging, and new building programs kept the librarians and collections in various states of confusion for much of the past two centuries. Yet it is precisely these upheavals that make the story interesting. Without them, librarians simply went about the work of acquiring new materials and making them available for students and faculty.

This chapter will sketch the origin and gradual growth of the two libraries that became one in 1959. Although the seminaries had libraries and faculty who served as librarians from the earliest years, rarely was any attention given to the library, as such. As a result, there are almost no records before the late nineteenth century. At that point seminary catalogs and bulletins, accession catalogs, patron records, board reports, printed recollections, and scattered correspondence emerge as primary sources. From the late nineteenth century to the 1950s, seminary catalogs are the only regular source of information about the size of the collection, the librarian, acknowledgments of gifts and funds, facilities, changes in service, and needs. Personal correspondence and anecdotal materials related to the library are scarce.

Not surprisingly, the story of the Seminary library begins in Europe.

Although publishing flourished in eighteenth-century America, pastors and teachers had to rely on the presses and booksellers of Europe for editions of the church fathers and the Reformers, complex lexicographical materials, and encyclopedias. Frank Dixon McCloy, librarian at Western Seminary in the 1950s, described the situation thus:

> There were no crumbling abbeys, no catacombs, no debris of ancient Christian cultures in the raw virgin land of America. It was in books, primarily, that the church's glorious past was enshrined. But the books which American seminary libraries needed were still in Europe, in great private collections or on the stalls of bookdealers whither they drifted following the dissolution of monastic libraries and the breakup of the *ancien regime* at the close of the eighteenth century. Toward the rich storehouses across the sea the vigorous and determined seminary founders turned for the literary traditions and legacies of historic Christianity.[1]

It was not the quest for books alone that prompted such long and arduous journeys. Books were one component of a broader spiritual fellowship, which included fund-raising, recruiting ministers for America, and the exchange of news of God's work between the Old and New Worlds.

Pittsburgh-Xenia and Western Seminaries, and the denominations they represented, were products of this fellowship. Ironically, the Seminary's ancestors could be one in the Spirit with brothers and sisters across the ocean but not necessarily so with other Presbyterians a few blocks away. Catalogs from Western and Pittsburgh-Xenia do not acknowledge each other's existence until the 1920s.[2] What is particularly revealing is that, in an effort to recruit students to the North Side of Pittsburgh, both seminaries went out of their way to call attention to nearby library resources. The Pittsburgh and Carnegie libraries get repeated mention in the catalogs, but neither seminary ever mentions the other's library. At first one might think that reciprocal library privileges were so obvious

---

1. Frank Dixon McCloy, "The Founding of the Library of the Pittsburgh Theological Seminary," *Pittsburgh Perspective* 5, 3 (September 1964): 5. (See the whole article, pp. 4-12.) This is perhaps the most accessible account of the contributions of John Mitchell Mason and Alan Ditchfield Campbell.

2. In the mid-1920s mention of athletic competition between the two seminaries found its way into the catalogs. Not until the 1930s is there mention of the possibility of cross registration and of attending lectures at the other seminary (particularly during World War II).

that they were assumed. This was not the case. Rather, a strong sense of self-sufficiency on both parts led to the existence of two quite similar libraries, no more than a few blocks apart, both struggling to grow. As a result, it is almost inevitable that this chapter follow two independent histories until the late 1950s when those histories began to merge.

Allegheny/Pittsburgh/Pittsburgh-Xenia Seminary

When the Allegheny Theological Seminary opened in December 1825, the founders spent $150 on a library for the use of Professor Joseph Kerr and his four students. Nothing is known about the size or scope of that collection. Presumably it moved along with the Seminary, first being housed at the Associate Reformed Church in Pittsburgh until Kerr's death in 1829, then in Circleville in Westmoreland County, Pennsylvania, until 1832, when it moved to the First Associate Reformed Church, Allegheny. It occupied that site until 1856, when the seminary building opened at the corner of North Avenue and Buena Vista Street. There the collection and reading room for students and faculty were on the second floor — a vast improvement over the damp basement of First Church, Allegheny.

Allegheny Seminary moved into a new five-story home in 1899, at a time when the collection numbered about 5,000 volumes. The library and reading room shared the first floor with "the large chapel . . . the parlor, the Faculty's study, the gymnasium, and the janitor's home."[3] That same year the Seminary received a gift of $15,000 from the estate of James Law of Shushan, New York, to be used as an endowment for what became the James Law Library. During those years efforts were made to secure funds to support a full-time librarian who would manage the collection and offer bibliographic instruction to students. Unfortunately, biographical information on the nonfaculty librarians, many of whom had degrees in library science, is scarce.[4]

3. Allegheny Seminary Catalog, 1898-99, p. 17.
4. Precise dates for many of the librarians are not available. The dates below are taken mainly from catalogs, and the reader should keep that in mind. The list of known librarians is as follows: Elisabeth McMillan, 1903-1906; James D. Palmer, 1906-1907; Mary R. Grier, 1908-1913; Agnes D. McDonald, 1913-1920; Harry E. Kelsey, 1920-1922; Eloise Reed, 1922-1925; Mary B. Clark, 1925-1928; Mary Nagy, 1930-1933; Elizabeth Randles, 1933-1943; Margaret E. Orr, 1943-1946; Dorothy J. Vorhis, 1946-

The best source on the books that were in the James Law Library is two copies of the American Library Association *Standard Accession Books.* Beginning sometime after 1887, when these books were published, entries were made chronologically until the late 1930s. Unfortunately, many of the entries are not dated; those that are, however, shed light on holdings and acquisition patterns.[5] As interesting as the titles themselves are the records of the sources of the books. Many were purchased outright, but the majority appear to have been acquired from individuals associated with the seminary. Gifts of books and funds were the backbone of the library, and this probably accounts for the regular listing of donors in the seminary catalog beginning in the earliest years. For example, the 1890 catalog mentions that "the large and valuable libraries of the late Doctors J. T. Cooper and D. R. Kerr, and many valuable books from the library of the late Dr. John Forsyth, have come into the possession of the Seminary."[6] Little more than a decade later, the seminary received a 2,500 volume collection from Samuel Rutherford Kerr.[7]

In 1896 Joseph Buchanan presented to the library for safekeeping the diary of John Cuthbertson (1718-91). Cuthbertson, a Covenanter minister, traveled 70,000 miles during his long career and kept a record of marriages and baptisms involving over 5,000 different families. To this day, his diary prompts a steady stream of inquiries and visits, mostly from individuals doing genealogical work. In 1969, the diary was encapsulated to protect its faded and deteriorating pages.[8]

1948; Mrs. Harold E. Kurtz, acting librarian, 1948-1949; Mrs. W. Robert Caldwell, acting librarian, 1949-1950; Agnes Ballantyne, 1950-1959. Prof. Oliver J. Thatcher was librarian from 1890 to 1892, and Prof. John A. Wilson was librarian from 1894 to 1903. Prof. James Leon Kelso was the library supervisor from 1930 to 1940. In 1943 a library committee of the faculty was established.

5. These volumes provide space for approximately 22,000 title entries, all of which are filled. There were no entries between 1930 and 1935 (a busy time for the library), and the last entries were in 1938, when the collection measured approximately 34,000 volumes.

6. Allegheny Seminary Catalog, 1890-91, p. 15. The *Accession* volumes indicate that the following persons were among those who made substantial gifts to the seminary library: Dr. Alex Young, Dr. J. B. Dales, Joseph T. Cooper, Rev. Alexander Sharpe, Henry Gordon, Dr. J. Barnett, Miss Steele, David R. Kerr, John A. Wilson, A. S. Aiken, John A. Douthett, and Huger Ferguson.

7. A special bookplate with biographical information on Kerr was designed for this collection. A good number of these volumes are still circulating in the Barbour Library.

8. See William L. Fisk, Jr., "The Diary of John Cuthbertson, Missionary to the

The year 1907 saw the arrival of Allegheny Seminary's most significant gift, the Mason Collection.[9] Some 2,000 volumes were collected in
Europe a century earlier and came to Allegheny after the closing of the
Newburgh Seminary in Newburgh, New York. The New York Associate
Reformed Presbyterian Church sent John Mitchell Mason (1770-1829)
to Great Britain in 1801 to encourage divinity students, upon graduation,
to labor in the Synod of New York; he was also to raise funds for a library
and a building for the seminary the Synod intended to create.[10] Mason
was "authorised to purchase a library for said seminary; and a collection
of those books which are most needful and useful for this Synod, to be
distributed among their ministers and students, as shall hereafter be
directed; using the advice and counsel of judicious and godly ministers
with regard to the selection; and that he solicit donations in books for
both these uses."[11] Mason spent more than a year in England, Scotland,
and Ireland visiting Presbyterian leaders and preaching in their congregations. Donors included William Wilberforce and John Erskine. Most of
the funds raised by Mason were in turn spent on books for the library,
and a number of books were donated, either for the library or for him
to sell in order to buy more desirable books.

Mason's first report to the Synod contains almost nothing about the
library he collected and quite a lot about his efforts to solicit divinity
students to come to America.[12] However, the committee that processed
the library Mason collected gave its report in 1804. The approximately
2,000 books sent back by Mason were grouped in the following categories:

1. The Scriptures, in various languages.
2. Expositors.

Covenanters of Colonial Pennsylvania," *The Pennsylvania Magazine of History and Biography*,
October 1949, pp. 441-58.

9. The most detailed source on the Mason Collection is Agnes L. Ballantyne's
M.L.S. thesis, "The Newburgh Collection of Theological Books of the 16th, 17th, and
18th Centuries with a Description of the Works of Fifty Authors" (Western Reserve
University, 1951).

10. For a sketch of Mason, see William B. Sprague, *Annals of the American Pulpit*,
vol. 4 (New York: Robert Carter and Brothers, 1858), pp. 1-26.

11. *Extracts from the Minutes of the Acts and Proceedings of the Associate-Reformed Synod*
(New York, 1801), p. 14.

12. *Extracts from the Minutes of the Acts and Proceedings of the Associate-Reformed Synod*,
pp. 37-61.

3. Biblical Literature.
4. Christian Ministry.
5. Systematic Theology.
6. Polemical Theology, comprising controversies:
    1st. The Deistical
    2d. The Socinian
    3d. The Arminian
    4th. The Popish
    5th. The Episcopal and Independent
    6th. The Baptist
7. Miscellaneous Theology, Sermons, &c.
8. Moral and Political Science.
9. Metaphysics.
10. Belles Lettres.
11. History:
    1st. Sacred History
    2d. Civil History
12. Natural Philosophy.
13. Grammars and Dictionaries in various languages.[13]

Gifts of books and funds arrived at the seminary long after Mason's trip, further evidence of the bonds between the church in the Old and New Worlds.

Although the Synod now had a suitable library for a seminary, it lacked a faculty and a building. Not surprisingly, Mason was elected to be the first professor, and the Synod rented a room adjacent to his living quarters for the books. The seminary continued in Mason's home, and he continued to buy books for the library until failing health forced him to resign. Without his strong leadership, the seminary floundered, so that by 1821 a controversial motion carried to merge the Associate Reformed General Synod into the Presbyterian Church (into which Mason had led his congregation several years earlier).

With the merger, and with the consolidation of the New York Seminary into Princeton Seminary, Professor Mason's collection of books and funds were soon on their way to New Jersey. This move was challenged

---

13. *Extracts from the Minutes of the Proceedings of the First General Synod of the Associate-Reformed Church in North America* (New York, 1804), p. 19. See pp. 35-41 for a list of donors from Mason's trip.

by a remnant of thirteen ministers and twenty-two congregations who intended to keep their denomination alive. They argued that the books and funds were given for an Associate Reformed body. At first, Princeton Seminary refused to return the books and funds, but after several years of litigation it did comply. Then 2,400 books and $150.00 were returned to the Associate Reformed Synod's new seminary in Newburgh, New York. While other volumes gradually trickled in from Princeton, Rev. Robert Forrest gave his substantial library to Newburgh Seminary.

The Newburgh books were back in court eight years later when the Associate and Associate Reformed churches united to form the United Presbyterian Church of North America (1858). A minority of the Associate Reformed denomination rejected the merger and sought to retain possession of the library by using the same argument that worked two decades earlier. This time, however, a judge ruled that the merger was legitimate in spite of the reservations of the minority. After years of effort to stay open, the doors of the Newburgh Seminary were finally closed in 1878. It was not until 1901 that a decision was made to divide its assets

Pittsburgh-Xenia Seminary, reading room, Library, Long Administration Building.
The Newburgh Collection is on the shelves to the left.

between the other two seminaries. The transfer did not take place until 1907, when Allegheny Seminary was given the Mason Collection and Xenia the Forrest Collection. The Mason and Forrest collections were reunited in 1930 when the then Pittsburgh Seminary merged with Xenia to form Pittsburgh-Xenia Seminary. When the Mason Collection arrived in Allegheny, it was housed in a special apartment. In later years much of the collection was kept in virtual storage, subject to water damage, dirt, and extremes of heat and humidity. During the 1940s and 1950s various volumes, presumably duplicates, were sold or given away.[14]

Since a substantial number of books from Xenia came to Pittsburgh in 1930, a brief discussion of the Xenia library is appropriate. The story begins with the eight hundred volumes collected for John Anderson at Service Seminary in 1794.[15] The library moved from Service Seminary to Canonsburg, Pennsylvania, in 1821, then to Xenia in 1855, where it spent the longest time of its history. In 1863, the 2,000- to 3,000-volume library was housed on the second floor of the Xenia building. "Many of the most valuable of these books, it is believed, were sent by the mother Church in Scotland, while the Seminary was in its infancy."[16] By 1907, the 7,000-volume library was on the first floor of the newly constructed Anderson Hall. In the same year the library received its share of the books from the Newburgh Seminary, bringing the total to approximately 7,500.[17] Six years later, it received a substantial collection from James Price, D.D., of Philadelphia. His books pushed the total to 10,000

14. Librarian Agnes Ballantyne recalled, "When we were desperate for space at the Northside building, Dr. [Theophilus Mills] Taylor pulled out a great number of duplicates, all not necessarily Newburgh books. These we sold to students or gave away. . . . Then when I began cataloging books in boxes, Dr. Taylor again discarded a great many. . . . Another mass disappearance of books occurred when there was a flood in the basement. When I returned from library school, I found that hundreds of the books that had been stored off the old gym, were laid out all over the gymnasium floor to dry. Many of these were so ruined that I couldn't tell what they were. I am sure many of these were Mason and Forrest books. Then, you remember, we sold over $1000 worth of the rare books — duplicates. In deciding which ones to sell, I usually picked the Forrest ones, although keeping the one in best condition was also a factor." (Letter to Mildred Cowan, 21 June 1969, Pittsburgh Theological Seminary Archives.)

15. See the brief history of the seminary in the Xenia Seminary Catalog, 1906-7, pp. 18-19.

16. *An Address Delivered to the Students of the United Presbyterian Theological Seminary, Xenia, Ohio, by Rev. Thomas Beveridge, D.D. . . . Together With a Catalog . . . of the Institution* (Cincinnati, 1863), p. 32.

17. *An Address . . . by Rev. Thomas Beveridge,* pp. 32ff.

Pittsburgh-Xenia Seminary, Library reading room. Framed seals of Presbyterian Churches on the walls are now in the Barbour Library.

volumes, some 2,000 more than the Xenia Public Library.[18] The move to St. Louis in 1920 was designed, in part, to situate the seminary in the orbit of Washington University and its library. During the nine years in St. Louis, the seminary had its first librarian, Dr. J. H. Webster, professor of Greek exegesis and New Testament literature, librarian, and secretary to the faculty. "Under the direction of the Librarian of the Faculty, the students use these [the collection of 15,000] books for the investigation of assigned subjects."[19] James Leon Kelso served as assistant librarian, a role he would take with him to the new Pittsburgh-Xenia Seminary.

The consolidation of the Xenia and Pittsburgh collections was one

18. The Annual Catalog of the United Presbyterian Theological Seminary (UPTS) of Xenia, Ohio, 1913, p. 32.

19. Annual Catalog of the UPTS, 1925, p. 52.

of a number of changes in the newly created Pittsburgh-Xenia Seminary. A new stack room and a vault for rare books were opened to accommodate the collection, which had doubled in size. The old reference room was converted into a reading room, which proudly displayed approximately one hundred periodical titles. The Sixth United Presbyterian Church of Pittsburgh donated funds to create a new reference room. Above the shelves around the wall were banners from the Second Council of the Alliance of the Reformed Churches Holding the Presbyterian System of Government, held in Philadelphia in 1880. Mary B. Clark, one-time librarian and secretary to President John McNaugher, recalled how the banners ended up in Pittsburgh: "Dr. McNaugher was at the [First] Council in Scotland. . . . When he returned he spoke of the Reformed faith banners that would be coming, but did not say definitely they would be a gift. They hung over the Council meeting Chamber he said. . . . I know he was very proud of them and felt honored to have them however he came by them."[20]

During the 1930s and 1940s the library section of the seminary catalogs makes repeated reference to standards. In 1939 the seminary was admitted to membership to the American Association of Theological Schools.[21] There is evidence of increased investment in older and out-of-print books, giving an indication that the library was interested in general improvements.

When the plans for a new campus in East Liberty were announced in the late 1940s, there were high hopes for the library. Librarian Agnes Ballantyne supervised the transfer to the new campus, salvaging furniture and shelving wherever possible. The new reading and office area were on the first floor of the new building (in what is now the dean's wing) and stacks on the ground floor (now offices, mail room, and bookstore areas). The seminary catalog boasted, "The beautiful new reading and reference room has seating capacity for seventy-six patrons. The chairs and tables,

---

20. Mary B. Clark to Mary Ellen Scott, n.d., Pittsburgh Theological Seminary Archives. At the present time, the banners hang in the seminar room in the Barbour Library. Across the courtyard, one can see a number of the seals from the banners in the stone work above the windows of what is now the large lounge. Speaking of Dr. McNaugher, the 1925 *Pitheosem Book,* published in the centennial year, records the following in the section on seminary antics: "Miss Reed objects if one takes too many books from the library, while Dr. McNaugher worries if not enough are taken. Its a great life, if you don't weaken" (p. 63).

21. Minutes of the UPCNA, 1939, p. 941.

selected for beauty and comfort, are new and harmonize with the new shelving. A separate alcove for the librarian ensures quiet for readers, apart from the noise of typing and the confusion of other library business. A new card catalog and new magazine racks are conveniently placed. Some 130 current magazines of popular and general interest, along with technical, theological and Biblical journals are provided."[22] The new library would also serve as a depository for the records of the United Presbyterian Church and its antecedent bodies.[23]

In the opening words of her 1951 thesis, Agnes Ballantyne wrote:

> The new appointee to the librarianship of the Pittsburgh-Xenia Seminary was given to understand that as soon as immediate library needs had been taken care of, she would be expected to catalog some twelve thousand books received as gifts or legacies, and, because of insufficient help, left uncared for since 1907. Among these are about three thousand valuable, handsomely-bound books of the 16th, 17th, and 18th centuries, mostly classical, which had been bought for the seminaries of the Associate Reformed Synod.[24]

In 1957 she was still waiting for that opportunity. Miss Ballantyne did have a new library to be proud of, but her article about it in *The United Presbyterian* is built almost entirely around the Mason Collection.[25] Unfortunately, she would not have an opportunity to catalog her beloved Mason Collection.[26] Her disapproval of the consolidation of the two Presbyterian denominations led to her premature resignation. But even had she stayed, she would have faced the daunting task of incorporating the larger Western collection and seeing a new library through its planning and construction.

22. Pittsburgh-Xenia Seminary Annual Catalog, 1955-56, p. 22.

23. Until the completion of the Barbour Library, such historical records, as well as seminary archives, were stored in a large, warm, stuffy vault on the ground floor of the Long Administration Building.

24. Ballantyne, "The Newburg Collection," p. ii.

25. *The United Presbyterian* 115, 23 (9 June 1957): 12-13.

26. Two items in the seminary archives could provide the basis for a substantial bibliographic description of the Mason Collection. One is a 125-page handwritten catalog and booklist of the books in the library at Newburgh compiled by R. D. Williamson, dated February 22, 1905. It contains both the Mason Collection and the Forrest Collection. The other is a 100-page catalog of John Mason's library, undated.

Western Seminary

Although Western Theological Seminary can trace its roots to John McMillan's course of theological lectures and the books in his library, the story of Western's library begins with the decision to create a seminary in Allegheny City. The first session was held on November 16, 1827, where four students sat under the instruction of Rev. Joseph Stockton and Rev. Elisha Pope Swift. Western's library grew around two major collections. One was collected by a student of John Mitchell Mason, Rev. Allan Ditchfield Campbell (1791-1861), who visited Great Britain in 1829 to "beg a library for the institution"; the second was donated by Alexander Henry at the encouragement of Dr. Francis Herron.[27] Henry's collection was "an extensive and valuable assortment of historical and exegetical works which previously had been gathered in Europe."[28]

Campbell prepared for his trip by securing letters of introduction from President Andrew Jackson, his former parishioner, and from Western's Board of Trustees. The trustee letter notes that four-fifths of the population of approximately 4,000,000 people in the United States were without the benefits of clergy and that servicing them with clergy was difficult because of the size of the Mississippi Valley — 1,800,000 square miles. The need for a Western Seminary was apparent, and requests for funds received most of the attention. However, in a postscript, we read: "Donations of Theological or Scientific Books will be thankfully received. It is requested that the Donors will write their names in the title pages of the books they may be pleased to bestow."[29]

Campbell left from New York in May 1829 and began his "preaching mission" in Great Britain the following month. Introductions in London led to meetings with sympathetic spirits in Scotland and Ireland. One minister, a Rev. Dr. Buchanan, welcomed Campbell just as he had welcomed John Mitchell Mason three decades earlier. He not only gave books

27. Allan Ditchfield Campbell, "The Founding and Early History of the Western Theological Seminary," *The Bulletin of the Western Theological Seminary* 20, 1 (October 1927): 49. This article is one part of Campbell's extensive history of the early period of the seminary's history, which was not published until 1927.

28. William Wilson McKinney, *The Challenge of a Heroic Past* (Western Theological Seminary, n.d.), p. 24. See also Samuel Black McCormick, "One Hundred Years," *The Bulletin of the Western Theological Seminary* 20, 3 (April 1928): 25-26.

29. Campbell, "The Founding and Early History," pp. 51-52.

from his library; he also "went to Mr. Oliphant's bookstore and purchased Milner's Church History for the Seminary."[30] Campbell recalled,

> The exact number of books collected I do not now recollect, but there were upwards of 2,000 volumes brought to America by myself or were sent to the Seminary after my return home. If it had been compatible with my sense of duty to my family to have stayed longer in Great Britain I could have collected a very large number of books for the Library, but what I did met the approval of the Directors and friends of the Seminary. . . . In honor of the donors it was styled by the Directors the English and Scottish Library.

As important as the books and the funds were, the goodwill evoked by the trip was more crucial. It "gave confidence and shewed that the resignation of no individual connected with the Seminary could nullify the prayerful effort of Assembly and friends in establishing the institution."[31]

Campbell's trip was completed before Western had a building. At the 1830 meeting of the General Assembly funds were appropriated for the "Seminary, viz., $3000 towards the erection of the building, $2,300 towards the salary of the professor and teacher."[32] That building was erected in 1831, with provision for the library, which by 1838 numbered approximately 6,000 volumes.[33] In 1852, Dr. Luther Halsey loaned to the seminary his library of 2,000 volumes, and that loan was made permanent twenty years later. Regrettably, the building on Monument Hill was destroyed by fire in 1854. Although the loss of the building was a hardship, Campbell stressed that "the great loss was in the destruction of so many of the books out of the Halsey and the English and Scottish Libraries, many works of rare value which could not be easily picked up again. Bricks and mortar might be got, house or houses erected, insurance recovered on the property and books destroyed, but all these would not repair the loss of valuable standard works, theological, etc."[34] An insurance

---

30. Campbell, "The Founding and Early History," p. 79.

31. Campbell, "The Founding and Early History," pp. 82-83.

32. *Minutes of the General Assembly of the Presbyterian Church in the United States of America* (Philadelphia: Presbyterian Board of Publication, 1930), p. 297.

33. *Annual Catalog of the Officers and Students of the Western Theological Seminary* (Pittsburgh, 1838), p. 10.

34. Campbell, "The Founding and Early History," p. 107.

payment of $5,000 did take some of the sting out of the fire and became the basis for a library endowment.[35]

The library received its own building in 1872 at a cost of $25,000. Library Hall, on Ridge Avenue, was touted as "a carefully built, fire-proof structure, lighted from the roof, with alcoves on the first and second floors, and a reading room at the front, the entire width of the building."[36] Records indicate that it was designed to hold 100,000 volumes, but before the collection was half that size the building would be deemed inadequate and a new library would be underway.

The "Reference Catalog of the Library of the Western Theological Seminary" is a four-volume list of the approximately 17,000 books in the collection. The volumes are dated 1879, and the first one is an index to the collection, with entries by author and subject. The other three volumes list the location of the items in the collection, with a classification system designating the book's alcove in the library, shelf number, and item number.[37] Regrettably, the "Reference Catalog" does not list materials by source or date of acquisition.

In the 1880s, an appeal went out from Western for funds for acquisitions and a librarian.

> The amount of the Library Fund is [currently] Eight Thousand One Hundred Dollars. . . . The melancholy significance of these figures is, that this vital interest of the Seminary must continue to languish so long as these figures remain as they are. The age, position, standing and importance of the Seminary fairly entitle it to the best Theological Library west of the Allegheny mountains. An absolutely essential condition of the Seminary's progress on the plane of higher scholarship and of wider influence is that there should be an adequate annual income to be expended in enriching the alcoves of the Library with the best treasures of theological learning in all departments. . . . Who will perpetuate his name and his influence for all time to come by

---

35. McCormick, "One Hundred Years," p. 26.

36. *Annual Catalog of the Western Theological Seminary,* 1897-98, p. 14. In *The Bulletin of the Western Theological Seminary, Catalog Number,* 9, 3 (February 1917): 23, the 1872 library is described as being "poorly adapted to library purposes."

37. A word on book classification systems is appropriate here. Western moved from its in-house system to the Union Theological Seminary classification system, which it retained until the consolidation. Pittsburgh-Xenia moved from an in-house system to Dewey Decimal to Library of Congress. One of the most time-consuming tasks of the consolidation was recataloging the Western collection in the Library of Congress system.

Western Seminary, reference room of Library, Swift Hall

endowing the Library in the sum of Fifty Thousand Dollars? The sum of Five Thousand Dollars will endow an alcove which will bear the name of the benefactor.[38]

By the late nineteenth century, the size of the collection alone demanded more attention than the library committee and the faculty member who served as librarian could give it. Faculty could continue to give instruction in bibliography and "attempt to train students in the practical use of books."[39] But managing a collection of over 20,000 volumes required a professional librarian, and during these years the Western trustees looked to remedy this need.[40]

38. *The Western Theological Seminary: An Historical Summary, A Statement and an Appeal* (Pittsburgh, 1881), pp. 16-17.

39. *The Bulletin of the Western Theological Seminary* 1 (1908-9): 28.

40. It is difficult to determine whether Western's librarians were full- or part-time and whether they were trained as librarians or not. Western librarians include the following: Rev. John Launitz, 1874-1884; Franklin N. Riale, 1884-1886; Jesse L. Cotton, 1886-1888; Rev. H. T. McClelland, 1888-1891; S. B. McCormick, acting librarian,

Seminary catalogs often detailed significant new acquisitions, specified periodical holdings, and spoke of improvements in service. For example, the 1908-9 catalog remarks that the library acquired three volumes of Doumergue's *Life of Calvin* and the *Opera Omnia* of Albertus 'Magnus and completed its set of Migne's *Patrologia Latina,* among many other books. It also listed the eighty-one periodical titles on file. A few years later, "increasing attention has been given to those writers who deal with the great social problems and the practical applications of Christianity to the questions of ethical and social life."[41] The most immediate social problems were created by the large influx of immigrants, and seminary students had many opportunities to work in settlement houses, as they were called. One great social problem that was not mentioned was industrial pollution, which took its toll not only on the books but also on patrons' eyes and respiratory systems. The 1908 catalog reports that the "usefulness of the Library has been greatly increased by the introduction of electric lights."[42] Keep in mind that electric lights in smoky Pittsburgh did not mean evening hours for the library (they would come later); rather, it meant that the library was now more usable during the day!

The 1910 catalog noted that the reference collection had been relocated to another part of Library Hall to promote greater quiet and better light. This was an early sign that the building was deficient in spite of electric lights. "It is hoped that the generosity of friends will, in the near future, permit the modernizing of the stack system, and increase the capacity of the Library and the accessibility to the departments and their preservation."[43] In 1915 a new campus building opened its doors, and

---

1889-1890; S. B. Groves, acting librarian, 1890-1891; W. E. Allen, acting librarian, 1891-1892; Rev. R. D. Wilson, 1891-1893; J. L. Lowes, 1893-1894, acting librarian, 1891-1892; J. M. Wilson, 1894-1895; James A. Kelso, 1895-1896 and 1897-1909; C. A. McCrea, 1896-1897; J. M. Oliver, 1896-1897; Rev. S. J. Fisher, D.D., 1909-1913; Rev. D. E. Culley, acting librarian, 1913-1919; and Rev. Frank Eakin, 1919-1927 (*General Biographical Catalogue, Western Theological Seminary of the Presbyterian Church* [Pittsburgh, 1927], p. 26). Subsequently, Agnes D. MacDonald was assistant to the librarian, 1926-1930, and librarian, 1930-1944. Prof. Frank Dixon McCloy served as librarian from 1945 to 1958. He was replaced by Prof. James S. Irvine, who served from 1958 to 1966.

41. *The Bulletin of the Western Theological Seminary, Catalog Number,* 2, 3 (February 1910): 28.

42. *Catalog* 1, 1 (1 October 1908): 28.

43. *The Bulletin of the Western Theological Seminary, Catalog Number,* 3, 2 (January 1911): 24.

Library Hall was abandoned a year later. To mark the occasion, "a circular letter was sent out to 650 clergymen and educators residing in Pittsburgh and vicinity, inviting them to avail themselves of the advantages of our theological library."[44] The library's new home was in a building at the rear of a proposed quadrangle of buildings. The stack area was designed to hold 165,000 volumes, triple the size of the collection at that time. The Medieval-Gothic Reference Room, with a capacity of 10,000 volumes, and library offices were on the second floor. A large room used as a chapel and a smaller seminar room were on the first. Prof. D. E. Cully, acting librarian, gushed that, with the new building, "our hopes have already been realized even beyond our former dreams. The new building is conceded to be one of the most beautiful in the country and ample provision has been made to take care of the growth of our collection for many generations to come."[45] In approximately fifty years it would fall to the bulldozer, the victim of the merger and of urban redevelopment.[46]

The acquisition of a substantial hymnology collection in 1916 was a fitting way to celebrate the new library. "The James H. Warrington Memorial Library: History of Hymnody" was one of the largest and finest libraries on psalmody, hymnology, and church music anywhere in the country. There has been some confusion about the size of this acquisition because it was not the first such collection assembled by Warrington, a Philadelphia accountant.[47] Hartford Seminary had the Silas H. Paine Hymnological Collection, which was purchased from Warrington in 1899 for $5,000. Warrington continued to acquire materials destined for Hartford. However, for reasons that remain unclear but that possibly had

44. "Report of the President to the Board of Directors," *The Bulletin of the Western Theological Seminary* 3, 5 (July 1911): 38.

45. *The Bulletin of the Western Theological Seminary* 8, 5 (July 1916): 52.

46. On the impending consolidation with Pittsburgh-Xenia, Western President Clifford E. Barbour indicated one more reason why the new Pittsburgh-Xenia campus was chosen to be the home of the new Pittsburgh Theological Seminary: "The proposed athletic stadium for the North Side will mean the loss of Herron and Swift Halls. . . . This may accelerate the program for merger — Western will need help — but, until merger, we can function in the three buildings on the north side of Ridge Avenue." *Western Watch* 9, 4 (15 December 1958): 4.

47. Issues of the *Bulletin* from the years immediately following the addition of the Warrington Collection refer to the number of volumes as between nine and ten thousand volumes. This may refer to the entire collection acquired by Warrington — that is, the Hartford and Pittsburgh collections. In any case, Western's Warrington Collection was not that large.

something to do with default of payment, Warrington broke off negotiations with Hartford and sought a new home for his later collection.[48]

David R. Breed, professor of homiletics, and Charles N. Boyd, professor of church music, were instrumental in getting Warrington's later collection to Pittsburgh. Breed recounted how the offer to buy the collection came during the 1913 Capital Campaign. "But the trustees realized the importance of securing it, and Mar. 20, 1914, advanced $250.00 to secure the option. I at once appealed to Mr. Carnegie. . . . Our appeal, however, was rejected and we were compelled . . . to make little effort towards the purchase price of $20,000.00. But with the death of Mr. Warrington we were favored by his widow with a most generous offer. Dr. Kelso visited her in our behalf, and it was agreed that the library should be ours upon the payment of $5,000.00 cash and an annuity bond of $10,000.00 with other favorable features which I need not recount."[49]

Agnes M. Armstrong, associate librarian, supervised the moving of the Warrington Collection to Western in June 1916. After processing, the collection was found to be 3,890 volumes and pamphlets and 1,280 pieces of music pasted in notebooks and ledger books.[50] This number does not reflect the enormous number of notes and cards. There are tens of thousands of note cards slowly deteriorating due to heavy acidity of the paper. One can only imagine what Warrington could have accomplished with a computer! C. N. Boyd, a former director of the Pittsburgh Musical Institute, arranged the purchase from Mrs. Warrington and later added his library to the Warrington Collection. Hymnology was occasionally described as a collection emphasis in the Bulletin, but the Warrington Collection received little care and attention until the 1960s.[51]

48. "Biographically, James Warrington proves to be an extremely elusive figure. He was born in Colchester, England, in 1841, and died in Philadelphia on October 4, 1915. The letterhead which he used in 1912 gives this information: 'Public Accountant and Auditor. New York and Philadelphia. Sometime Lecturer at the University of Pennsylvania. Member of a Commission to simplify Post Office Accounts, etc.'" Theodore M. Finney wrote these words about Warrington in his introduction to the reprint of Warrington's Short Title of Books Relating to or Illustrating the History and Practice of Psalmody, Bibliographia Tripotamopolitana, no. 1 (Pittsburgh: Clifford E. Barbour Library, 1970), p. [i].

49. "The Ministry and Music," The Bulletin of the Western Theological Seminary 9, 1 (October 1916): 10.

50. The Bulletin of the Western Theological Seminary 9, 3 (1917): 25.

51. The Pitcairn Crabbe Foundation gave several gifts in the 1960s for rebinding the Warrington Collection.

In the middle years of this century the librarians at Western settled into productive patterns of slow, steady growth and collection maintenance. From 1926 to 1944 Agnes D. MacDonald served as a librarian at Western. Her many Board reports were brief and to the point, yet they also reveal her steady efforts to manage and preserve the collection as well as to encourage its use. The office of librarian reverted to a member of the faculty in 1944 with Frank Dixon McCloy. At the end of McCloy's tenure as librarian, the catalog proclaimed, "The library of 70,000 volumes is one of the glories of the Western Seminary."[52] James S. Irvine replaced McCloy in 1958 and led the Western Library through the consolidation with Pittsburgh-Xenia and the building program of the Barbour Library.

Pittsburgh Theological Seminary

When talk of merger heated up between the Presbyterians and the United Presbyterians, it gradually became clear that Western and Pittsburgh-Xenia were destined for consolidation. A statement issued after a joint meeting of the Boards of Trustees indicated the goal:

> The ideal plan for theological education in the Pittsburgh area would include the emergence of one great theological institution or university of theology which would have several schools, including at least a graduate school of theology, a theological school granting the B.D. [Bachelor of Divinity degree], and a school of Christian education or a vocational school. This institution should become one of the outstanding centers of the theological education in the world.[53]

Consolidation of the two seminaries affected the libraries, not simply in the obvious sense of combining two collections, but also in terms of direction and the kind of materials to be acquired because an extensive graduate program was planned.[54] When Agnes Ballantyne resigned in September 1959 as a sign of displeasure over the consolidation, losing

52. Catalog, 1958, p. 11.
53. Quoted in "President Barbour Writes . . . ," *Western Watch* 9, 2 (15 May 1958): 22. See also Theophilus Mills Taylor, "The Future of Theological Education in Pittsburgh," *Western Watch* 9, 4 (15 December 1958): 1-4.
54. The libraries are featured prominently in a "Report of [the] Special Committee

her at that critical juncture was painful. In retrospect it meant that James Irvine would be the head librarian alone at the new Pittsburgh Theological Seminary. Irvine inherited the unenviable job of merging two collections and reclassifying the Western books, with the full realization that all shifting would only be temporary until a new library building could be built. The first catalog of the newly created Pittsburgh Theological Seminary reported a collection of over 100,000 volumes. This was 25,000 more than the library, barely five years old, could hold. After its trip across town, the Western library was shelved in various parts of the administration building, including the student recreation center.

Plans for a new library were made during the 1960-61 academic year.[55] Named for the acting president of the new seminary, the Clifford E. Barbour Library opened with great fanfare in September 1964. To mark the opening, Karl Barth donated his desk to the library. Barth's biographer, Eberhard Busch, explains: "The desk at which he sat [in the mid-1960s] was no longer the one which he had taken over from his father and at which he had written out by hand the whole of the *Church Dogmatics*. He now had a splendid new desk, given by the Presbyterians in Pittsburgh in exchange for the old one (which has become a museum piece there with an inscription)."[56] Martin Niemöller gave the opening address and spoke on the folly of thinking that the days of Christianity have passed. The church would have to rethink its message in light of the claims of agnostics, atheists, and secularists, and to do that, according to Niemöller, the church would need access to the resources of the Christian tradition.

---

on the Study of Presbyterian Theological Education in the Pittsburgh Area," prepared by the two seminaries with assistance from an outside committee (April 24, 1959). Among many recommendations, the needs for a new library building and enlarging the staff were most conspicuous. This report is included in "Minutes of the Board of Directors of the Pittsburgh-Xenia Theological Seminary, January" (28 January 1958–17 November 1959), Pittsburgh Theological Seminary Archives.

55. See the 1960-61 Librarian's Annual Report, p. 4. The campaign brochure *1 +1 = 1: The Mathematics of a Dream* displays an architect's early plan for the library. It differs markedly from the present structure by the inclusion of a substantial wing for faculty offices. Gifts of $675,000 from both the Sarah Mellon Scaife and the R. K. Mellon Foundations paid for the construction and furnishings of the library.

56. Eberhard Busch, *Karl Barth: His Life from Letters and Autobiographical Texts* (Philadelphia: Fortress Press, 1976), p. 475. Barth wrote the inscription (in English) that is on the desk in the library foyer. See *Karl Barth — Letters 1961-1968*, ed. J. Fangmeier and H. Stoevesandt, trans. G. W. Bromiley (Edinburgh: T. & T. Clark, 1981), pp. 351-52.

Pittsburgh Seminary. Martin Niemöller, President Donald G. Miller, and Dr. Barbour at the Karl Barth desk on the day of the dedication of the Clifford E. Barbour Library

The times have gone, when any student of theology, when a minister or a missionary could have all the literature in his own library. This new building is intended to become the house for 300,000 volumes. Nobody will ever be able to know them all or even a considerable part of them. But whoever tries to work in a special field in order to prepare the spreading of God's saving word under certain and still unknown conditions, he simply cannot do so without a technically most perfect and organized library.[57]

A publicity postcard for the Barbour Library from the period proclaims it as "the scholar's workshop to match a distinguished faculty."[58]

57. Martin Niemöller, five-page untitled address, September 21, 1964, p. 5. Pittsburgh Theological Seminary Archives.
58. Contained in the Pittsburgh Theological Seminary Archives.

Now, finally, the seminary had a building worthy of recognition, and efforts to fortify the collection were in place. What they lacked was a staff to create that "technically most perfect and organized library." By 1964, the staff had grown to seven persons, with plans to add five more: "A reference librarian and secretary, a bibliographic assistant, a cataloger with foreign language proficiency and secretary are essential for the support of a serious graduate program."[59] Although grateful for the new library building, Irvine now had to contend with less tangible but no less real needs, such as a larger book budget. "The steady progress of the library program through the vicissitudes of merger and building should not blind us to the fact that the library still has many problems to solve, new worlds to conquer and much painful toil to undergo in the service of the Kingdom."[60]

James Irvine left the seminary in June 1966 to join the staff of Princeton Theological Seminary's Speer Library. Dikran Y. Hadidian was called as librarian by President Donald Miller from a number of distinguished faculty who were about to be casualties of the breakup of the Hartford Theological Seminary. With Irvine's plans in place to build the staff, Hadidian's first annual report takes us to the heart of his mission: "The task of implementing the decision to make the Barbour Library a worthy center for study and research and eventually one of the major theological libraries in our country has brought me to Pittsburgh."[61] A functional and spacious building, a sizable general collection with several significant special collections, and new funds earmarked for acquisitions — the ingredients for a great library were falling into place.

By 1967, the graduate component of the theological university had shifted to a cooperative doctoral program with the University of Pittsburgh. This was not to affect acquisitions for the library. After mentioning the various benefits of the program to the seminary, the catalog adds, "Already the Seminary library has earmarked large sums of money for the building up of book collections in the fields in which the Doctorate will be offered. This, again, of course, will strengthen the Bachelor of Divinity program."[62] For Hadidian, this meant immediate efforts to strengthen the reference and bibliographic collections, particularly foreign

59. Librarian's Report to the Board of Trustees, 1964, p. 3, Pittsburgh Theological Seminary Archives.
60. Librarian's Report, 1964, p. 2.
61. Annual Report to the Board of Trustees, 1966-67.
62. Catalog, 1967-68, p. 89.

language materials. The number of periodicals received also increased drastically, in part because the size of the faculty was expanding. Donald Miller was a "library president," and Hadidian was grateful to him as the one "who persuasively convinces the Trustees that the library is at the heart of the academic endeavors!"[63]

In the late 1960s, Hadidian began to address the problem of the lack of what he thought was a responsible use of the library, and he continued to do so for most of his tenure as librarian.

> In these years of restlessness on the campuses one wishes that students would decide to "sit-in" the library more and search for a proper perspective on life. . . . May we hope that in the immediate future our faculty would take the *lead* in directing the student's attention not to matters of the moment which tend to change each month of the academic year but to the very content of our faith which in turn obliges us to refer back to the "sources" of our faith — the Bible, the history and doctrine of the Church, and the corporate life of the Church as it is lived in this world.[64]

One of Hadidian's joys was his working relationship with Theodore Finney. After Finney retired in 1968 as head of the department of music at the University of Pittsburgh, he served as a volunteer curator of the Warrington Collection until his death in 1978. During those years he organized the collection and added many of his own volumes to it. In 1971, during the breakup of the Hartford Theological Seminary Library, Finney labored unsuccessfully to get the first Warrington Collection to Pittsburgh. As a tribute to his many contributions, the home of the Warrington Collection was named the Finney Room in 1970.

With Harold Lancour, Dean of the Graduate School of Library and Information at the University of Pittsburgh, Hadidian established a program between the seminary and the university leading to a joint Master of Divinity and Master in Library Science.[65] Although the program has had few students since its beginning in 1968, the relationship between the seminary and the library school continues to be a good one.

The seminary acquired a treasure in the second edition of Napoleon's *Description de l'Egypt*. In the early 1960s the twenty-six volumes

63. Hadidian, in the catalog, 1969-70, p. 7.
64. Board Report, 1968-69, p. 1.
65. Catalog, 1969-70, p. 88.

were removed from the American College for Girls in Cairo for safekeeping. They found their way to the Barbour Library thanks to friends who knew of the seminary's rare book collection, connections to Egypt, and commitment to archaeology.[66] In November 1975 the library acquired a major collection of rare books and bibliographic materials belonging to Louis Grier (1891-1973), an executive at Alcoa and, for forty years, an avid bibliophile. The collection spans over four hundred years and has been kept intact as a memorial to Grier.

In spite of these acquisitions and the promising start of the bibliographic series *Bibliographia Tripotamopolitana* in 1970, the seventies were years of uncertainty.[67] Rising inflation and the devaluation of the dollar put the brakes on acquisitions. Still, the collection remained strong, and it continued to bolster the library's reputation. The staff, whose numbers dropped from ten in 1972 to six by the end of the decade, recataloged many of the rare and antiquarian volumes housed in the Anderson Room and were among the first in the Pittsburgh area to catalog using OCLC, a national online bibliographic utility.

The 1980s were years of stabilization after the difficult seventies. The library celebrated the acquisition of the two hundred thousandth volume in 1984. Gifts continued to supplement regular acquisitions. Dr. Caroline Anderson donated a substantial collection of Byzantine and Russian art, theology, and literature. An anonymous gift led to the endowment of a chair for the librarian and professor of bibliography. Hadidian retired from the library in 1985 and, with his wife Jean, continued to use his talents as the editor of Pickwick Publications.

When I became librarian in 1987 I was given the goals of automating the library and increasing its use by students. Ironically automation opens the floodgates of information at precisely the time in the history of North American theological education when older and busier second-career students lack the background and time to use these resources. Just how this will work itself out over the next twenty years is anyone's guess. Regardless of that future, plans are already being made to acquire materials for patrons who will celebrate the seminary's tercentenary.

66. See the letter dated September 28, 1987, from Kenneth E. Bailey to Rev. Willis McGill recounting the story, in the Pittsburgh Theological Seminary Archives. The precise date of the set's arrival is unclear, probably sometime in 1969.

67. Ford Lewis Battles gets credit for the name of the series, "Tripotamopolitana," which means "City on the Three Rivers." Approximately ten volumes have been published in the series.

The 1990s will also see ongoing efforts to protect and promote the seminary's rare and antiquarian materials, to preserve the general collection, and to cultivate gifts of manuscript and book collections. The Barbour Library and its antecedent libraries have been and continue to be the only research-level theological collections in the area. This is a heavy burden but one that is always gladly borne. Pressures to acquire widely in nontheological areas will need to be resisted if the Barbour Library is to maintain its place as a research-level theological collection. Fortunately, the Oakland Library Consortium is only a few miles from the seminary, and its millions of volumes complement the holdings of the Barbour Library.

As this chapter has shown, library work, past and present, proceeds best when librarians are not distracted by needs for adequate funds, buildings, and staff. The present building will take the library well into the next century and quite possibly beyond. Substantial efforts are being made to strengthen acquisitions through endowment funds for the library. So the Barbour Library is in an enviable position in every respect but one. Life in an automated library environment and attentiveness to patron service require an adequate number of highly trained staff. In future years, the library staff will be turning its attention to this, the chief need of the Pittsburgh Seminary Library at the beginning of its third century.[68]

68. I wish to thank the staff of the Barbour Library for their patience during and assistance in this project. Special thanks to Mary Ellen Scott, cataloger on the Barbour Library staff for twenty-five years and now volunteer archivist, for her help and encouragement during the research of this chapter.

CHAPTER NINE

Pittsburgh Theological Seminary in World Mission

Charles B. Partee

Reflection on the history of Pittsburgh Theological Seminary in world mission provides abundant opportunity for bicentennial celebration. So many graduates went forth from the academic halls of this institution to the mission fields of the world, however, that it is quite impossible to know or tell the whole story. Some of those who crossed seas and cultures spent many years proclaiming the good news revealed in Jesus Christ; others died within a few weeks of landing; still others because of various circumstances were forced to return to America, their mission unfulfilled. Without a doubt, hidden away in diaries and letters home, there must be countless wonderful and inspiring tales of their self-sacrificing devotion, but the complete narrative is known to God alone — and will remain so.

Although the Presbyterian churches trace their theological identity to the Reformation of the sixteenth century, their major concern for world mission began near the close of the eighteenth century. Perhaps the fact that Protestantism in its first three centuries directed almost no efforts toward global evangelism may be explained by the overpowering need first to survive and then to become established. In any case, it is strange to note that both Martin Luther and John Calvin believed that the Great Commission to "go . . . and make disciples of all nations" (Matt. 28:19) applied only to the early church.[1]

Among Protestants, the modern world mission enterprise was

---

1. See Gustav Warneck, *Outline of a History of Protestant Missions,* 3rd ed. (New York: Fleming H. Revell, 1906), pp. 8ff.

generated by the pietistic movement, powered by the industrial revolution, and swept along by the European scramble for global empire. Especially ascendant in the nineteenth century was the political and commercial might of the British Empire, with missionaries sometimes preceding, but more often following, empire builders. Thus at about the time of the founding of Pittsburgh Seminary's oldest predecessor institution (1794), "the great missionary campaign of English-speaking Evangelicalism [began] an expansion which was to dominate all Christian missions up to World War I, and provide what was, until the war, the most spectacular diffusion any body of ideas had experienced in world history."[2]

The nineteenth century, roughly extending from the French Revolution to World War I, can be called the great century of world missions. In 1900 there were 13,600 Protestant missionaries, of whom 5,900 were British and 4,100 were American.[3] A good number of these American missionaries were graduates of Pittsburgh Seminary. In fact, in the seminary's first fifty years, one out of seventeen Western Seminary graduates went to the mission field. Indeed, the missionary consciousness was still so central that the centennial (1827-1927) issue of *The Bulletin of the Western Theological Seminary* not only celebrated the inauguration of an alumni chair of religious education and missions but also devoted two of its six chapters to missions — one to world missions and one to home missions.[4]

This passion for the world-encompassing mission of the church is well represented by Elisha P. Swift (1792-1865), who dedicated his life to missions but instead of going on the mission field himself became the first instructor at the Western Seminary and the chief founder of the Western Foreign Missionary Society.[5] According to the Society, "the missionary obligation is the obligation of the Church in her essential character and . . . every member of the church is committed to this obligation. The Presbyterian Church owes it as a sacred duty to her glorified Head to yield a far more exemplary obedience . . . to the command . . . 'go ye into all the world and preach the gospel to every creature.'" Swift, a zealous advocate of world missions, believed no pastor should "be told

2. James Hastings Nichols, *History of Christianity 1650-1950* (New York: The Ronald Press Company, 1956), p. 306.

3. Nichols, *History of Christianity*, p. 307.

4. *The Bulletin of the Western Theological Seminary* 20 (April 1928): 62ff., 81ff., 124.

5. A plaque on the wall outside the President's office in the Long Administration Building commemorates this latter event.

that, according to the Word of God, and the constitution of the Church, he has a right to come and consume hours of time in trifling litigation" while "a world of benighted men" has not yet heard the good news that Jesus Christ is Lord.[6]

This chapter offers a few selective profiles, but it is intended to honor all the good and faithful servants of the Great Commission who graduated from Pittsburgh Theological Seminary.

Pittsburgh Seminary in China:
Calvin Wilson Mateer, Class of 1861

The first Presbyterian missionaries to China were Joseph S. Travelli and Robert W. Orr of the class of 1836. Because they were not allowed to enter China itself, they worked in Singapore. Among other early notables was Andrew P. Happer, class of 1844, who spent fifty years in China, and Samuel I. J. Schereschewsky, class of 1858, who became an Episcopal bishop, a biblical translator, and author of a Mongolian dictionary. Pittsburgh Seminary also contributed to the martyrs of China. When the murderous fire-storm of the Boxer uprising swept across north China, Frank E. Simcox, class of 1893, was last seen on June 30, 1900, with his wife by his side and their three small children clinging to his hands in the midst of the flames of their burning house outside the walls of Paotingfu.

Of the "Three Great Pioneers" of the Presbyterian mission in Shantung province, two were from Pittsburgh Seminary. The tireless Hunter Corbett, class of 1863, spent fifty-seven years in evangelism, "traveling through eastern Shantung for more than half a century until there was hardly a village in all that area where his kindly, bearded face was not known."[7] His

---

6. Robert E. Speer, "The Western on the Mission Field," in *The Bulletin of the Western Theological Seminary* 20, 3 (April 1928): 66.

7. B. A. Garside, *One Increasing Purpose: The Life of Henry Winters Luce* (New York: Revell Press, 1948), p. 82. For Hunter Corbett (1835-1920), see James R. E. Craighead, *Life of Hunter Corbett: Fifty-Six Years a Missionary in China* (New York: Revell Press, 1921); and Harold Frederick Smith and Charles Hodge Corbett, *Hunter Corbett and His Family* (Claremont: College Press, 1965). Corbett was moderator of the General Assembly in 1907. The third founder was John Livingston Nevius; see Helen S. Coan Nevius, *The Life of John Livingston Nevius: For Forty Years a Missionary in China* (New York: Fleming H. Revell, 1895).

formidable colleague, Calvin Mateer, is called the founder and father of modern education in China.

Calvin Wilson Mateer was born January 9, 1836, and grew up on a succession of farms in the Harrisburg, Pennsylvania, area. His mother, Mary Diven Mateer, was the greatest influence in his life, keeping the ideal of missionary service before all her children and living to see four of them in China. "Mary Mateer taught her children that piety is the first of virtues and that dutifulness is piety's ethical expression. In her judgment their particular duty was to go to the ends of the earth as Christian missionaries."[8]

In 1860, while on a preaching assignment in Ohio, Calvin Mateer met Julia Ann Brown, a quiet, thoughtful, pretty girl with a strength fully equal to his. They were married late in 1862. "Where Calvin had the ability to command respect from people, Julia seems to have moved them to love. She meant a great deal to him from the first, and her quick response, her trust in him, and his half-formed resolution, were all immeasurable comforts to him." While Calvin was dithering about their missionary vocation, thinking about North India or Africa, Julia simply packed up everything they owned, and the Mateers sailed for China on July 3, 1863, the same afternoon that America's future was being determined at the Battle of Gettysburg within earshot of Calvin's boyhood home.[9]

After a thoroughly miserable six-month voyage across the Pacific Ocean (from which the health of Hunter Corbett and Julia Mateer never fully recovered) and a hazard-filled journey inland, the Corbetts and Mateers arrived in Tengchow, five hundred miles from Shanghai. "Both Mateer and Corbett were indefatigable preachers and pastors and traveled widely in Shantung spreading the Christian message and building up churches."[10] For Mateer, the first ten years in China (1864-74), dealing with the complex language and the xenophobic people, was intensely frustrating. Carrying a pistol to protect himself and being called a "foreign devil" thousands of times, Mateer — unlike Corbett — was never a great

---

8. Irwin T. Hyatt, Jr., *Our Ordered Lives Confess: Three Nineteenth Century American Missionaries in East Shantung* (Cambridge: Harvard University Press, 1976), p. 142. Mary Mateer is buried in Wooster, Ohio. The biology building at the College of Wooster carries her family name.

9. Hyatt, *Our Ordered Lives Confess,* p. 145.

10. Kenneth Scott Latourette, *A History of Christian Missions in China* (New York: Macmillan Company, 1929), p. 367.

*Julia Brown Mateer, missionary in China with
her husband, Calvin Mateer, 1863-1898*

success as an itinerating evangelist. Even Corbett could hardly get a hearing
in the 1860s and was attacked by hostile mobs. Still he persevered, and
in 1907 on a five-hundred-mile tour he spoke 265 times to large and
attentive audiences.[11]

In the earliest picture included in her biography, Julia Mateer seems
to be gazing at the world with bold merriment. In China she was later

11. Latourette, *History of Christian Missions in China,* p. 570.

described as "this noble daughter of the heavenly King."[12] To her profound regret, if not deep sorrow, she and Calvin had no children, but in a very real sense Julia Mateer was mother to the entire China Christian mission. For example, one young woman remembered when her missionary father had taken his three young, and now motherless, children to "Auntie 'Teer," and "she loved and mothered us with all the strength and sweetness of her great heart. Her days were already crowded to overflowing with her work for the Chinese, but we children never for a moment suspected that we were an added burden. I remember especially the evening hours, when we gathered around her knee and listened to her stories or told her all that was in our hearts."[13] Fanny Corbett Hays said of Julia Mateer: "Never lived a missionary who more lovingly and conscientiously entered into the details of the common daily life of the people who pressed upon her."[14] In his address at her funeral, Dr. Watson M. Hayes wryly remarked, "When the Chinese pastors, helpers or teachers came to Tengchow to report their work, they did not go first to Dr. Mills or to Dr. Mateer or to me, but you would find them sitting in Mrs. Mateer's room giving her a detailed account of every discouragement and every success."[15]

Julia and Calvin committed their lives to Christian mission in China. Thus after she arrived in China, Julia would see her Ohio home only twice again. Among other things, she worked almost alone for thirty years for the education of Chinese girls. She spoke of having "plenty and more than plenty of delightful work which by God's blessing had been prospering more and more year by year."[16]

She appealed to other women to come to China:

> In the United States there must be at least one minister for every two or three thousand persons, besides all the Sabbath-school teachers and other Christian men and women who are working and praying for the unconverted. In China, counting ministers, and male and female teachers, native and foreign, there is scarcely one religious teacher of any grade for a million. Women in Christian lands can never know what

12. Robert McCheyne Mateer, *Character-Building in China: The Life-Story of Julia Brown Mateer* (New York: Revell, 1912), p. 36.

13. Mateer, *Character-Building in China,* p. 36.

14. Mateer, *Character-Building in China,* p. 97.

15. Mateer, *Character-Building in China,* p. 142.

16. Mateer, *Character-Building in China,* p. 81.

they owe the Bible until they see the deep, utter degradation, — mental, moral, and physical — of heathen women. And the wretched heathen women are our sisters, as good by nature as we, and as deserving of God's favor. If, then, we have been singled out to receive such blessings, shall we 'deny to them the lamp of life'? If the watchman failed to warn the city, the guilt was his. (See Ezekiel, thirty-third chapter.) I could write a volume on the need of teachers here, especially earnest, self-denying women. How shall I compress it into the space of one letter! . . . I do not forget the longing that every true woman has for a home, for I have been a homeless orphan; nor would I underestimate the happiness of married life — no happy wife can. I know, too, that it is no light thing for a woman to leave friends and home and all the blessings of a Christian land, and go out alone, to bear the toils and cares, the responsibilities and disappointments, the weariness and loneliness of a missionary life in China. But God will give grace even for this *to every one whom he calls to it.* They who endure to the end will find deep and abiding happiness in this work.[17]

Calvin Mateer was "busy all his life at 'an amount of work that would have killed most men,'" primarily as an author, translator, and teacher. In addition he was "a scientist, an inventor, and a kind of backyard industrialist, [making] his greatest mark, however, by founding and developing what was debatably the first — but almost certainly was the best — of the nineteenth-century China Christian Colleges." As a result of his educational and literary efforts, Mateer's influence permeated the life and work of practically every young Protestant missionary north of Shanghai.[18]

From the beginning Mateer threw himself into a variety of work, because his way of resting was to take up a new task. "In the early years, in addition to his own house (the first two-story house in China), Mateer built everything from false teeth to coffins for fellow missionaries." His

17. Mateer, *Character-Building in China,* pp. 168, 169, 171.
18. Hyatt, *Our Ordered Lives Confess,* pp. 139-40. The first General Conference of Protestant missionaries held in Shanghai (May 1877) gave Mateer the opportunity to defend his conviction of the effectiveness of education as missionary outreach against those who disparaged education in favor of direct evangelism and medical efforts. Mateer's *Course of Mandarin Lessons,* published in 1892, was an immediate success and remained the starting point of most English-speaking arrivals in north China for a generation. Among his numerous works Mateer published a Mandarin Bible. His last book in Chinese was a translation of the Westminster Shorter Catechism.

workshop included machinery for "turning, blacksmithing, plumbing, screw-cutting, burnishing, electroplating, casting, and so forth." This workshop "was a kind of microcosm of Calvin Mateer's personality; it harnessed his energy, or his abhorrence of inactivity." On later furloughs "he toured locomotive factories, sketched industrial exhibits, and took cram courses in medicine and dentistry [spending a month, for example] in Machinery Hall at the 1893 Chicago World's Fair. . . . On his last furlough in Siberia in 1902, he was finally called upon to fix a locomotive." Once Mateer pumped out a flooded coal mine, and for "the lower classes he fixed eyeglasses and bicycles and treated toothaches, burns, broken legs, and cholera."[19]

The range of Mateer's activities is staggering, but his heart was mainly involved in the college to which he chiefly devoted his life in China. That is to say, Mateer found the proper focus for the exercise of his considerable talents and industry when he began to help Julia in the little school that she had established during their early years in China. After he joined her and channeled his immense energy into it, this school eventually became Tengchow College. Calvin fought many battles to improve their school and then to preserve it. He was especially concerned that instruction be given entirely in the Chinese language. He spent the first twenty-five years learning the language and learning about the people, "getting his ideas straight, initiating lines of work, and training others to take over in each. In the last two decades the local enterprise largely ran itself, leaving him free to write and promote."[20] Toward the end, Mateer's increasing responsibilities made it imperative that he relinquish the presidency to his younger friend, colleague, and devoted admirer Watson McMillan Hayes (class of 1882), who spent sixty years in China.

For his college and for China, Mateer produced all kinds of textbooks. Once he wrote home, "I have collected a large number of lists of subjects for terms in chemistry, physics, mathematics, astronomy, geology, metallurgy, photography, watchmaking, machinery, printing, music, mental and moral philosophy, political economy, theology, and so forth."[21] He also wrote hymns and helped to establish in Shanghai a printing press, which was later taken over by his brother Robert.

19. Hyatt, *Our Ordered Lives Confess,* pp. 192-93.
20. Hyatt, *Our Ordered Lives Confess,* pp. 202-3.
21. Daniel W. Fisher, *Calvin Wilson Mateer: Forty-Five Years a Missionary in Shantung, China* (Philadelphia: Westminster Press, 1911), p. 160.

Calvin Mateer, known on campus as *Lao Hu* or "Old Tiger," taught all science classes except mental arithmetic, as well as classes in religion (moral science) for the older boys. According to the school's *Alumni History,* his classroom performances soon inspired "god-like awe . . . for his mental faculties, his intense activity, and his good judgment." More comprehensively, "they loved him like a father. When someone transgressed a rule he punished severely; but once past, he forgot it at once and did not remember it. When someone was in difficulty, he would find a way [to help] generously, appropriately, and without partiality."[22]

For all his famous stubborn tough-mindedness, Calvin had a tender side, at least toward Julia. Once when she was separated from Calvin for a while in seeking better health, Julia registered this mock complaint: "I cannot even have the satisfaction of a good cry, for Calvin would hear of it, and how worried he would be to hear of tears that he could not wipe away!"[23] Julia Brown Mateer died February 18, 1898, and was buried in Tengchow. In 1900 Calvin married Ada Haven, an accomplished scholar in Chinese. When Mateer died in 1908, however, the casket of his beloved Julia was disinterred and placed by his side in Chefoo.

In later years the leadership in Presbyterian-sponsored higher education in China was assumed by younger missionaries, especially the energetic Henry Winters Luce (1868-1941), whose son, Henry Robinson Luce, the founder of *Time, Life,* and *Fortune* magazines, was baptized by Mateer.[24]

As Calvin Mateer grew older, many of the views that he had long advocated — such as the exclusive use of the Chinese language — were not favored by the new missionaries. Mateer believed passionately that evangelism and education should work from the "bottom out." In contrast, many of the new missionary generation preferred the softer and lazier method of working from the "top down."[25] As Mateer's biographer puts it, this is "only another instance of a state of things so often recurring;

22. Hyatt, *Our Ordered Lives Confess,* p. 169.

23. Mateer, *Character-Building in China,* p. 157.

24. Garside, *One Increasing Purpose,* p. 86. It may be said that Henry Winters Luce, in the role of educational financier, was Calvin Mateer's successor and rival as the most influential American Presbyterian missionary in China. Mateer's true heir, however, was Watson McMillan Hayes, Pittsburgh class of 1882, who arrived in China in 1883 to work with Mateer. Hayes wrote twenty-four textbooks in Chinese on mathematical, scientific, biblical, and theological subjects.

25. Hyatt, *Our Ordered Lives Confess,* pp. 228, 293n.4.

that is, of a man who has done a great work, putting into it a long life of toil and self-sacrifice, and bringing it at length to a point where he must decrease and it must increase; and where in the very nature of the case it must be turned over to younger hands, to be guided as they see its needs in the light of the dawning day." Thus in a letter dated December 21, 1907, Calvin Mateer resigned both as president and as director of the college because, as he put it, "I could not conscientiously carry out the ideas and policy of a majority of the mission. It was no small trial, I assure you, to resign all connections with the college, after spending the major part of my missionary life working for it."[26] Nevertheless Mateer wrote, "I have never been homesick in China. I would not be elsewhere than where I am, nor doing any other work than what I am doing."[27]

Mateer's Shantung compound was the site of Langdon Gilkey's book recounting the story of incarceration by the Japanese during World War II. It was here that Henry R. Luce was born, and it was here that Eric Liddell, the now legendary 1924 Olympic gold medalist and missionary hero of the movie *Chariots of Fire,* died.[28] Calvin Mateer was a tough-minded man of furious energy. He always stood during public prayer. He had a consuming desire to serve the cause of Christ in China. He was not easy to live with, yet his contribution deserves to be remembered by all Christians, and his name should be honored especially by those who, like him, are graduates of Pittsburgh Seminary.

Calvin Mateer died at 10:25 on the morning of September 28, 1908, at age 72. He was buried near John L. Nevius. "One of the great regrets incident to the burial was that Dr. Corbett, who had come out to China with him on that first long voyage, and who had been his close associate on the field in so much of the work, and who cherished for him the warmest regard, could not be present. He was away in a country field when death came to Dr. Mateer, and the news did not reach him in time for him to return to the funeral." Corbett wrote, "Personally I shall ever esteem it one of the greatest blessings of my life that it has been my privilege to have enjoyed the friendship, and of being a colaborer with this great man for nearly fifty years."[29]

26. Fisher, *Calvin Wilson Mateer,* pp. 232-33.
27. Fisher, *Calvin Wilson Mateer,* p. 39.
28. Russell W. Ramsey, *God's Joyful Runner* (S. Plainfield, NJ: Bridge Publishing Inc., 1987). See also Langdon Gilkey, *Shantung Compound* (New York: Harper & Row, 1966).
29. Fisher, *Calvin Wilson Mateer,* pp. 327-29.

Calvin Mateer's last audible words were, "Holy! Holy! Holy! True and Mighty." Among Mateer's papers a little book was found in which he had written the following private prayer:

> Permit not the great adversary to harass my soul, in the last struggle, but make me a conqueror, and more than a conqueror in this fearful conflict. I humbly ask that my reason may be continued to the last, and if it be Thy will, that I may be so comforted and supported that I may leave testimony in favor of the reality of religion, and Thy faithfulness in fulfilling Thy gracious promises, and that others of Thy servants who may follow after, may be encouraged by my example to commit themselves boldly to the guidance and keeping of the Shepherd of Israel. And when my spirit leaves this tenement, Lord Jesus receive it. Send some of the blessed angels to conduct my inexperienced soul to the mansion which Thy love has prepared. And oh, let me be so situated, though in the lowest rank, that I may behold Thy glory.[30]

Pittsburgh Seminary in India: John C. Lowrie, Class of 1832, and James C. R. Ewing, Class of 1880

Divinity students paraded through the streets of Princeton, New Jersey, rousing Professor Irenaeus Prine from his sickbed, shouting exultantly, "Lowrie is off for India!" The subject of their excitement, John C. Lowrie, Pittsburgh Seminary class of 1832, was to be the first American Presbyterian missionary to the Asian subcontinent. Of course, men and women like John and Louisa Lowrie who left home and kindred to serve the cause of Christ in a far country required deep commitment and sound learning, but they also needed remarkable courage. Because of the hazards of primitive travel and the swift and ever-present dangers from tropical diseases, great personal sacrifices were often exacted of those who would proclaim the gospel in distant lands.

On the afternoon of May 29, 1833, the Lowries, along with William Reed, class of 1832, and his wife Harriet, boarded the *Star*, which was anchored in the Delaware River and bound for Calcutta. Pale with emotion, they said good-bye to family and friends, not knowing if they would ever see them again in the land of the living.

30. Fisher, *Calvin Wilson Mateer*, pp. 324-25.

On the six-month sea voyage Louisa Lowrie's health became greatly impaired. For that reason, when the *Star* reached India, the Lowries transferred to a smaller and more comfortable boat to make their way up the Ganges River to Calcutta. After the Reeds joined them, they consulted with more experienced India missionaries, the Scots Joshua Marchman and Alexander Duff, and decided to locate at Lodiana in the most remote part of the Protected Sikh States of the northwestern provinces. Being the first American missionaries to attempt to form stations in Upper India, Lowrie and Reed decided that their efforts should be primarily educational, since education allowed access to the minds of the indigenous peoples without arousing their religious hostilities. According to Lowrie, the English language would become to India what Latin had once been in Europe, the learned language of the educated. Therefore, with God's blessing and grace, the Americans expected to accomplish their great object, to train up a race of native preachers by means of academic instruction. Lowrie wrote:

> I could not look in any direction without seeing multitudes of people "without God, — without hope in the world," through our Lord and Savior, Jesus Christ. I could not receive the Sacred Scriptures as the guide of my own faith, the means of my own hope of eternal life, without at the same time believing a knowledge of them to be equally necessary to the dark-minded people around me; nor could I doubt the solemn obligation resting on all Christians, to use all proper means for making known the glad tidings of salvation to every creature.

Lowrie concluded that foreign missionaries always labor under great disadvantages.

> Their numbers are too small; they are and ever must be regarded as foreigners, imperfectly acquainted with the language, the usages and the habits of mental association of the people; they cannot live but at great expense, compared with the cost of supporting a native missionary . . . : these and similar considerations will ever preclude the hope of the conversion of the Hindus by a purely foreign agency, and they show the necessity of directing our endeavors to the training of a native ministry, on whom must finally devolve the great work of evangelizing India.[31]

31. John C. Lowrie, *Two Years in Upper India* (New York: Robert Carter, 1850), pp. 70, 136. Walter Lowrie left the U.S. Senate to become Dr. Swift's successor as

On November 21, 1833, only six weeks after arriving in India and nine months after her wedding, Louisa Ann Lowrie died at the age of twenty-four. Of that event her grief-stricken young husband wrote, "I have forborne to speak of my own feelings in this time of deep affliction. There are dispensations in the lives of most men, whose desolating severity no language can describe. There are hours of cold despair, which nature could not long endure. The blessed gospel is our best and our only real solace in such time of trial."[32] Of Louisa Ann Lowrie a minute of the Western Foreign Mission Society reads, "There to proclaim as she sleeps on India's distant shores the compassion of American Christians . . . and to invite others from her native land to come and prosecute the noble undertaking in which she fell."[33]

Shortly thereafter, William Reed became gravely ill. He made his way back down the river from Calcutta, but he died three weeks after bidding farewell to Lowrie. His colleague wrote of him:

> His hopes were all disappointed, his plans all set aside, his fervent desire of usefulness . . . not granted — I do not say, not accepted nor rewarded. For He, whose eye saw His servant's purpose to assist in building the spiritual temple, would in his case, as in that of David, accept the desire and vouchsafe a gracious reward. It is not what our hands perform that chiefly receive His favor, but what our hearts, influenced by His grace, devise and desire to accomplish. And if this dispensation appeared as dark as it was severe to us all, yet we were assured that what we knew not then we should know hereafter, and that we should yet praise God for all His dispensations towards our-

---

secretary of the Western Foreign Missionary Society. He gave three sons to global mission: John to India and two others to China — one to a martyr's death. See Arthur Judson Brown, *One Hundred Years* [of Presbyterian Missions] (New York: Fleming H. Revell, 1936), p. 52.

32. Lowrie, *Two Years in Upper India,* p. 56.

33. Robert E. Speer, *Sir James Ewing: A Biography of Sir James C. R. Ewing: For Forty-Three Years a Missionary in India* (New York: Fleming H. Revell, 1928), p. 27. To a friend, Louisa wrote, "[I] bid you farewell, with no hope of seeing you until, with all our beloved friends, who have gone before us, we meet around the throne above. . . . if the Lord shall regard my desires and accept of my weak services, it is my fixed intention to spend my life among the heathen" (p. 90). Barbour Library has a rare copy of *Memoirs of Mrs. Louisa A. Lowrie, Wife of the Rev. John C. Lowrie, Missionary to Northern India: Who Died at Calcutta, Nov. 21st, 1822, Aged 24 Years,* compiled by Ashbel G. Fairchild, with an introduction by Elisha P. Swift (Pittsburgh: Luke Loomis, 1836).

David E. Campbell, Western Seminary, 1849, martyred with his wife and two children in India, 1857

Maria Irvine Campbell, graduate of Female Seminary, Steubenville, Ohio, 1850; martyred, 1857

selves and towards His cause. Thus in faith we parted, no more to meet on earth, but with firm hope of meeting in a better world.[34]

The mortal remains of William Reed were consigned to the waters of the Bay of Bengal, and his young widow crossed the ocean to home alone.

Within a few months Lowrie himself took sick, and he was informed by physicians that he could not expect to survive if he remained in India. Nevertheless, without companions and under sentence of death, Lowrie pushed on to Lodiana, twelve hundred miles away, at the edge of British rule, where he had intended to spend his life. His purpose now was to survey this territory for the benefit of those missionaries who would follow him into India. While there, Lowrie was invited to visit the kingdom of Ranjit Singh, "the Lion of the Punjab." He traveled part of the way by elephant.

Lowrie was forced to go home in December of 1835. There he

34. Lowrie, *Two Years in Upper India*, p. 67.

became Secretary of the Board of Foreign Missions of the Presbyterian Church, U.S.A., from 1838 to 1891.[35] Before he left India, he was gratified to welcome the second wave of American Presbyterian missionaries to India. One of these was James Wilson (Pittsburgh class of 1833), and another was John Newton (class of 1834).

Newton lived in India for fifty-seven years. He was one of the holiest and best beloved men the Punjab had ever seen. He wrote a grammar and dictionary before translating the New Testament into Punjabi. He was followed by his two daughters and his sons Charles (class of 1867), who spent forty-seven years in India; Frank (class of 1870), who lived in India forty-one years; and Edward (class of 1873), who spent forty-five years in India. Together the Newton men devoted nearly two centuries to India.

Two decades later the native Indian troops revolted because they believed that the cartridges they were using were greased by religiously unclean animal fat. Among those murdered in the Sepoy Mutiny were the Reverend Mr. and Mrs. Albert O. Johnson (class of 1855) and Rev. David and Mrs. Maria Campbell (class of 1849), who with their two children were shot on the parade ground at Cawnpore on June 13, 1857.[36] After the death of Albert Johnson, his brother William F. Johnson (class of 1860) came to India, mastered the language, and produced over six hundred titles in Christian literature during sixty-two years. Probably no other missionary ever performed so much literary work. The wonderfully whimsical Johnson had a famous snake story that he would relate in exquisite detail until his audience was absolutely captivated. And then he would stop! No amount of earnest pleading or dire threats ever persuaded him to reveal the conclusion.[37]

James Caruthers Rhea Ewing (class of 1880), who spent forty-three years in India, was one of those fortunate men who have the gratification of seeing their services appreciated during their lifetimes. He was born June 23, 1854, in Rural Valley, Armstrong County, Pennsylvania. He studied at Pittsburgh Seminary under B. B. Warfield, and he was especially

---

35. Lowrie Hall, a building that still stands on Ridge Avenue, was named for John C. Lowrie. Its initial purpose was to house missionaries on furlough. Later, faculty and married students lived there.

36. J. Johnston Walsh, *A Memorial of the Futtehgurh Mission and Her Martyred Missionaries* (Philadelphia: Joseph M. Wilson, 1859), chaps. 10, 11, 12, 14.

37. Speer, *Sir James Ewing,* p. 48.

influenced by Professors A. A. Hodge and S. H. Kellogg — both of whom had served in India.

During his first years of district evangelistic work, Ewing learned thoroughly the language and thought of the Indian people. For a while he was a theological teacher in the seminary at Saharanpur, and later he spent thirty years as principal of Forman Christian College at Lahore. "Theologically he was a firm conservative as to the great evangelical convictions and was known to be such, but he was known also to be a man of great catholicity of spirit and entire openness of mind and absolutely just and fair." Dr. Ewing's administration of Forman College was remarkable for its effortless discipline, to which his burly size (he was six feet two inches tall) but genial personality and keen sense of humor greatly contributed.[38]

Ewing wrote a life of Alexander Duff, a Greek-Hindustani dictionary of the New Testament, and *A Prince of the Church in India: The Life of Rev. Dr. Kali Charan Chatterjee.* In his time James Ewing was the foremost missionary in India, respected, trusted, and honored by all classes, British, Muslim, Hindu, and Sikh. He was three times Vice-Chancellor of the Punjab. Then as Secretary of the India Council he was the general advisor on all the work of the mission board in India. Returning to America in 1922, he became president of the foreign mission board, where he brought to his duties a solid judgment, a thorough acquaintance with the problems and the sound principles of missionary work, and a deep sympathy and full understanding of the mind and spirit of the missionaries.

In 1924 Ewing was made a Knight Companion of the Indian Empire for unequaled service to education, progress, and popular well-being in the Punjab, the first American missionary to be so honored and, so far as we know, the only graduate of Pittsburgh Seminary ever to be knighted. For all his high honors, Ewing was "noted for his approachability. He was never too busy to stop to listen to the humblest brother who wished a word with him and never failed to give a kind reply."[39]

The Reverend Dr. Sir James C. R. Ewing died on August 20, 1925. "So fell at length 'that tower of strength that stood foursquare to all the winds that blew.' But fell to stand, here and forevermore." The funeral services were held in Saltsburg Presbyterian Church, near his boyhood home, where his father had been an elder for thirty-eight years, and from

38. Speer, *Sir James Ewing,* p. 244.
39. Speer, *Sir James Ewing,* p. 245.

which he himself had gone out as a missionary forty-six years before. His body was laid to rest beside his father's and mother's until the Resurrection.[40]

Included in the flood of tributes that poured in from around the world was this one:

> The Board mourns the death of so great and good and wise a man and thanks God for the memory of his rich and fruitful life and for the happy fellowship of the golden years at its close. It extends the assurance of its loving sympathy to Mrs. Ewing and to her children, especially to the two daughters who are carrying forward their father's service in India.[41]

Pittsburgh Seminary in Egypt:
Andrew Watson, Class of 1861

Recognizing the strategic importance of Egypt for both the Middle East and Africa, the General Synod of the United Presbyterian Church, meeting in Pittsburgh on May 21, 1853, voted that "our missionaries be instructed to occupy Cairo at their earliest convenience."[42] The task that the little Christian army faced in "occupying" Egypt was considerable in a country that was ninety-seven percent desert and had a population that was ninety percent Muslim, to say nothing of such implacable enemies as cholera. The indigenous Coptic Church, traced by legend to St. Mark and fallen from its ancient glory of the times of Clement and Origen, had been cruelly persecuted by its Muslim conquerors in recent centuries. The American Mission in Egypt estimated that there were at least twelve million people within the intended sphere of its evangelistic efforts, extending from the Mediterranean Sea to the first cataract of the Nile. The Coptic Church, numbering about 250,000 in 1855, was regarded as in desperate need of enlightenment. The American Presbyterians hoped that a revitalized Egyptian church would become a mighty evangelistic force

40. Speer, *Sir James Ewing*, p. 241.

41. Speer, *Sir James Ewing*, p. 243.

42. Earl E. Elder, *Vindicating a Vision: The Story of the American Mission in Egypt 1854-1954* (Philadelphia: Board of Foreign Missions of the United Presbyterian Church of North America, 1958), p. 16.

in East Africa. And if so, the Americans purposed to go with the Egyptian missionaries into Sudan and Ethiopia.

The first two Americans to heed this call were Thomas McCague (class of 1853), who reached Egypt on November 15, 1854, and James Barnett (class of 1844), who arrived twenty days later from Damascus, where he had spent the preceding ten years; Barnett thus had the advantage of being already able to preach the gospel in Arabic. In his diary for June 1855 Barnett offered this prayer for Egypt: "Thou seest that here are many precious souls; we have come from a far country to do them good; do Thou open up doors of usefulness to us."[43]

In the early years the work in Egypt was often frustrating. It was a time of small beginnings and slow returns. A later historian of the mission complains that no one "realizes more keenly than our missionaries in Egypt how lacking their history is in exciting drama. Farther into the interior of Africa there are lions, venomous reptiles, and crocodiles, also naked savages with spears and shields."[44] Of course, Christians are more concerned about obedience than about drama. Nevertheless Gulian Lansing insisted that it was easier to walk from one end of Africa to the other than to learn to speak Arabic.[45] Grace Giffen compares the missions in Egypt and Sudan this way:

> During the twenty years of our missionary life in Egypt we, like all the rest in Egypt, worked hard and tried to do our duty, and in addition to the burden of work we carried a load of worry and anxiety that was more trying than the work itself. This worry we do not have here [in Sudan]. To be sure, we are often perplexed, and very often are in doubt as to what should be done and what left undone; but when night comes we go to bed to sleep and not to lie with eyes wide open staring into the darkness, and with brain throbbing, trying to work out some problem or method, or scheming for the accomplishment of some work or staring at some great catastrophe that has befallen the work.[46]

The accomplishments of the first decade included the first English worship service (Christmas Day, 1854), and the first Arabic service

43. Elder, *Vindicating a Vision*, p. 23.
44. Elder, *Vindicating a Vision*, p. 8.
45. Gulian Lansing, *Egypt's Princes: A Narrative of Missionary Labor in the Valley of the Nile* (New York: Robert Carter, 1865), p. 8.
46. J. Kelly Giffen, *The Egyptian Sudan* (New York: Fleming H. Revell, 1905), pp. 194-95.

(January 21, 1855); the first cholera epidemic endured (1855); the first boys' school opened in Cairo (1855); the first evangelistic tour taken up the Nile (1857); a missionary settled in Alexandria (1857); the first girls' school opened at Alexandria (1858) and at Cairo (1860); and, after five years of evangelism, the first converts (four in all) admitted to the Protestant Church (1859). In addition, the first bookstore was opened (1859), the first presbytery was organized (1860), property was purchased for the mission (1862), and the first class was held in the Egyptian Theological Seminary (1864). A great price was paid for these achievements, however, since the first death among the American Mission family occurred on May 2, 1857: the McCagues' baby died of smallpox. A later minute reads: "The hearts of Mr. and Mrs. McCague were again filled with grief at the loss of their dear Mary Barnett, on May 31 (1860), the second child whose little form was laid in Egyptian soil."[47]

It should also be noted that the first single woman missionary arrived in Egypt in 1858. Sarah B. Dales had crossed the ocean on the same ship with the McCagues but had spent four years in Damascus. The record speaks of her "natural vivacity, tact, intelligence, and Christian earnestness."[48] She was associated with the Lansings in Syria and again in Egypt. After Maria Lansing and her baby died of cholera in 1865, Sarah became Mrs. Lansing.

Sarah Dales Lansing was closely involved in the "Great Romance" of the American Mission. Duleep Singh, the son of the fabulously rich Ranjit Singh, last king of the Punjab (whom Lowrie had visited in 1832), had become a Christian under the influence of American Presbyterians in India. Being forcibly retired to England (albeit with a generous pension), Duleep Singh bore the title "Maharajah," and since he was of royal blood, he stood next in social rank to the family of Queen Victoria. In 1864 Duleep Singh visited the American Mission Girls' School and asked the missionaries to recommend a Christian girl, native to the East, to be his wife. Bamba Müller, about fifteen years old, was the illegitimate, although acknowledged, daughter of a wealthy German father and an Abyssinian slave mother. One can imagine the unsophisticated teenager's anxiety at so strange a providence that led from her mother's slave quarters to the little Presbyterian school for girls and then to mingle with royalty in London. From this point on, Bamba led a rather troubled life, but the

---

47. Elder, *Vindicating a Vision,* p. 51.
48. Elder, *Vindicating a Vision,* p. 27.

interest and support from the American Mission in Egypt was constant. According to Andrew Watson, the Maharani "Bamba died at her own home in 1887, in the humble and strong faith in which she lived. Mrs. S. B. Lansing, who had been her teacher and life-long friend, was by her bedside when she fell asleep in Jesus."[49]

Neither of the pioneers spent their entire careers in Egypt. McCague returned to America in 1861 and Barnett in 1875. Both became home missionaries on the great plains of the American West. Before they left, however, another Pittsburgh graduate arrived who would devote thirty-eight years to Egypt. Writing in 1920, Anna Milligan offered this assessment of Andrew Watson, class of 1861:

> Andrew Watson was a scholar, teacher, statesman, and preacher. He arrived in Egypt in 1861, when there were only six members of the infant church. Today (1920) there is a native Protestant Community of 40,000, containing nearly 15,000 communicants. He helped to establish a theological seminary in 1864, and was soon made the professor of systematic theology. In 1892 he became the head of the school. Through his classroom passed the pastors and preachers of the church. . . . He counted them his sons. His life was built into their lives. They are his monument — and there is little need for any other.[50]

It may be true that the history of Egyptian evangelism is not very dramatic. It may be likewise true that the "story of the American Mission in Egypt is not a tale of a few brilliant personalities who dominate the scene."[51] If not exactly dramatic and brilliant, however, a lot of sturdy Christians — many of them from Pittsburgh — devoted their quietly obedient and softly luminous lives to the cause of Christ in Egypt.

49. Andrew Watson, *The American Mission in Egypt 1854-1896* (Pittsburgh: United Presbyterian Board of Publications, 1898), p. 469. See also Michael Alexander and Sushila Anand, *Queen Victoria's Maharajah: Duleep Singh: 1838-93* (New York: Taplinger, 1980).

50. Anna A. Milligan, *Facts and Folks in Our Fields Abroad* (Philadelphia: United Presbyterian Board of Foreign Missions, 1921), p. 205.

51. Elder, *Vindicating a Vision,* p. 18.

Pittsburgh Seminary in Sudan:
John Kelly Giffen, Class of 1881

In Sudan a rain shower during the dry season, especially one accompanied by thunder and lightning, was a great surprise. Since April 6, 1932, had been an intensely hot day, an old Sudanese woman claimed, "This storm is a sign that a saint or a prince is dying." Very shortly the church bell began to toll announcing the sudden death of J. Kelly Griffen, a prince among men and a saint of God. The people he had served for fifty-one years in Egypt and Sudan thought that even the African skies wept for his passing.[52]

The American Presbyterians, working in Egypt since 1854, had often dreamed about establishing Christian missions deep in Sudan, a land that was becoming known as the result of such legendary explorers as Burton, Speke, the Bakers, Schweinfurth, and the redoubtable Alexandrine Tinne. Indeed, Sudan seemed a natural evangelistic outreach for the indigenous Egyptian Christian Church. For that reason a special agent was sent to Khartoum in 1882 as a colporteur and evangelist to explore possibilities for further work.

The Mahdist Rebellion (1881-85), however, made Sudan entirely unsafe for missionaries. It was later estimated that one-half to three-quarters of the population died during these years.[53] In any case, the Mahdists had already slaughtered several armies when Brigadier General Charles George Gordon (who had put down the Taiping Rebellion in Calvin Mateer's China) shook Kelly Giffen's hand in Assiut, Egypt

---

52. Ried F. Shields, *Behind the Garden of Allah* (Philadelphia: United Presbyterian Board of Foreign Missions, 1937), p. 9. The first American Presbyterian missionary from Pittsburgh to black Africa was probably John Cloud, class of 1833. He died in Liberia on April 9, 1834. A. C. Good, class of 1882, spent twelve years in Gaboon (French Congo). His son Albert, class of 1909, was also a missionary to Africa. See Ellen C. Parsons, *A Life for Africa: Rev. Adolphus Clemens Good, Ph.D.* (New York: Fleming H. Revell, 1897). At his death, Dr. Good left no converts, but he had prepared a vocabulary to be used by his successor, William Caldwell Johnston (class of 1895), who served in West Africa for forty-two years. The first convert was made in 1900. By 1950 there were more than 72,000.

53. Giffen, *The Egyptian Sudan,* p. 230. See Rudolf Karl Freiherr von Slatin, *Fire and Sword in the Sudan: A Personal Narrative of Fighting and Serving the Dervishes 1879-95,* trans. F. R. Wingate (London: E. Arnold, 1896); and Father Joseph Ohrwalder, *Ten Years' Captivity in the Mahdi's Camp,* trans. F. R. Wingate (London: Sampon Low Marston, 1892).

(1884), on the way to a heroic and immortal death in Khartoum. After a siege of 321 days Khartoum fell on January 26, 1885, and Gordon's head was carried off to the Mahdi and onto the world's outraged conscience. According to Giffen, terrible as it was, "Gordon's death was one of the necessary sacrifices in the redemption of the [Sudan]."[54]

To avenge Gordon and restore their national honor, the British laboriously built a railroad across six hundred miles of desert in order to bring Kitchener's great army into contact with the Mahdi's forces. The Mahdists were defeated at the battle of Omdurman (1898), which included — in the charge of the 21st Lancers — a very young Winston Churchill. Giffen describes this battle as memorable in its awful carnage.[55] As soon as Sudan was reasonably safe, the American Mission was ready to move south. In December of 1899, Andrew Watson and Giffen went up the Nile for a missionary reconnaissance arriving at Khartoum, where the unbelievable savagery and indescribable squalor of the Mahdi's reign were still visible.

In 1900 the Giffens and a medical couple, the H. T. McLaughlins, were appointed missionaries to Sudan. At age forty-seven and after nearly two decades as a missionary in Egypt, Giffen was not thrilled with his new assignment, which he described as "the severest trial of all. On former occasions youth and hope and ignorance of all that was before me softened the trial of those former partings. But now nineteen years of my best strength and manhood had been given to Egypt, and the ties thus formed with the missionaries and native pastors and teachers were to be severed. It was not a light thing to leave the work and associations of these years and begin a work entirely new and unknown."[56]

In the beginning, the British government of Sudan refused to permit evangelism among the Muslim population but approved work among the black tribes. Therefore the Giffens and the McLaughlins traveled south of Khartoum six hundred miles up the Nile system into the Sobat River above Malakal to choose a mission site.

54. Giffen, *The Egyptian Sudan,* p. 33.
55. Giffen, *The Egyptian Sudan,* p. 28.
56. Giffen, *The Egyptian Sudan,* p. 62. Due to his wife's ill health, Dr. McLaughlin came back to America in 1911. Charles R. Watson, author of several books on Egypt, was born to the Andrew Watsons in Cairo on June 17, 1873. After studying at Pittsburgh Seminary he returned to Egypt and became president of the American University of Cairo (1916-45). The copy of Watson's book used for this essay was donated to Barbour Library by Mrs. H. T. McLaughlin.

As a pioneer missionary Giffen admitted that it was extremely difficult to get started because there was no one with experience in the south
Sudan whose judgment could be trusted on the countless important details
that one needed to know in order to live there. Moreover, "so much
depended on the first year or two. We dared not act rashly, for our one
great fear was *failure;* a failure that, perhaps, might prove fatal to the
undertaking [and] discourage others [if] interpreted to mean that the
maintenance of a mission on the Sobat by white missionaries was not
even a possible thing."[57]

In 1902 a Christian outpost was founded at Doleib Hill among the
Shulla people. Giffen had already begun to preach the gospel in south
Sudan when an explorer wrote that almost the only large spot in the Nile
basin remaining unexplored was the district occupied by the Dinka, Nuer,
and Shulla.

On one occasion at Doleib Hill, a Shulla chief was told by a visitor
that Sudan now had a good and righteous government, which would
protect and help the Shullas, and the missionaries would teach the
children, help in the cultivation of fields, and teach of God from "The
Book." After a good deal of pipe-smoking deliberation, the chief replied:

Master, you speak well. We had here the Turks [the old Egyptian
government] and they said "Be submissive to us; we will protect you,
we will fight your battles for you, we will teach you of God." But they
took our cattle, they destroyed our villages, and carried away our
women and children into slavery, and they are gone. Then came the
Ansar [the Mahdists] and they said: "Come with us, we have a great
army; we will care for you and protect you; we will give you plenty to
eat, and a good place to live; we have The Book and we will teach you
the truth and teach you of God." But they slew our men, and right
here where these missionaries built their houses many of our men fell
fighting for their women and children. They took away our cattle,
destroyed our villages, carried off our women and children, and they
too have gone. Now you come and say: "We will care for you; we will
protect you, we will fight for you, we have The Book; we will teach
you." Master, you speak well; but we will see.[58]

57. Giffen, *The Egyptian Sudan,* p. 71.
58. Giffen, *The Egyptian Sudan,* p. 120.

As the years of the twentieth century advanced and the number of missionary graves increased at Doleib Hill, the Shullas had reason to know that the American Presbyterians came to serve, not to exploit.[59]

Not long after establishing the Christian mission at Doleib Hill, the Giffens were due for a furlough in America. Grace Giffen wrote:

> Mr. Giffen and I were talking of our leaving [Doleib Hill] for our furlough, and I, at least, was surprised at the heartache which came with the thought that we must leave. The black [mud] walls of our house mean home to us now; and the black faces of the people are the faces of friends; and we feel that we have been able to do so little of the great work that needs to be done for them. It is not that we have been careless or negligent, but as you know work always seems slow at the beginning. Ah, well. If we are to come back [to Doleib Hill] we will be able to do more. If not, then someone else will do it, better perhaps than we.[60]

After furlough the Giffens returned to Khartoum and spent the remainder of their missionary careers there. They were replaced at Doleib Hill by Ralph E. Carson, class of 1895, who arrived in 1903, and George A. Sowash, class of 1896.[61]

In his book about the Anglo-Egyptian Sudan (1905), Giffen pointed out that in Arabic-speaking north Sudan there were only five Protestant missionaries, and in all of south Sudan there were only two missionary couples (at Doleib Hill). Changes, he said, are occurring rapidly in Sudan, and many people will come to risk their lives for financial gain. To Christians he offered this challenge: "Surely then there will be men and women courageous enough to take similar risks, whatever they be, to bring these Sudanese tribes the glad tidings of salvation."[62]

John Kelly Giffen, Pittsburgh Seminary class of 1881, was born on June 3, 1853, in St. Clairsville, Ohio. In the year 1922, after forty-one years of missionary service, Giffen, a member of the Presbytery of Sudan, was elected moderator of the United Presbyterian Church of North Amer-

59. Among those buried at Doleib Hill is J. Alfred Heasty, class of 1918, who served there from 1920 until his death in 1951.

60. Giffen, *The Egyptian Sudan,* pp. 198-99.

61. On Sowash, see my *Adventure in Africa: The Story of Don McClure* (Grand Rapids: Zondervan, 1990), pp. 435-36, note 15.

62. Giffen, *The Egyptian Sudan,* pp. 240-41.

ica. He died on April 6, 1932, and was buried in Khartoum, where his grave bears this inscription:

JOHN KELLY GIFFEN
1853-1932
PIONEER MISSIONARY
Lover of God and All Things Fair
Friend to Little Children
He Served All Men as His Brothers
With Love Unfeigned.[63]

Thomas A. Lambie wrote, "Words can never express the high regard I have always had for Doctor and Mrs. Giffen. They were all that missionaries should be. . . . Ever kind-hearted and cheery, always unselfish, always willing by every way to make Christ known, there was nothing of sanctimoniousness about them — just pure goodness shone out of every word and act."[64]

Pittsburgh Seminary in Ethiopia:
William Donald McClure, Sr., Class of 1934

The primary task of Pittsburgh Theological Seminary has always been to prepare pastors for the American church. The tributary to mission overseas, however, which flowed so powerfully during the nineteenth century, dwindled to a trickle in the twentieth. The world, and with it the world mission of the church, changed drastically. According to Nichols, the Edinburgh Conference of 1910 marked the point at which the history of global evangelism became an aspect of the ecumenical enterprise.[65] Others

63. Partee, *Adventure in Africa,* pp. 529-31, note 7.
64. Thomas A. Lambie, *Doctor Without a Country* (New York: Fleming H. Revell, 1939), p. 22.
65. Nichols, *History of Christianity,* p. 320. One of the speeches given at this important meeting was by Arthur H. Ewing, the founder of Ewing College in Allahabad, who graduated with the Pittsburgh class of 1890. In 1893 he and his brother James walked 710 miles around India. Arthur was one of the most scholarly of the India missionaries; he earned the Ph.D. degree from Johns Hopkins University in Sanskrit and philosophy. While devoting his efforts primarily to education, Dr. Ewing went abroad with the largest missionary purpose, but after only twenty years in India he died in 1912.

see the end of World War I as the culmination of the great century of world mission expansion. Still others regard the demise of colonialism after World War II as the major shift away from world mission as it had been known. In any case, and for whatever reasons, the interest in and support for global evangelism has declined sharply in mainline Protestant denominations.

This decline is represented here by the fact that only this final profile concerns a missionary who graduated from Pittsburgh Seminary in the twentieth century. Don McClure, born in 1906, was animated by the same evangelistic convictions that informed earlier generations of Pitts-

W. Don McClure, Pittsburgh-Xenia Seminary, 1934, meeting Emperor Haile Selassie of Ethiopia. McClure was missionary in Sudan and Ethiopia, 1954 to 1977, when he was martyred by guerrillas.

burgh missionaries. His colleagues speak of him as the last of the pioneers. Like the other pioneers profiled, McClure was prepared to do whatever was necessary to preach the gospel effectively. He traveled to isolated and dangerous places, hunted for food, built houses and schools under primitive conditions, did basic medical and educational work, and, above all, learned to speak unwritten languages and to preach the gospel in them. Don McClure went to Africa in 1928 as Kelly Giffen's distinguished missionary career was drawing to a close. And as Giffen served in two countries, Egypt and Sudan, McClure devoted his life to Sudan and Ethiopia. When Don McClure began his career, the remoter mission stations could be reached only by canoe. By the time he was murdered, they were being served by airplanes. A fuller account of his fifty-year career is contained in my book *Adventure in Africa: The Story of Don McClure.* [66] These paragraphs, therefore, will not attempt to survey his remarkable contribution but will only bring this chapter to a fitting close.

The American Mission of the United Presbyterian Church of North America began its work on the African continent in Egypt (1854) and expanded south into Sudan at Khartoum and Doleib Hill (1900). In 1913 the Nasir station, farther up the Sobat among the Nuer people, was established by Thomas A. Lambie, M.D. (University of Pittsburgh, 1907), and Elbert McCreery (Pittsburgh Seminary, 1906). Later, after a surveying trip with the Giffens, Lambie moved into Ethiopia to help with a devastating influenza epidemic. Thereafter, the first Christian outpost in Ethiopia was founded among the Oromos (or Gallas) at Dembi Dollo (1920). In 1938 Don and Lyda McClure began work with the Anuak people on the Sudan border and later moved over into Ethiopia.

This letter summarizes Don McClure's evangelistic passion:

Dear Mother:

I sometimes wonder if we will ever get our houses built. More and more people are coming in for help everyday, some of them from as far away as thirty and forty miles. Today I had 148 patients. Among them was a woman whose whole foot is rotting away. She crawled on her hands and knees several miles through the forest to get here. A man staggered in, carrying two sick children who should never have been moved from their home. They were burning up with the fever of

66. For the publication information, see note 61 above.

small pox. Their little bodies were covered with sores and black with flies. They cried and squirmed in their efforts to escape from the flies. Where the father had held them in his arms the sores were bleeding and raw. To protect them from the flies he had covered the children with cow dung before he left his village. But the village is several miles away and the dung had been rubbed off so that thousands of flies were eating away at each sore. I washed the children and then sprayed them with insecticide. For the first time in days they were free of the flies digging away at their bodies.

I had to treat the usual cases of yaws, dysentery, malaria, infected eyes, sores and wounds. Daily I have twelve lepers who come in for their medicine. Most of them do not need anything more than just three daily pills; their sores have dried and healed and I no longer need to dress their hands and feet or cover the sores from flies. But I have learned that I cannot give them more than one day's medicine at a time. Even then it is almost necessary for them to take the three pills all at once instead of morning, noon, and night. As sure as they carry a pill or two back to the village, someone there will beg one of the pills for some kind of illness. I once gave the lepers sufficient pills for a week so they would not need to come in so often, but I discovered that they in turn became the doctors in the villages. Everyone wanted to share the pills. The poor lepers had to hand them out one by one and did not get their proper treatment. Some of them walk several miles a day for the medicine. I just do not have time to get out to see the sick who are dying all about us. The need for a real physician is tremendous, but I am here alone and my seminary courses did not include tropical medicine. Still, I must do what I can for the people I can reach.

Several days ago a man came in from a distant village and asked me to go to see his little girl. It was a twenty-mile walk because the roads were closed by the heavy rains, and I just did not see how I could go. I did not know what the child was suffering from so I gave the man some aspirin and sent him back. The next morning he was in again pleading with me to go and see his daughter for she was dying. Again I put him off, pointing out that many others nearby were dying and I could not see all of them. So I gave him some more medicine and sent him home. He must have walked all night, for the next day he was back again with the girl's mother. They threw themselves prostrate on the ground before me. Grasping my feet, they begged and begged for me to go to their village and see their sick daughter. Apparently the girl was too big to carry even if she had been well enough. Their pleas melted my heart and I had to go. I gathered a bag of medicines and we started on the long hike back through the woods and swamps. We arrived at the village after six hours in the hot sun and I marvelled how that father had walked over that same path six times in three days in his bare feet.

As I crawled into their little grass hut, I could hear the girl's strained breathing and I feared the worst. As I knelt over her emaciated form and felt the burning face I knew I was too late. I told her who I was and that I had come to help her. She opened her eyes and said to me in the Anuak tongue, "Why didn't you come long ago?" My heart flamed within me. Why hadn't I gone immediately? I am a minister of the gospel, not a doctor of medicine, but I might have been able to help her.

Those words of that dying girl will never leave my ears and heart. I wish I could shout them in every church and into the ears of every American Christian. Over the last nineteen hundred years God's children all over the world have been crying out, "Why have you waited so long?" I cannot rest or spare myself until I have used every ounce of my energy and strength in sharing the gospel of Christ with these children of Africa.[67]

With relentless energy for nearly half a century in Africa Don McClure preached the good news from God revealed in our Lord Jesus Christ. On March 27, 1977, at 2 a.m., he stood with his beloved son (Pittsburgh Seminary, class of 1965) for the last time. Confronting them were three Somali guerillas with rifles leveled at their chests. At point-blank range the guns fired, and the Reverend Dr. W. Don McClure (Pittsburgh Seminary, class of 1934) was called home by a bullet through the heart. A heart that had always bled for the pain of Africa began to bleed in actuality and mix with the soil on which he had served his Lord for so long.

Conclusion

Pittsburgh in its early years marked the western frontier of the young nation. Vast tracts of land that would in time become the United States

---

67. Nichols, *History of Christianity,* pp. 325-26.

of America had barely been explored and were inhabited by people who had not heard the gospel. The Pittsburgh Seminary Centennial reflection contained two chapters on missions: one on those graduates who served the cause of Christ overseas, and the other on those intrepid ministers who worked in far-flung "home missions." This bicentennial volume has devoted one chapter to missions. If the decline in evangelistic outreach continues, the tricentennial volume may well have none.

It is therefore fitting that this chapter does not merely celebrate a glorious past but also reminds each reader of the need to find ways and means to continue the commitment to the Great Commission to go into all the world.

CHAPTER TEN

Archaeology and the James L. Kelso Bible Lands Museum

Nancy L. Lapp

It is particularly fitting that we look at archaeology at Pittsburgh Theological Seminary and its parent institutions on this two hundredth anniversary. Biblical archaeology has been a part of our seminaries for almost a century, and recently there have been efforts to make archaeology a vital part of the next hundred years. There is now an endowed chair of Bible and archaeology — but that comes toward the end of the story, not at the beginning.

A Professor of Biblical Archaeology

The determination that an ancestor of Pittsburgh Theological Seminary was the first Protestant seminary in this country to have a professor of biblical archaeology has never been challenged.[1] Beginning in 1908, the Reverend M. G. Kyle, pastor of a United Presbyterian church in Philadelphia, went to Xenia Theological Seminary in Xenia, Ohio, for one

---

1. A history of archaeology at Pittsburgh Theological Seminary first appeared in an article written by Professor Howard Jamieson in *Pittsburgh Perspective* in 1965, and he wrote an updated account ten years later. In 1984 I presented a revised and updated history on the occasion of the celebration of sixty years of archaeological research and biblical studies; this was again updated in September 1986 for a new edition of the *Museum Manual*. The present chapter is greatly indebted to all of these.

semester each year as lecturer in biblical archaeology. Kyle became president of Xenia Seminary in 1922.

Also in 1922, Dr. James A. Kelso, president and professor of Hebrew and Old Testament literature at Western Theological Seminary in Pittsburgh, went to Jerusalem to serve as lecturer at the American School of Oriental Research (ASOR) for one year. The director, William F. Albright, was most appreciative of the presence of Dr. Kelso and members of his party, which included his wife and Mrs. William M. McKelvy. Mrs. McKelvy made possible the excavation of some tumuli near Jerusalem.[2] In 1924 President Kyle of Xenia Seminary and Director W. F. Albright initiated the first of several field projects sponsored jointly by the parent institutions of Pittsburgh Seminary and by the ASOR in Jerusalem.

The man most responsible for the seminary's involvement in archaeology, M. G. Kyle, was a versatile churchman. He was pastor of a large congregation in Philadelphia and was president of the United Presbyterian Board of Missions from 1889 to 1922. As a scholar, in addition to his teaching and presidency at Xenia Seminary, he served as editor-in-chief of the religious and sociological review *Bibliotheca Sacra Theologia Eclectic* and as revision editor of the *International Standard Bible Encyclopedia*.

When Kyle made frequent trips to Egypt in connection with his work for the Board of Missions, Professor Max Mueller of the University of Pennsylvania, one of the best-known Egyptologists of the time, asked Kyle to look up archaeological data for him. His friendship with Mueller aroused Kyle's own interest in archaeology.

Kyle also became a strong friend of Sir Flinders Petrie, one of the pioneers in field archaeology in the Near East. Petrie introduced the systematic recording of all finds and led the way in using pottery for dating purposes. He developed his scientific techniques in Egypt and then transferred his methodology to Palestine. At Tell el-Hesi in southwestern Palestine, Petrie cut vertical sections and noted the precise level from which every potsherd came. This fundamental principle of sequence dating of pottery in Palestine is the foundation on which ceramic chronology has been developed. Petrie could give rough absolute dates to several of the pottery periods at Tell el-Hesi by identifying potsherds with wares already found in datable Egyptian burials.

Kyle's early archaeological research for Mueller had also been in

2. *Bulletin of the American Schools of Oriental Research (BASOR)* 10 (April 1923): 2. A "tumulus" is an ancient sepulchral mound.

*M. G. Kyle, Xenia Seminary (Professor, President 1914-1930,
and noted archaeologist)*

Egypt, but he too did not confine his interest. After World War I, an opportunity came to work in Palestine with W. F. Albright. An expedition to Moab and the Dead Sea was the first joint undertaking of the ASOR in Jerusalem with a stateside institution. Albright wrote at the conclusion of the project:

> The joint undertaking of Xenia Theological Seminary and the American School of Oriental Research may be considered a great success, which we owe largely to the fine spirit of President Kyle. Let us hope that other institutions will see the opportunity for similar joint expeditions,

where we can promise scientific results and interesting experiences quite out of proportion to the modest expenditures.[3]

This cooperative venture in which Xenia Seminary provided the funds and the ASOR the expertise was the beginning of a policy in which institutional members of the ASOR corporation join forces in fielding excavations and surveys, a policy that has continued until today,[4] and Pittsburgh Theological Seminary, like its antecedents, has continued to be a participant.

Kyle and Albright had become great friends. Kyle, a conservative scholar, had supported Albright's appointment to the ASOR in Jerusalem even though Albright was a student of Paul Haupt, one of the most liberal scholars of the time. Kyle's comment was one of his typical witticisms: "Albright is young enough to learn better." On Kyle's death, Albright wrote:

> To few men is it given to combine such ecclesiastical and scholarly distinction as Dr. Kyle attained with such simplicity and purity of character. Still fewer men possess that spiritual reach which enables them to unite charity with knowledge and zeal, so as to form a tolerance that is due neither to ignorance nor to indifference. Dr. Kyle was one of the very few really tolerant men whom the writer has known. He possessed that rarest of all qualities, the instinct and art of befriending those whose religious and scholarly views diverged sharply from his. Often he converted enemies and ill-wishers to warm friends and admirers, wholly through the cumulative force of personal contact. . . . There can be no doubt that our constant association with the ever-recurring opportunity for comparing biblical and archaeological data has led to increasing convergence between our views, once so far apart. To the last, however, Dr. Kyle remained staunchly conservative on most of his basic positions, while the writer has gradually changed from the extreme radicalism of 1919 to a standpoint which can neither be called conservative nor radical, in the usual sense of the terms.[5]

Kyle introduced at least two other new policies to Palestinian archaeology. He had suggested to Albright an ecumenical makeup to the staff of

3. Albright, "The Archaeological Results of an Expedition to Moab and the Dead Sea," *BASOR* 14 (April 1924): 11, 12.

4. P. J. King, *American Archaeology in the Mideast: A History of the American Schools of Oriental Research* (Philadelphia: American Schools of Oriental Research, 1983), p. 73.

5. Albright, "In Memoriam," *BASOR* 51 (September 1983): 5, 6.

their joint operations; thus they consisted of Jews, Catholics, and Protestants. In addition, earlier digs had usually been super-secret affairs and did not allow visitors. Guards had even been posted with guns. But Kyle and Albright did away with the guards and welcomed visitors, expert and amateur alike. Well-known archaeologists such as L. H. Vincent and Roland DeVaux were frequent guests. This policy has continued on excavations in Palestine until today.

Archaeological Fieldwork

In reviewing the role of Pittsburgh Theological Seminary in archaeology in 1965, Howard Jamieson could write that this seminary "has actually been engaged in more archaeological explorations than any Protestant seminary in the world. Both Jewish organizations and Catholic orders have done more work; but among Protestant seminaries Pittsburgh is at the front in archaeological research in Palestine."[6]

Since 1924, Pittsburgh Seminary and its parent institutions have participated in fourteen excavations in connection with the ASOR in Jerusalem and three at Ashdod in connection with Carnegie Museum of Pittsburgh and the Israeli Department of Antiquities. Since 1970, the seminary has also participated in four seasons of excavation with the Expedition to the Dead Sea Plain through the contribution of funds and staff.

Expedition to Moab and the Dead Sea

The first joint expedition to Moab and the Dead Sea in 1924 was to investigate an area that was still an archaeological *terra incognita,* the southern Ghor of eastern Palestine — that is, the southern and southeastern shores of the Dead Sea and their immediate hinterland. The primary purpose of the joint expedition was to secure evidence throwing light on the problem of the Cities of the Plain, especially Sodom, Gomorrah, and Zoar, which biblical tradition locates at the southern end of the Dead

6. Jamieson, "Pittsburgh Theological Seminary and Archaeology," *Pittsburgh Perspective* 6, 4 (December 1965): 5.

Sea.[7] Dr. Kyle raised the money for the expedition, so perhaps he recognized that a search for the wicked cities of Sodom and Gomorrah had "sales value"!

The descriptions of their preparation, the logistics of camp life, and the wonders of the land they explored are fascinating. Theirs were the first visas ever granted by the newly designated Consular Agent for the Trans-Jordanian government in Jerusalem.[8] All provisions had to be taken with them, from tents and a cook, to pots, pans, and several hundred pounds of canned goods. Though their travel began in early-model Fords, roads were poor or nonexistent. The trip from Jerusalem to Amman, which in 1966 took slightly more than an hour, was a day's trip in 1924; the trip to Kerak, partially along the route of the Hejaz railroad, took another day. From there horses and mules were hired to carry the staff and equipment down to the Dead Sea. Wadis (often dry river and stream beds, sometimes deeply eroded) were difficult to negotiate, and one mule was lost over the precipice, while two others stumbled over the edge and rolled downhill until stopped by boulders.[9]

Kyle describes learning how to eat lunch on horseback, getting the shells off his eggs, and alternating bites of bread and chocolate without letting the egg fall or swallowing the shells! In the bottoms of the wadis it was rather easy going. The vivid colors of the rocks, from the white and yellow of the limestone bases to gorgeous hues of the red sandstone, towered above. Although already fifty feet below sea level, they had some twelve hundred yet to go. Camping places were beside rushing streams before irrigated fields of fig orchards, vineyards, clover, dura, and indigo.[10]

Their explorations around the southern end of the Dead Sea, and particularly for the Old Testament site of Zoar, revealed many ancient reservoirs, aqueducts, sugar mills, much pottery, and even coins, but all of these were from Byzantine and early Arabic times. Albright and Kyle could only conclude that Zoar as well as Sodom and Gomorrah was submerged beneath the Dead Sea, which had risen significantly in recent years.

They spent a few days exploring the Lisan, the "tongue" that reaches into the Dead Sea and which today virtually cuts the Dead Sea in half toward its southern end. Here, too, the remains were late, and it was only when

7. *BASOR* 14 (April 1924): 2. See Genesis 13:12, 13; 19:23-30.
8. M. G. Kyle, *Explorations in Sodom* (New York: Fleming H. Revell, 1928), p. 22.
9. *BASOR* 14 (April 1924): 3.
10. Kyle, *Explorations in Sodom,* pp. 49-51.

their expedition was about to return to Kerak that they found their first really ancient remains. Ascending from the Lisan about five hundred feet above the Dead Sea, some ancient burials of the Early Bronze age[11] were found, leading them to a large open-air settlement, then a large walled acropolis, and finally a group of seven fallen limestone monoliths. No deposit of debris was found, so it was concluded that it was not a town, but that the site, Bab edh-Dhra', was an open-air sanctuary with *masseboth* (the large monoliths, probably dragged for miles to the site) to which the people from the Cities of the Plain came on pilgrimages. The numerous surface remains of hearths and enclosures would represent booths and camping sites, and the fortress stood to protect the pilgrims. The pottery dated to around 2000 B.C. according to Albright, while some of the specimens may have gone back to the first centuries of the Early Bronze age.[12] The seminary's Bible Lands Museum has a small collection of the pottery that had been gathered on this early expedition, all dating to the Early Bronze IV period (2300-2050 B.C.) and forming the basis of the seminary collection of that time.

Very gratifying to Kyle was "the fact that the evidence of pottery sets the end of the settlement at Bab edh-Dhra' at about the time when biblical sources place the catastrophe of the Cities of the Plain."[13] This was no doubt an impetus for his future archaeological work.

11. Archaeologists designate periods of antiquity by "ages." These archaeological periods may be equated with our B.C./A.D. chronology as follows:

2 million years ago	Paleolithic	"Old Stone Age"
10,000 B.C.	Mesolithic	"Middle Stone Age"
8000-4300	Neolithic	"New Stone Age"
4300-3200	Chalcolithic	"Copper-Stone Age"
3200-2050	Early Bronze Age	
2050-1900	Middle Bronze I	
1900-1550	Middle Bronze II	
1550-1200	Late Bronze	
1200-918	Iron I	
918-587	Iron II	
587-539	Exilic	
539-332	Persian	
332-63	Hellenistic	
63 B.C.–A.D. 330	Roman	
330-630	Byzantine	
630-1516	Arabic	

12. *BASOR* 14 (April 1924): 4-7.
13. M. G. Kyle and W. F. Albright, "Results of the Archaeological Survey of the Ghor in Search for the Cities of the Plain," *Bibliotheca Sacra* 81 (July 1924): 280.

Tell Beit Mirsim

In Kyle's day the debate concerning the date of the Exodus was between an early one (1600-1500 B.C.) and a later one (the thirteenth century B.C., during Rameses the Great's reign in Egypt). Kyle was convinced that the solution lay in the study of the many sites in Palestine associated with the biblical account of Joshua's conquest. At the time Albright was fascinated with a very attractive *tell*,[14] Tell Beit Mirsim, in southern Palestine, thirteen miles southwest of Hebron, six hours from Hebron by horse or camel. He identified it with Debir or Kiriath-sepher, meaning "Book Town," and it had been suggested that this name might mean there was a library of cuneiform tablets here.[15] So both Albright and Kyle agreed that Tell Beit Mirsim would be an ideal site to work, and it proved better than either had dreamed.

The first expedition to Tell Beit Mirsim took place in 1926. Kyle, though not in good health, was president of the campaign. James L. Kelso, also of Xenia Seminary, began his archaeological career as assistant to Albright. Albright praised his staff, who did their work in spite of dust and heat, fleas, earwigs, and scorpions. One day a terrific wind and dust storm forced them to suspend work, and all had to rescue the tents, which were badly damaged.[16]

In terms of archaeological methodology the digs at Tell Beit Mirsim were some of the most important ever made in Palestine, for from the findings Albright was able to outline the chronology of Palestinian pottery from before Abraham's time to the period of Nebuchadnezzar. In the first campaign the director wrote that he had not seen anywhere in Palestine

> such ideal conditions for precise stratigraphical results. The site is free from encumbrances, and exhibits three very strongly marked burn levels, belonging to three complete destructions of the city by fire. Thanks to the careful study of the pottery from the successive strata and sub-strata, it is possible to describe the history of the town already,

14. A *tell* is a mound of debris that has built up over the years from a series of occupations, the layers being in reverse order, the oldest civilization at the bottom on natural soil.

15. W. F. Albright, "The Excavations at Tell Beit Mirsim," *BASOR* 23 (October 1926): 3.

16. Albright, "Excavations at Tell Beit Mirsim," p. 14.

Tell Beit Mirsim archaeological dig, 1932
(seated, James L. Kelso, W. F. Albright, M. G. Kyle, Nelson Glueck)

though names and personalities naturally elude us as yet, owing to the fact [that] no inscriptions have been found.[17]

It was because Tell Beit Mirsim had been inhabited, conquered, and reinhabited over and over again that results were so significant. There were twelve levels of occupation, with only one major break between occupational periods. Petrie had some periods of occupation at Tell el-Hesi, but there were some major breaks, long periods the extent of which could not be known without cross-references. Tell Beit Mirsim provided the cross-references.

There were four seasons at Tell Beit Mirsim: in 1926, 1928, 1930, and 1932. The cost of the first two campaigns and over half that of the third and fourth campaigns was borne by Dr. Kyle, who earned practically all the amount by indefatigable writing and lecturing. The agreement was that he should preside over the staff and should take charge of all publicity, while Albright had full control of the excavation proper and the scientific

17. Albright, "Excavations at Tell Beit Mirsim," p. 3.

publication. Four *Annuals* of the ASOR (vols. 12, 13, 17, and 21-22) presented the final results. The first two deal with the pottery finds. The third volume is a report on the Bronze Age city, and the fourth volume centers on the Iron Age. The frequent references in archaeological studies to the pottery finds at Tell Beit Mirsim give ample evidence of their significant contributions. This is not to say that pottery chronology has not been significantly refined since these excavations and publications, and most scholars no longer consider Tell Beit Mirsim the site of Old Testament Debir. But Tell Beit Mirsim has provided a foundation and starting point for many students and studies in archaeology. Most important to Pittsburgh Seminary is the fact that many artifacts from these excavations have come to Pittsburgh through the efforts of Professor Kyle and his successor, James L. Kelso, and they are now an important part of the museum and study collections.

Bethel

M. G. Kyle died in 1933. Kelso and Albright arranged for a memorial dig at Tell Beit Mirsim in 1934 in honor of Kyle. Following Kyle's pattern, all the money Kelso raised for the dig came from individual church members and from congregations. When the dollar was devaluated, however, its worth was cut in half, and it was too expensive to continue work at Tell Beit Mirsim. A site was chosen near Jerusalem, where the depreciated dollar could accomplish the most work.

Bethel, about fifteen miles north of Jerusalem, is mentioned more often in the Old Testament than any city except Jerusalem. Although Bethel had been identified with the village of Beitin by Edward Robinson in 1840, archaeological evidence was still needed to know whether occupation went back to Canaanite times. In November 1927, Albright had directed a trial excavation at Beitin. His test trenches revealed pottery that dated back as far as 2000 B.C., with strata of the Middle and Late Bronze Ages, Iron I and II, Hellenistic, and occupation down to medieval times. Moreover, he could report that nearly four acres of the site were free from modern buildings and were thus awaiting the "fortunate excavator of Bethel."[18]

18. W. F. Albright, "A Trial Excavation in the Mound of Bethel," *BASOR* 29 (February 1928): 10, 11.

Professor James L. Kelso of Xenia Seminary had become such a disciple of Kyle that he had come to think like him. Kelso, too, figured that sin still had "sales value." If the archaeologists could find Jeroboam's temple at Bethel, it would be much easier to raise more funds. After all, it is hard to top Jeroboam's sinful accomplishments: he did "evil above all those who were before [him]" and caused Israel to commit sin.[19] After four campaigns at Bethel, however, in 1934, 1954, 1957, and 1960, the temple continued to elude the archaeologists. But the 1960 campaign did produce a cultic area in the bedrock high place dedicated to the Semitic god El, an ancestor of the Baal of Jeroboam's day. This sanctuary was in use as early as 3500 B.C. and continued to be used for nearly a millennium and a half, when a temple was erected immediately above it.

After the 1934 campaign at Bethel, Pittsburgh-Xenia Seminary's excavation program suffered severe financial depression. It was not until 1954, and again in 1957 and 1960, that work was renewed at Bethel, now under the direction of Professor Kelso.

Bethel had a long history lasting until the Muslim conquest of Palestine. Middle Bronze II and the Late Bronze Ages showed particular prosperity. A huge burn level yielded the best evidence yet for destruction by the Israelites at the end of the thirteenth century B.C. Albright reported after the first campaign:

> Somewhere in the thirteenth century B.C. the second phase of Late Bronze was destroyed by a tremendous conflagration . . . to the height of a metre and a half, on the average, by a solid mass of fallen brick, burned red, black ash-filled earth, charred and splintered debris. We have never seen indications of a more destructive conflagration in any Palestinian excavation. . . . When we consider the masonry, building plans, pottery, and culture of the following three phases, which are in these respects homogeneous, the break becomes so much greater that no bridge can be thrown across it, and we are compelled to identify it with the Israelite conquest.[20]

The culture of Iron I that followed was very crude in comparison with the preceding Canaanite city. The poor construction continued until the tenth century. In Iron II uninterrupted occupation continued for

19. See 1 Kings 14:9, 16, and numerous references in chapters 12–14.
20. W. F. Albright, "The Kyle Memorial Excavation at Bethel," *BASOR* 56 (December 1934): 9, 10.

more than three centuries, when it was destroyed by a great conflagration sometime in the sixth century.[21] When the town was reoccupied, there is evidence of prosperous intertestamental, New Testament, and Byzantine periods.

The final report of the four campaigns was published in the *Annual* of the ASOR (vol. 39). Pittsburgh-Xenia received its share of the finds from the excavations, and this material has added substantially to the museum collections, particularly in the later periods.

Tulul Abu el-'Alayiq and Khirbet en-Nitla

Kelso returned to Jerusalem in 1949 with adequate funds in hopes of returning to Tell Beit Mirsim. He requested and received a military permit to visit the site, but the trip revealed that it was now in "no man's land" and not available for archaeological research — just for target practice. This forced a decision to work elsewhere, and Tulul Abu el-'Alayiq, New Testament or Herodian Jericho, was selected. The excavation was carried on in January, February, and March of 1950.

Kelso's return to Jerusalem was just after the creation of the state of Israel and an armistice dividing Palestine between Jordan and Israel. Professor Ovid Sellers of McCormick Theological Seminary was the director of the ASOR most of the year, but he was severely burned when the commercial plane in which he was traveling was shot down by an Israeli plane. Kelso replaced Sellers as director of the institute. Neither Israel nor the Arabs were respecting the armistice. One night heavy shelling just west of the school lasted from 7 p.m. until 3 a.m., but Kelso could not lose a day of work. The next day he continued his excavation at Tulul Abu el-'Alayiq. Mrs. Kelso was more often caught in the firing, for while Dr. Kelso was digging in the Jordan Valley, she was looking after the affairs of the school in Jerusalem. A totally new city government had been established after the partition, and all new utilities had to be set up. The school itself needed renovation because the United Nations had used it as military headquarters in 1948.

Tulul Abu el-'Alayiq yielded evidence of a Hellenistic fortress, probably the work of the Hasmoneans. Roman Jericho has proven to be one of the most unique cities of that time east of Rome. Herod the Great and

21. Albright, "Kyle Memorial Excavation," pp. 11-14.

his family secured architects, engineers, and builders from Rome. With these craftsmen the same type of architecture was reproduced at Jericho as Augustus was using to rebuild Rome. Jericho is the only city east of Italy yet excavated where *opus reticulatum* architecture is used. *Opus reticulatum* is a concrete wall whose face is made up of small, square-based, pyramidal blocks laid with the side at a forty-five degree angle from the vertical, giving a net (reticulum) pattern. Luxury was everywhere in Roman Jericho, and the magnificent natural setting along the Wadi Qelt matched the buildings, gardens, and pools built by Herod. Pompeii shows the same architecture, but it lacked the tropical luxury of Jericho.[22] Subsequent excavation has shown that the Roman occupation of Tulul Abu el-'Alayiq probably lasted more than a century.

The Jericho dig presented one problem probably never before encountered by a Palestinian archaeologist: an overabundance of free labor. Two thousand workers were offered for the work at Jericho by the United Nations Commission seeking employment for Palestinian refugees. But the United Nations specified that refugee workers could be employed only for two-week periods, causing a constant turnover of workers. But Kelso felt that the workers were very adaptable, and the work suffered little.[23]

The surplus of labor made it possible to carry on a minor excavation at a ruin three kilometers east of Tulul Abu el-'Alayiq. Nitla had attracted explorers as a possible identification with Gilgal. Four soundings by Kelso exposed Byzantine or Early Arabic walls of unpretentious character. The fifth revealed the ruins of a church that had undergone many changes from the fourth to the ninth centuries.[24] There was a basilica-type church with two aisles, a small chapel-like church, and a two-story church. The floors of the chapel and its narthex were mosaics with Greek inscriptions and scenes of birds and grapes.

The final reports of the campaigns at Tulul Abu el-'Alayiq and Nitla are published in the 1955 *Annual* of the ASOR (vols. 29-30). This was one of the first publications to present dated Byzantine and Arabic pottery. The seminary's share of the finds provides the basis for the museum's exhibitions of these periods.

22. See the preliminary report, J. L. Kelso, "The First Campaign of Excavation in New Testament Jericho," *BASOR* 120 (December 1950): 19.

23. Kelso, "First Campaign of Excavation," p. 13.

24. James L. Kelso, "Excavations at Khirbet en-Nitla near Jericho," *BASOR* 121 (February 1951): 6.

James L. Kelso

While Professor Kelso was director of the American School in Jerusalem, he was appointed president of the trustees of the Palestine Archaeological Museum. The policy of that museum, built by a Rockefeller grant, had to be reworked after the end of the British Mandate. Until 1966 it was governed by an international Board of Trustees. In 1967 it was taken over by the government of Israel, who refer to it as the Rockefeller Museum.

The policy that Albright and Kyle had initiated of training young archaeologists on their digs was continued by Kelso. Many students and faculty members from Pittsburgh Seminary received archaeological experience in the field and in research. Students from other institutions in the United States and residents at the Jerusalem institutes also joined in the American excavations. Some staff members went on to further archaeological endeavors and biblical studies, including such scholars as Nelson Glueck, Ernest Wright, James Pritchard, A. Ben Dor, Ovid Sellers, Henry Detwiler, William Steinspring, John Bright, James Muilenburg, William Brownlee, and Joseph Callaway.

Kelso continued the study of the Palestinian artifacts brought back to Pittsburgh through the city's outstanding research facilities. Major research involved the study of the ceramic material brought to the United States from Tell Beit Mirsim. Professor J. Thorley, a specialist in ceramics, did the technical studies, and Kelso handled the archaeological features. Thorley demonstrated that the ancient Palestinians knew most of the ceramic techniques ever used in working with clay. By the time of Isaiah and Jeremiah, the potters had invented modern assembly line techniques, and were using standardized sizing of their wares, as well as trademarks. The ASOR published the results of the Thorley-Kelso studies in a monograph entitled *The Potter's Technique at Tell Beit Mirsim,* and for many years this was the only study of the technical production of pottery in Palestine.[25]

Assisted by professors from Carnegie Institute and the University of Pittsburgh and by staff chemists from the United States Steel Corporation, Kelso studied ancient metallurgy. Scientific analysis of pottery, metallurgy, and all artifacts is now a part of every archaeological excavation.

25. Reprinted from the *Annual* of the American Schools of Oriental Research, vols. 21-22, New Haven, 1943.

Kelso's early training as a pharmacist was helpful in his pioneering efforts in this area.

Kelso's great contribution to archaeological studies at Pittsburgh Theological Seminary has found lasting results in the Bible Lands Museum. Kelso brought together the various artifacts that have formed the basis for the museum's collections.

Later Fieldwork

Ashdod

In the summer of 1962 Pittsburgh Seminary continued its program of archaeology with an excavation at Tell Ashdod. This was a cooperative effort involving the seminary, Carnegie Museum of Pittsburgh, and the Department of Antiquities of Israel. Professor David Noel Freedman was the director of the Ashdod excavation project, and Dr. James L. Swauger of Carnegie Museum was associate director. Dr. Moshe Dothan, representative of the Department of Antiquities, directed the fieldwork. This dig was financed through U.S. State Department counterpart funds and generous gifts from supporters and friends of the Holy Land Exhibition Fund.

Ashdod covers more than one hundred acres. In 1962, four acres, mainly in the southwest portion of the tell, were excavated. Finds ranged from the Late Bronze period (sixteenth-fifteenth centuries B.C.) to the Byzantine level. The most sensational discovery of the first season was the recovery of three fragments of a basalt stele commemorating the victories of the Assyrian King Sargon II.

The second season at ancient Ashdod took place in 1963. Participants on the project came from twenty different countries, speaking a dozen languages. More extensive and detailed information about the history of the site became known. Significant finds included a cylinder seal inscribed in Old Babylonian cuneiform and the identification of two Philistine occupation levels.

The third season, in 1965, was again a cooperative effort of the seminary, Carnegie Museum, and the Israeli Department of Antiquities, and most of the funds expended on the site were counterpart funds channeled through the Smithsonian Institution. With Moshe Dothan director of excavation and James Swauger director of the Ashdod project, there was a trained staff of about twenty-five. Faculty and students of Pittsburgh Seminary, including Donald Gowan and A. Vanlier Hunter of the biblical faculty, participated in the excavation. The 1965 season extended the history of the site back to about 3000 B.C. with the discovery of a thick Early Bronze level. The cultural influence of the Philistines was noted as late as 800-700 B.C., and Persian period ceramics were uncovered.[26]

Tell el-Fûl

In the summer of 1964, Pittsburgh Seminary again formed a joint excavation with the ASOR in a campaign at Tell el-Fûl, three miles north of Jerusalem. Paul Lapp, director of the American School, was director of the dig, and James L. Kelso was president.[27] In these later years of Kelso's life, the organization model was that of Kyle's digs with Albright. Albright had excavated Tel el-Fûl in 1922 and 1933 and identified it as Gibeah of Saul in Benjamin. Questions had again been raised concerning its occupation. The 1964 campaign confirmed Albright's conclusion regarding Iron I occupations (about 1200 and 1000 B.C.) and a fortress belonging to Saul. Also uncovered was a sizable occupation belonging to Late Iron II and the Exilic period, the late seventh and sixth centuries B.C. The Exilic pottery groups provided information about a little-known period in Palestinian archaeology. A second extensive occupation was in the Hellenistic period, especially in the second century B.C. I published the results of the 1964 campaign in the 1981 *Annual* (vol. 45) of the ASOR.

A fund supporting biblical archaeology had been established at Pittsburgh Theological Seminary beginning with the excavation at Tell el-Fûl in 1964. In honor of the two who had made archaeology an integral part of the seminary's program, the fund was known as the Kyle-Kelso Fund for Archaeological Research. With the active interest of President Donald G. Miller and through the efforts of Professor Howard Jamieson, the fund provided resources for work in the Bible Lands Museum and

26. The final reports of the Ashdod excavations are slowly being published in a series of volumes of *'Atiqot. Ashdod I* has appeared in *'Atiqot,* vol. 7, and *Ashdod II* in *'Atiqot,* vols. 9-10.

27. I was with my husband Paul and usually tended to the school building and its affairs when he was in the field.

for field projects in Palestine. Many individuals and churches contributed to the fund. A generous, sizable contribution was secured by David Molyneaux, senior minister of the First Presbyterian Church of Flint, Michigan. As a member of the seminary Board of Directors, Dr. Molyneaux enlisted the aid of a number of members and friends in Flint who responded to the opportunity to be involved in biblical archaeology.

Tell er-Rumeith

In 1966-67, Howard Jamieson, professor of biblical theology, spent his sabbatical year in Jerusalem, Jordan. The Molyneaux contribution to the Kyle-Kelso Fund made possible a major effort at Tell er-Rumeith during the spring of 1967. Under the direction of Paul W. Lapp, then professor of ancient Near Eastern history and archaeology of ASOR, this excavation was jointly sponsored by Pittsburgh Seminary and ASOR. The budget was provided by the former and the equipment and a contribution toward transportation by the latter. Jamieson served as codirector, as treasurer, and as a field supervisor.

Tell er-Rumeith is located east of the Jordan River near the Syrian border at the juncture of the Irbid-Baghdad highway with the Damascus-Amman road. A sounding had been made at the site by Lapp in 1962. The six weeks of work in 1967 produced the excavation of the northeast quarter of the fortress area plus some work in the southeast quadrant. The ceramic chronology for the site established in 1962 was confirmed in detail.

Stratum VIII, the earliest stratum at Rumeith, is dated to the time of Solomon. It was destroyed near the beginning of the ninth century B.C. The site was taken over by the Arameans, and the Stratum VII fortification was their border of defense. The end of Stratum VII occupation in the middle of the ninth century may be related to the campaign of Jehoshaphat and Ahab, or to that of Ahaziah and Joram.[28] The reconstruction of the site involved the building of a platform over the entire area defined by the Stratum VII fort wall. The Stratum VI occupation is also attributed to the Arameans. It came to a conclusion at the end of the ninth century B.C. This was the time when Joash defeated the Arameans at Aphek.[29] The

---

28. See 1 Kings 22:29-36 and 2 Kings 8:25-29.
29. See 2 Kings 13:14-25.

Stratum V occupation ended generally with an attack that may be attributed to Tiglath-pileser III's campaign of 733 B.C. This ended the
existence of the Northern Kingdom of Israel.[30] While material from the
Hellenistic, Roman, Byzantine, and Arab periods (Strata IV-I) was discovered, it was meager. Lapp wrote at the conclusion of the excavation
at Rumeith:

> The question of the identification of Tell er-Rumeith with Biblical
> Ramoth-Gilead has not been conclusively proved by the excavations,
> but the case is as strong or stronger than for many Biblical sites. The
> continuity of the name, the congruence of occupational history with
> that of the literary record, and its geographical position fit such an
> identification. If it is not Ramoth-Gilead, [Rumeith] is certainly one
> of the 60 towns 'with walls and bronze bars' controlled by Bengeber
> (I Kings 4:13). But this objective must be coupled with evidence for a
> larger site in the area with equally impressive claims if it is to replace
> Tell er-Rumeith as the most viable candidate for Ramoth-Gilead.[31]

Bab edh-Dhra'

During the winter of 1967, Pittsburgh Seminary was involved in the third
in a series of excavations at Bab edh-Dhra', the site that Kyle and Albright
had found during their expedition to Moab and the Dead Sea in 1924.
The three campaigns of the American School in Jerusalem in 1965 and
1967 were all under the direction of Paul Lapp. Howard Jamieson was
Pittsburgh Seminary's representative on the staff in February 1967.

When Albright and Kyle spent a few days at Bab edh-Dhra' in 1924,
they limited the Early Bronze occupation to a sacred area fortified for the
protection of the pilgrims and dated it toward the end of the third
millennium B.C. In the 1960s, Early Bronze pottery appearing on the
antiquities market in Jerusalem sent Paul Lapp and colleagues in search
of their origin. They finally were led to Bab edh-Dhra', and the discoveries
there boggled their imaginations. A vast cemetery over a kilometer long
and almost equally wide saw continual use from the thirty-second century
B.C. through the third millennium, indicating over a half million burials.

---

30. See 2 Kings 15:29; 16:5–17:6.
31. Lapp, *The Tale of the Tell* (Pittsburgh: Pickwick, 1975), p. 119.

In the second campaign the strongly fortified town site that flourished during the Early Bronze II (2850-2550 B.C.) period was also investigated.

The third campaign at Bab edh-Dhra' concentrated on tombs in the cemetery at the eastern edge of the Dead Sea Lisan. The material produced from those tombs provided Lapp with sufficient evidence to reach a number of challenging conclusions concerning life in Palestine in the Early Bronze Age, especially about 3200 B.C., a period designated as Early Bronze I A. He published a description and interpretation of Tomb A 76 at Bab edh-Dhra', a shaft tomb excavated under the supervision of Howard Jamieson.[32] The two chambers of this tomb were well preserved and untouched from the time the material was first deposited, so Lapp focused on this tomb as illustrative of the earliest shaft tombs of the cemetery. The final publication of Lapp's work at Bab edh-Dhra' appeared in 1989 through the work of staff members of the third campaign.[33]

Paul W. Lapp

In 1968 a number of factors combined to bring Paul Lapp to Pittsburgh Theological Seminary as professor of Old Testament and archaeology — the Six-Day War in Palestine, the need to provide for a young growing family, and his relationship with Howard Jamieson. There were high hopes that under Lapp's enthusiastic and able leadership new fields of involvement would appear as Pittsburgh Seminary pursued its program of combining biblical studies with archaeological research. Lapp thought that archaeological discovery might be even more important than space exploration, for perhaps it is more important for us to understand ourselves than to expand our world.

Four months after assuming his duties as a member of the seminary faculty, Lapp visited Egypt. From that study, plans were begun for a campaign at Hamra Dom in December and January of 1969-70. Adjacent to Hamra Dom is the cemetery consistently reported to be the site of the discovery of the Coptic Gnostic codices, including the Gospel of Thomas,

32. Lapp, "Bab edh-Dhra'," *BASOR* 189 (February 1968): 12-41.
33. R. Thomas Schaub and Walter E. Rast, *Bab edh-Dhra': Excavations in the Cemetery Directed by Paul W. Lapp (1965-1967),* Reports of the Expedition to the Dead Sea Plain, Jordan, I (Winona Lake, IN: Eisenbrauns, 1989).

which is probably the best known. The proposed campaign was designed to provide more information on the life and thought of the early Christian church in Egypt. Involved in the expedition were Professor James M. Robinson of Claremont, the American Research Center in Egypt, the Smithsonian Institution, and Pittsburgh Theological Seminary. In November 1969, however, Professor Lapp had to postpone the expedition indefinitely because of military restrictions.

Idalion

Another opportunity presented itself in January 1970 for fieldwork at a significant site in the eastern Mediterranean world. In association with the State University of New York in Albany, Pittsburgh Seminary was responding to an invitation of the Cyprus government to excavate at Idalion in central Cyprus. There were possibilities of securing new light on the origin and migrations of the Philistines and of refining Palestinian

Paul Lapp, Pittsburgh Seminary (Professor, 1968-1970) with archaeologists Pere Roland DeVaux (left) and Yigael Yadin (right)

ceramic chronology in the Persian period by relating sixth-fifth century B.C. occupation at Idalion. The decision was made to share in the excavation. The non-Cypriote staff of eighteen was to include Paul Lapp, Howard Jamieson, and students John and Jean Graham, Michael Brubaker, and David McCreery from the seminary. Because of the untimely death of Paul Lapp through drowning in the treacherous current off the north shore of Cyprus on April 26, 1970, Pittsburgh Seminary's involvement at Idalion came to an end. The students participated in the limited work of that season.

Although Lapp's time at Pittsburgh was less than two years, his influence on students was lasting, and he started several students on advanced degrees and careers in archaeology and biblical studies.[34] Thomas Schaub earned his doctorate in archaeology under the direction of Lapp and his colleagues on the faculty of Pittsburgh Seminary and the University of Pittsburgh. For a time Schaub was guest instructor at the seminary. He now teaches at Indiana University of Pennsylvania and continues the work at Bab edh-Dhra' as co-director of the expedition to the Dead Sea Plain.

Expedition to the Dead Sea Plain

Military restrictions in the region and then his premature death prevented Lapp's investigations of the Dead Sea area. Several years later, restrictions were lifted, and work was renewed in 1975 by Thomas Schaub and Walter Rast, who had been members of the 1967 staff and who were entrusted with the publication of the Bab edh-Dhra' material. Their explorations once again included the southeastern plain around the Dead Sea and southern Ghor, but only in investigating the low foothills to the east of the plain did they find evidence of the Early Bronze towns they were seeking. To continue their work, the expedition to the Dead Sea Plain was formed, and major archaeological campaigns took place in 1977, 1979, 1981, and most recently during the winter of 1989-90. With foreign staffs of as many as fifty participants, with a wide variety of

34. An issue of *Pittsburgh Perspective* (12 [Spring 1971]) contained "Essays in Memory of Paul W. Lapp." There were articles by many prominent archaeologists and a bibliography of Lapp's writings.

backgrounds, an attempt has been made to undertake comprehensive environmental studies as well as to search for cultural information with the most modern archaeological methods available. In investigating the total Early Bronze settlement pattern of the area, excavations have also been carried out: (1) at the site of Numeirah, an Early Bronze III (2550-2300 B.C.) town about ten kilometers south of Bab edh-Dhra'; (2) at Feifi, where there is a huge pre—Early Bronze and Early Bronze I cemetery and town occupation of the Iron Age on a mound at the edge of the Ghor south of the Dead Sea; and (3) at Khanazir, the farthest south of the Early Bronze sites of the region, where a huge Early Bronze IV cemetery on the plateaus above the Ghor was investigated in the 1989-90 campaign.

Funds for these campaigns have come largely through grants from the National Endowment for the Humanities, the National Geographic Society, and the Smithsonian Institution, with a number of contributions from universities, colleges, and seminaries, as well as from individuals. Due to the increased cost of excavation and the absence of large sums of money in recent years, Pittsburgh Seminary's participation in fieldwork has been limited to small contributions to larger projects. It is fitting that the seminary's support of fieldwork should be to an expedition to the Dead Sea Plain, as it was when it first participated in field archaeology sixty years ago. Faculty and students from the seminary participated in the 1977, 1979, 1981, and 1989-90 campaigns, and small financial contributions have been made. I was privileged to be a member of the field staff in 1979 and 1989-90, and I have continued study and publication of some of the excavated materials: one of the Early Bronze IV tombs I helped to excavate; the significant corpus of cylinder seals and impressions, as well as the incised sherds, that have come from the various campaigns; and the Iron Age occupation and pottery from Feifi.

The Bible Lands Museum

Since 1970 most of the seminary's archaeological interest and participation as a part of the educational program has centered around the Bible Lands Museum. I became curator of the museum in 1975. Although this is a part-time position, it represents the first time a Pittsburgh Seminary staff or faculty member has been given prime responsibility for the museum. During the past twenty years it has been possible to completely

James L. Kelso, Xenia, Pittsburgh-Xenia, and Pittsburgh Seminaries (Professor, 1923-1963) in the Bible Lands Museum, named in his honor

catalog the museum collections, develop new displays, carry out in-depth study of various materials in the collections, and provide special lectures and visitor programs. Archaeology classes have been taught on an intro-ductory level, and a number of students have fulfilled independent re-quirements in more advanced study. Students and vounteers have con-tributed many hours to the work of the museum and the study of its materials. Particular displays have been developed as student projects, such as those concerning the earliest tools of humankind, figurines in ancient Israel, scarabs and beads, coins, the dyeing and weaving industries, and the development of writing.

On the fiftieth anniversary of field archaeology, in 1975, a celebra-tion took place with guest lecturers Thomas Schaub and Walter Rast, and the first museum open house was held for the seminary and Pittsburgh communities. These open houses have continued to take place, sometimes in conjunction with an archaeology lecture. Along with the museum's regular collections, these occasions have also featured extended displays and "Archaeology in Action," with pottery making, archaeological materials, movies of excavations, and slide shows of Pittsburgh Seminary's early work in archaeology.

The museum received its own home in the Long Administration Building when space was made available by the dedication of the Barbour Library in 1964. Through Professor Kelso's efforts, an area on the ground floor was designated for the museum. Wall and table display cases suitable to the space were obtained and are still in use today. Kelso and his students were then able to exhibit items that Kyle and Kelso had collected over fifty years of their activity in biblical lands. Displays had previously been limited to classrooms, occasional hall exhibits, and the professors' homes and offices.

In 1975 the museum was renamed the James L. Kelso Bible Lands Museum in honor of the professor who had furthered the seminary's interest and participation in archaeology and the museum to such a great extent. Dr. Kelso's concern for the museum was maintained until his death in 1978. His widow, Adolphina Kelso, who had always assisted her husband in his archaeological projects both in Jordan and in Pittsburgh, continued support and contributed artifacts and much of their collection of memorabilia from the Holy Land to the museum. The archaeological program at the seminary lost great friends as the last of that pioneer generation passed away with Mrs. Kelso's death in 1981.

Since 1979 a portion of the museum budget has been allocated for an archaeological lecture. In 1991 the fifteenth annual lecture was held. The lectures have included archaeologists who have worked in Jordan, Israel, and Cyprus.[35]

In cooperation with the Clifford Barbour Library, a special project was undertaken in 1981 to catalog and copy the large collection of lantern slides pertaining to the Near East that had fallen into the hands of the seminary through the years. Some of the slides were commercially available in Jerusalem during the first quarter of this century, and a large

---

35. Lecturers who have not been mentioned elsewhere include James Sauer, Moyiweh Ibrahim, Yigael Shiloh, Nabil Khairy, Philip King, Larry Geraty, Marilyn Schaub (Duquesne University), Douglas Esse, Stuart Swiny, Ted Campbell, and Carol Meyers.

number are from the collections of Kyle and Kelso. Over 2,300 have been cataloged and indexed, and standard projector slides are available for borrowers of the seminary library. After Mrs. Kelso's death, Stanleigh McDonald, a nephew, gave the seminary the archaeological slides from the Kelsos' current collection, and others have also contributed slides to the seminary's collection.

Artifacts, collections, and displays are usually added to the museum through gifts of interested individuals. Accurate records have been kept in recent years. Many artifacts are on loan from the Lapp family collection, and pottery groups from Beth-zur, Shechem, and 'Araq el-Emir are available for study. Through the courtesy of the Jordanian Department of Antiquities, and with a gift from Mr. and Mrs. George E. Trotter, Jr., the museum received a tomb group from the 1968 excavation at Bab edh-Dhra', the pottery of Tomb A 75, which had been excavated by Howard Jamieson when he was on the seminary faculty. The tomb was reconstructed as found and is on display in the museum.

In 1984, at the celebration of the sixtieth anniversary of archaeological research first carried out near the Dead Sea, Drs. Rast and Schaub presented an illustrated lecture of their most recent excavations. In honor of the museum curator, they presented the museum with a second tomb group from the Bab edh-Dhra' cemetery, Tomb A 85, dating about 3200 B.C.

Museum displays and activities have expanded in recent years beyond the confines of the rather small museum area. In 1983 two displays on archaeology and the Old and New Testaments were developed for permanent exhibition in the Hicks Chapel foyer. The next year six displays were arranged in the Registrar-Admissions Lounge area on themes from the museum. Jeanette Rapp, seminary director of continuing education and special events, along with community and student volunteers, contributed much time and effort. On occasion, special displays have been placed in library exhibition cases. Larger and better areas for study, display, and storage are a part of the long-range capital development plans of the seminary.

In the meantime, the Bible Lands Museum continues to be visited by hundreds of people each year as individuals and school, church, and community groups, from preschool children to senior citizens, take advantage of the unique opportunities that are offered. An automatic slide presentation is given to museum visitors as an introduction to the museum and archaeology, and more detailed manuals and tapes are available.

Most importantly, the museum serves as an educational resource for the students, faculty, and friends of the seminary. Archaeological artifacts enlighten biblical history. With the introductory class offered each year and guided studies, interested students may further their understanding and even prepare for archaeological fieldwork. Beyond the seminary community, other scholars have researched our important collections of coins, seals, stamps, and forty cuneiform tablets.

Toward the end of 1989, the Jamieson-Trotter Endowment Fund was established through gifts of the Trotter family in honor of Dr. Jamieson, who had been their pastor in Santa Ana, California. The purpose of this fund is to supplement the archaeological program at Pittsburgh Seminary through scholarships for students to participate in field projects, to supplement the annual archaeology lecture so that highly qualified archaeologists may be presented, and to support the upgrading of the Kelso Bible Lands Museum through purchases or projects outside its regular budget. Through another endowment, the G. Albert Shoemaker Chair of Bible and Archaeology was established, and Professor Robert L. Kelley, Jr., was installed on April 3, 1990, as its first occupant.

On November 4, 1990, all of these recent events were celebrated. There were extensive archaeological displays and demonstrations. The annual archaeological lecture was presented. A reception honored the donors of the Jamieson-Trotter Fund, the first recipient of the G. Albert Shoemaker Chair, and alumni of the seminary who have made distinguished contributions to the seminary's archaeological program. These alumni included Howard Jamieson, class of 1943, Robert Kelley, Jr., class of 1951, and the annual archaeological lecturer, David McCreery, class of 1973. Mr. and Mrs. George Trotter, Mr. and Mrs. David Trotter, Dr. and Mrs. Jamieson, and Dr. Kelley were present for the occasion.

In the latter part of 1989, the seminary faculty called for the formation of a Museum Committee to serve as advisors to the museum and archaeology program. In 1991 this became a subcommittee of the newly formed Educational Resources Committee. With this academic recognition, the Jamieson-Trotter Endowment Fund, and the new Chair of Bible and Archaeology, the future for archaeology at the seminary in its third century looks very exciting. The Museum Committee is encouraging a return to extended fieldwork on the part of the seminary. It looks forward to expanded museum facilities, and it is advocating attention to the immediate needs of the museum. The valuable museum collections and the extensive biblical archaeology tradition of Pittsburgh Theological Seminary provide an inestimable contribution to the seminary's life and history.

□ EPILOGUE □

James Arthur Walther

The essays in this volume have skimmed over two centuries of the pursuit of theological education among the particular people who follow the Presbyterian and Reformed understanding of Christian faith. One conclusion should be clear: these folk have never felt that they have arrived at the ultimate goal. The book Dr. Slosser edited on the American Presbyterians, entitled *They Seek a Country,* took its title from Hebrews 11:14. But the text goes on to say, "they desire a better country, that is, a heavenly one" (v. 16). Each school antecedent to Pittsburgh Theological Seminary was a worthy accomplishment, and certainly the present institution is a notable achievement.

This moment of looking back, however, is only a pause on the threshold of the third century of the seminary's history. There is no need to emphasize the truism that the past is prelude to the future. Shall we prophesy? Except within the parameters of God's promises, that is a precarious venture.

The present quality of training at Pittsburgh Theological Seminary matches the standards set by the antecedent institutions. The character of the training has changed with the changing scene in the churches. Sometimes the seminary reflects changes; at least as often, it effects changes. The curriculum today is a far cry from that of McMillan and Anderson, but so is life in the land and in the churches. Change is essential to life and growth.

The makeup of the student body has changed radically. Two hundred years ago young men acquired theological training as a part of the advanced

263

education that was available on the frontier. One hundred years ago men prepared for ministry in a relatively formal and austere setting. At the end of two hundred years the whole aspect of the seminary classes is different. Most notable is the presence of women; in recent years women have made up more than forty percent of the student population. Closely related to this change is the presence of large numbers of second-career persons. And the average age of the students has crept upward until it is now in the mid-thirties. In the entering class of 1991, less than nine percent of the students came to the seminary directly from college. Nearly half of the students commute, which reflects on the makeup and concentration of the seminary community and its common life.

The demography of Pittsburgh is another strong evidence of change. The seminaries on the North Side (once Alleghenytown) were established in fashionable neighborhoods. Captains of industry had their luxurious homes along its streets. Long ago these elite families moved to other parts of the city and then to the suburbs. The growth of Afro-American and ethnic populations has had a profound influence on communities, on churches, on ministry in the churches, and thus on the seminary. These changes are reflected in the makeup of the student body and the faculty.

The change in America from colonial frontier to industrial centers, with clear reflections of world community, has affected the atmosphere and the substance of theological education. As such changes have touched all Christian bodies, the ecumenical effect in particular bodies has been profound. So teachers and students come to the seminary from peoples of the world who once were called "foreign missions" or who live in lands that were unknown two hundred years ago.

"The parson" was once "*the* person" in the community, one of very few learned leaders. The broadening and deepening of educational opportunity bring new challenges to the professional leadership in the church. So the curriculum changes in the seminary, and the demands upon the faculty and staff increase. The church, then, continues to look to its seminaries and their graduates for leadership.

Denominational support of the seminaries has varied throughout the years. The importance attached to theological education has been reaffirmed in recent times, and the Presbyterian Church has made new efforts to undergird its schools. It seems clear that the future of the church and the future of the seminaries are closely bound together. The quality and character of professional leadership in the church depend heavily upon the quality and character of the theological seminaries.

In the first decade of Pittsburgh Seminary's third century, we will enter a new millennium. When the first millenium turned into the second, there was widespread terror that it would produce "the end of the age." In the 1920s, James Snowden dealt with millennial controversies. Again we hear similar predictions about the year 2000. We respond that it will indeed be A.D., "in the year of our Lord."

Whatever is required to prepare persons to minister "in the year of our Lord," Pittsburgh Theological Seminary will teach by precept and by example. The task is still "to equip the saints for the work of ministry, for building up the body of Christ" (Eph. 4:12). The response of the seminary will surely be, in the popular cliche, "whatever it takes."

A venture into history such as we have undertaken here has some value as it collects and preserves data from the past. It may also prove valuable in providing guidance for the future. It is most important, however, as a contribution to our confession that we believe "in the communion of saints."

Name	Seminary	Years of Service
John Anderson	Service	1794-1819
John Mitchell Mason	Newburgh	1805-1821
John Banks	Philadelphia	1820-1826
James Ramsey	Canonsburg	1821-1842
Joseph Kerr	Pittsburgh	1825-1829
Jacob Jones Janeway	Western	1828-1829
Mungo Dick	Pittsburgh	1829-1831
Luther Halsey	Western	1829-1836
Luther Halsey (Emeritus Lecturer)	Western	1872-1880
John Williamson Nevin	Western	1829-1840
John Taylor Pressly	Allegheny	1832-1870
David Carson	Canonsburg	1834
Thomas Beveridge	Canonsburg	1835-1871
Moses Kerr	Allegheny	1835-1836
David Elliott	Western	1836-1874
Joseph Claybaugh	Oxford	1835-1855
Samuel W. McCracken	Oxford	1839-1840
Lewis Warner Green	Western	1840-1847
James Martin	Canonsburg	1842-1846
Alexander Taggart McGill	Western	1842-1854
James Lemonte Dinwiddie	Allegheny	1843-1846
Abraham Anderson	Canonsburg	1847-1855

Alexander Downs Clark	Allegheny	1847-1884
David Reynolds Kerr	Allegheny	1851-1887
Melancthon Williams Jacobus	Western	1851-1876
William Swan Plumer	Western	1854-1862
Samuel Wilson	Xenia	1855-1875
William Davidson	Oxford	1855-1858
Alexander Young	Oxford	1855-1874, 1876-1891
Samuel Jennings Wilson	Western	1857-1883
John Scott	Monmouth	1858-1874
Joseph Clokey	Xenia	1858-1873
William Miller Paxton	Western	1860-1872
Andrew Morrow Black	Monmouth	1864-1874
Archibald Alexander Hodge	Western	1864-1877
David Alexander Wallace	Monmouth	1867-1870
	Xenia	1883
James Harper	Newburgh	1867-1878
	Xenia	1878-1899
Joseph Tate Cooper	Allegheny	1871-1886
William Bruce	Xenia	1871-1880
William Henry Hornblower	Western	1871-1883
James Gillespie Carson	Xenia	1873-1888
William Gallogly Moorehead	Xenia	1873-1914
Jackson Burgess McMichael	Xenia	1973-1878
Samuel Thompson Lowrie	Western	1874-1877
Samuel Henry Kellogg	Western	1877-1886
William Hamilton Jeffers	Western	1877-1914
Benjamin Breckenridge Warfield	Western	1878-1887
Thomas Hastings Robinson	Western	1883-1906
David MacDill	Xenia	1884-1902
David A. McClenahan	Allegheny	1885-1921
Robert Dick Wilson	Western	1885-1900
James Alexander Grier	Allegheny	1886-1909
John McNaugher	Allegheny	1886-1943
Henry T. McClelland	Western	1886-1891
Matthew Brown Riddle	Western	1887-1916
Oliver Joseph Thatcher	Allegheny	1888-1892
Wilbert Webster White	Xenia	1889-1894
Robert Christie	Western	1891-1923

John A. Wilson	Allegheny	1893-1915
John Douds Irons	Xenia	1895-1905
James Anderson Kelso	Western	1897-1944
David Riddle Breed	Western	1898-1931
Joseph Kyle	Xenia	1899-1921
Jesse Johnson	Xenia	1903-1930
David Schley Schaff	Western	1903-1926
David Gregg	Western	1904-1909
John Elliott Wishart	Xenia	1905-1923
David Ernest Culley	Western	1906-1948
William Riley Wilson	Allegheny	1907-1940
Charles Frederick Wishart	Allegheny	1907-1914
William Robertson Farmer	Western	1907-1939
John Hunter Webster	Xenia	1908-1933
James Henry Snowden	Western	1911-1928
Melvin Grove Kyle	Xenia	1914-1930
James Doig Rankin	Pittsburgh	1914-1929
David Frazier McGill	Pittsburgh	1915-1931
Frank Eakin	Western	1915-1927
James Gallaway Hunt	Pittsburgh	1920-1926
Selby Frame Vance	Western	1921-1935
James Harper Grier	Pittsburgh	1922-1926
Robert McNary Karr	Xenia	1922-1949
James Leon Kelso	Xenia	1923-1963
George Boone McCreery	Xenia	1924-1946
Robert Nathaniel Montgomery	Pittsburgh	1926-1930
Donald MacKenzie	Western	1928-1933
Gaius Jackson Slosser	Western	1928-1958
Albert Henry Baldinger	Pittsburgh-Xenia	1931-1947
Clarence Joseph Williamson	Pittsburgh-Xenia	1932-1950
John Wick Bowman	Western	1936-1944
William F. Orr	Western	1936-1974
George Anderson Long	Pittsburgh-Xenia	1942-1955
Theophilus Mills Taylor	Pittsburgh-Xenia	1942-1962
Jarvis M. Cotton	Western	1944-1961
Frank Dixon McCloy	Western	1944-1967
Henry Alexander Riddle	Western	1944-1949
J. Carter Swaim	Western	1944-1954
Walter R. Clyde	Western	1945-1975

Addison Hardie Leitch	Pittsburgh-Xenia	1946-1961
Florence M. Lewis	Pittsburgh-Xenia	1947-1952
H. Ray Shear	Pittsburgh-Xenia	1947-1959
David Noel Freedman	Western	1948-1964
Gordon Edmund Jackson	Pittsburgh-Xenia	1949-1983
Ralph G. Turnbull	Western	1949-1954
John H. Gerstner	Pittsburgh-Xenia	1950-1980
Clifford E. Barbour	Western	1951-1962
Bessie M. Burrows	Pittsburgh-Xenia	1953-1971
James Arthur Walther	Western	1954-1983
Sidney O. Hills	Western	1954-1975
Robert Lee Kelley, Jr.	Pittsburgh-Xenia	1955-
Robert Clyde Johnson	Western	1955-1963
Howard M. Jamieson, Jr.	Pittsburgh-Xenia	1955-1970
John M. Bald	Pittsburgh-Xenia	1957-1977
Elwyn Allen Smith	Western	1957-1966
Walter E. Wiest	Western	1957-1987
Malcolm S. Alexander	Pittsburgh-Xenia	1958-1966
Harold E. Scott	Pittsburgh-Xenia	1959-1978
Howard L. Ralston	Western and	
	Pittsburgh-Xenia	1960-1972
William A. Nicholson	Western	1960-1975
James Sheppard Irvine	Pittsburgh	1960-1966
J. Gordon Chamberlin	(from	1960-1979
Gayraud S. Wilmore	this	1961-1965
Arlen P. Dohrenburg	point)	1961-1964
Edward D. Grohman	. . . .	1961-1964
David G. Buttrick	. . . .	1961-1975
Donald G. Miller	. . . .	1962-1970
George H. Kehm	. . . .	1962-
Dietrich Ritschl	. . . .	1963-1970
Markus Barth	. . . .	1963-1972
Edward Farley	. . . .	1963-1969
Lynn Boyd Hines	. . . .	1963-1972
Iain G. Wilson	. . . .	1963-1968
Douglas R. A. Hare	. . . .	1964-1993
Donald E. Gowan	. . . .	1965-
Jared J. Jackson	. . . .	1965-
H. Eberhard von Waldow	. . . .	1966-1993

Dikran Y. Hadidian	. . . .	1966-1985
Peter Fribley	. . . .	1966-1970
Robert S. Paul	. . . .	1967-1977
Ford Lewis Battles	. . . .	1967-1978
Neil R. Paylor	. . . .	1968-1982
Paul W. Lapp	. . . .	1968-1970
Robert M. Ezzell	. . . .	1969-
Ronald H. Stone	. . . .	1969-
John Wiley Nelson	. . . .	1971-1979
William H. Kadel	. . . .	1971-1978
Arthur C. Cochrane	. . . .	1971-1975
John S. Walker	. . . .	1971-1972
David T. Shannon	. . . .	1972-1978
M. Harjie Likens	. . . .	1973-
Samuel K. Roberts	. . . .	1973-1976
Gonzalo Castillo-Cardenas	. . . .	1977-
Ulrich W. Mauser	. . . .	1977-1990
Marjorie Suchocki	. . . .	1977-1983
Charles B. Partee	. . . .	1978-
Richard J. Oman	. . . .	1979-
Carnegie Samuel Calian	. . . .	1981-
Andrew Purves	. . . .	1983-
Ronald H. Cram	. . . .	1983-1985
John E. Wilson, Jr.	. . . .	1984-
Susan Nelson	. . . .	1984-
Byron H. Jackson	. . . .	1986-
Martha A. Robbins	. . . .	1986-
Keith F. Nickle	. . . .	1990-
Ronald Peters	. . . .	1991-

□ BOARD OF DIRECTORS □

Officers

Chairperson	James E. Lee
Vice Chairperson	Laird J. Stuart
Secretary	Henry C. Herchenroether, Jr.
Treasurer	Thomas D. Thomson
Assistant Secretary/Treasurer	Douglas N. Clasper
Legal Counsel	Henry D. Herchenroether, Jr.

Members

H. Pat Albright	Pamela L. Foster	Francis W. Park
Frank R. Bailey	Angela M. Freeman	Clark O. Parry
George W. Bashore	John T. Galloway, Jr.	F. Morgan Roberts
Gail E. Bowman	Nancy Hart Glanville	William A. Schenck, III
C. Samuel Calian	C. Kenneth Hall	Mercedes Shoemaker
John W. Caster	William S. Hansen	George W. Smith
Edwin V. Clarke, Jr.	Jean L. Kiskaddon	Laird J. Stuart
Robbin R. Clouser	James E. Lee	Thomas D. Thomson
Louise Dick	Russell E. Mase	Donald R. Vance
Robert D. Duncan	W. Craig McClelland	John E. White
David E. Epperson	LindaJo McKim	Theodore R. Williams
Richard M. Ferguson	Sandra J. McLaughlin	Marianne L. Wolfe
	Paul A. Neely	

□ CONTRIBUTORS □

Carnegie Samuel Calian — President and Professor of Theology, Pittsburgh Theological Seminary

Stephen D. Crocco — Director of the Library and Assistant Professor of Bibliography, Pittsburgh Theological Seminary

Howard Eshbaugh — retired pastor and writer

Dwight R. Guthrie — Emeritus Professor of Religion, Grove City College

Wallace N. Jamison — former President, New Brunswick Theological Seminary; former Dean, now Professor Emeritus, Illinois College

Robert L. Kelley, Jr. — Shoemaker Professor of Bible and Archaeology, Pittsburgh Theological Seminary

Nancy L. Lapp — Curator of the Bible Lands Museum; Lecturer in Archaeology and Hebrew, Pittsburgh Theological Seminary

Charles B. Partee — P. C. Rossin Professor of Church History, Pittsburgh Theological Seminary

James A. Walther — Emeritus Professor of New Testament Literature and Exegesis, Pittsburgh Theological Seminary

John E. Wilson, Jr. — Associate Professor of Modern European and American Church History, Pittsburgh Theological Seminary

□ SELECTIVE INDEX □ OF PROPER NAMES

NOTE: *Faculty names in this index are particularly selective.*
See the complete Historical Roll, pp. 267-71.